COMPUTER SIMULATION
AND MODELLING

COMPUTER SIMULATION AND MODELLING

FRANCIS NEELAMKAVIL

Department of Computer Science
Trinity College, Dublin
Ireland

JOHN WILEY & SONS

Chichester   New York   Brisbane   Toronto   Singapore

Library of Congress Cataloging-in-Publication Data:

Neelamkavil, Francis.
  Computer simulation and modelling.

  Includes index.
  1. Computer simulation.   I. Title.
QA76.9.C65N44   1986   001.4'34   86–9263

ISBN 0 471 91129 1
ISBN 0 471 91130 5 (pbk.)

British Library Cataloguing in Publication Data:

Neelamkavil, Francis
  Computer simulation and modelling.
  1. Digital computer simulation   2. System analysis
  I. Title
  003'.0724   QA76.9.C65

ISBN 0 471 91129 1
ISBN 0 471 91130 5 (pbk.)

Typeset by Photo·Graphics
Printed and bound in Great Britain

To
my parents who made it all possible
and
my son Arun, who missed a lot of fun

Contents

Preface

This book is about modelling and simulation of systems with the aid of computers. Both modelling and simulation (continuous and discrete) aspects are covered in sufficient detail; however, the emphasis is on digital computer simulation of discrete systems.

Modelling and simulation is not a clearly defined subject; it has its roots in several fields and derive its strength from the concepts, theories, and techniques developed in all the major disciplines over the last several decades. It is more than an art, but not a fully developed science. Human judgement, experience and computer programming skill still play an important role in the formulation and solution of problems by this method. Earlier applications of modelling and simulation centred around the problems arising in science and engineering, and it has now become clear that modelling and simulation can make a significant contribution in solving problems in economics, management, social and behavioural sciences.

A number of books on modelling and simulation have appeared on the market during the past 15 years, and the classroom trial of these books highlighted several deficiencies in the structure, organization, presentation, and practical orientation of various aspects of computer modelling and simulation. This book describes all important aspects (concepts, techniques, tools, strengths, and weaknesses) of computer-aided modelling and simulation in a single volume suitable for adoption as a textbook for an undergraduate or a postgraduate course on the subject. Concepts and theories have very little meaning unless they are illustrated through diagrams and examples, which make both teaching and learning enjoyable. Diagrams, numerical examples, sample program listings (Pascal, CSMP, GPSS, SIM-SCRIPT) and output from actual computer runs are the main features in the presentation of various topics. The emphasis is on practical problem-solving and not on theorem-proving. Unnecessary proofs and theoretical derivations are avoided and more theoretically motivated readers are referred to selected additional reading materials which in turn will lead to further sources.

This is the age of microprocessors and supercomputers. Interactive computer graphics, animation, artificial intelligence, and expert systems have become usable tools. The computer is no longer a luxury and micros are currently accessible to the vast majority of students, researchers, and other practitioners. The use of microprocessors for modelling and simulation, and the availability of micro-based simulation software have been stressed throughout the book so as to make simulation an attractive tool for problem-solving in a wide range of disciplines.

Reading is a necessary first step in learning the subject, but what is more important is the actual construction and implementation of simulation models and interpretation of results. The summary and exercises given at the end of each chapter are designed to encourage reading and 'learning by doing', and thus gain experience and confidence in the practice of modelling and simulation.

The reader of this book is assumed to be familiar with basic algebra, calculus, statistics, and at least one of the computer programming languages such as Pascal, Fortran, Basic, etc. No previous knowledge of simulation languages is required. Students in computer science, engineering, natural sciences, operations research, management science, and social sciences will find this book particularly useful. The bulk of the material can be covered in a standard 1-year university course. People from industry and other fields, who are engaged in modelling and simulation projects, should also find this book helpful. A brief outline of topics covered in various chapters appear in Section 1.7 of Chapter 1.

Several people have aided me directly or indirectly in writing this book. In particular, I would like to thank my colleagues at the Department of Computer Science, Trinity College, Dublin and University of Kansas (1984–85) for their constructive criticisms and suggestions; Stella Coughlan for her help in the preparation of the manuscript, and all my students who served as a test population during the last so many years. Finally, I am grateful to A. Mullarney of CACI, Dublin, for his comments on SIMSCRIPT in Chapter 9.

Francis Neelamkavil

1

Introduction and Overview

1.1 Background

A system is a collection of interacting elements or components that act together to achieve a common goal. Systems can be studied by direct experimentation, by building prototypes, or by building mathematical/logical models. The experimentation with the prototype or the real system is highly undesirable due to a variety (expensive, impractical, risky, or time-consuming) of reasons, and these methods are not dealt with in this book. The purpose of systems study through modelling is to aid the analysis, understanding, design, operation, prediction, or control of systems without actually constructing and operating the real thing. The mathematical/logical models which are not easily amenable to conventional analytic or numeric solutions form a subset of models generally known as *simulation models*. A given problem defined by a mathematical/logical model can have a *feasible solution*, *satisfactory solution*, *optimum solution*, or *no solution* at all. Computer modelling and simulation studies are primarily directed towards finding *satisfactory solutions* to practical problems. In Figure 1.1, points inside the shaded area are all feasible solutions and any point close to the optimum solution can be treated as a satisfactory solution.

Modelling and Simulation emerged (revived) as an identifiable numerical problem-solving technique during World War II when the so-called *Monte Carlo methods* (Hammersley and Handscomb, 1964) were successfully used by John Von Neumann and Stanislaw Ulam of Los Alamos scientific laboratory for solving neutron diffusion problems. Simulation need not necessarily involve computers. However the evolution of modern computers and high-level simulation languages popularized (Zeigler, 1979) the application of modelling and simulation for solving real-life problems in several disciplines, and the expected advances in computer technology indicate that this trend will continue.

Computer modelling and simulation was introduced into university curricula in the 1960s, and books (Tocher, 1963; Forrester, 1961) and periodicals (Ören, 1974, 1976) on the subject began to appear around the same time. The multidisciplinary character of modelling and simulation is evident from

1

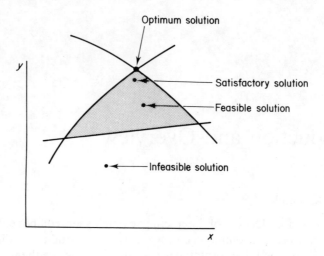

Figure 1.1   Types of solutions to a problem.

the fact that the subject is taught by different departments in different universities around the world.

1.2   Principle of computer modelling and simulation

The method of problem-solving by computer modelling and simulation can be best explained by a simple example. In Figure 1.2 the shaded area A bounded by the non-negative function $y=f(x)$, the x axis and the vertical lines at $x=b$ and $x=c$ is given by the definite integral

$$A = \int_b^c f(x)\mathrm{d}x \tag{1.1}$$

where $0 \leqslant f(x) \leqslant h$ and $b \leqslant x \leqslant c$.

The area A is a portion of the total area enclosed by the rectangle R with base (b,c) and height h. If a point P is dropped at random on R (this can be visualized as the throwing of a dart P from a distance on to the plane R so that the probability of hitting any point on R is the same), then the probability p of the point P falling in the area A is given by

$$p = \frac{A}{h(c-b)}$$

If the point P is dropped N times and K times it fell within the area A, then

$$p = \frac{K}{N} = \frac{A}{h(c-b)} \quad \text{when N} \to \infty$$

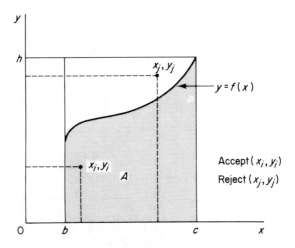

Figure 1.2   Area under the curve $y = f(x)$.

or

$$A = \frac{Kh(c-b)}{N} \qquad (1.2)$$

Figure 1.3 shows a simple flowchart to determine the area A by computer simulation, using the model defined by equation (1.2). A Pascal program and the actual computer (VAX 11/780) output are given in Figure 1–4 where $N=3000$, $b=0$, $c=h=1$, $y=f(x) = \sqrt{1-x^2}$ and a standard library routine MTH\$RANDOM is generating random numbers in the range (0,1).

The computer modelling and simulation method of problem-solving (here, the evaluation of a definite integral) becomes attractive only when it is difficult, time-consuming, expensive, hazardous, or impossible to solve the problem by conventional analytic, numeric, or physical experimentation methods. It must be clear by now that simulation results are likely to be less accurate than analytic solutions.

1.3   Simulation versus Monte Carlo simulation

The city of Monte Carlo is well known for its gambling (roulette wheel) activities, and hence this name has come to be associated with simulation (Von Neumann gave the code name Monte Carlo for his military project at Los Alamos) which involves the generation and use of random or chance variables. Some authors use the terms *Monte Carlo simulation* and *simulation* (discrete system simulation) synonymously. However, there is a distinction between the two. Both simulation and Monte Carlo simulation (Shreider, 1966) imply that the simulation model is influenced by random events;

4

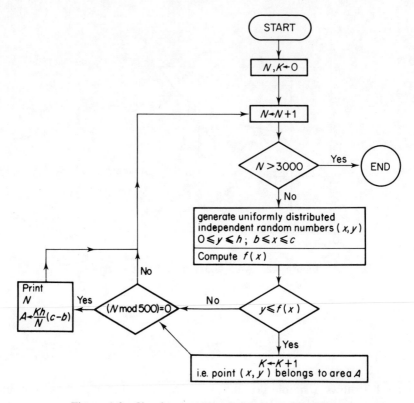

Figure 1.3   Simple example of computer simulation.

however, the system being modelled is deterministic in the case of Monte Carlo simulation, and stochastic (presence of random phenomena) in the case of simulation. In other words, Monte Carlo simulation is performed by using an approximate stochastic simulation model of a deterministic system whereas in simulation both the real system and its model are stochastic in nature.

Referring to Section 1.2, when $f(x) = \sqrt{1-x^2}$, $h=c=1$ and $b=0$, the definite integral of equation (1.1) can be evaluated analytically as follows.

$$A = \int_0^1 \sqrt{1-x^2}\, dx$$

Substituting, $x = \sin\theta$ and $dx = \cos\theta\, d\theta$, we get

$$A = \int_{x=0}^{x=1} \cos^2\theta\, d\theta$$
$$= \tfrac{1}{2} \int_{x=0}^{x=1} (1 + \cos(2\theta))\, d\theta$$

```
PROGRAM SIMULATION (INPUT,OUTPUT);
 (*evaluation of definite integral by simulation *)
 (*  y =  f(x) = (SQRT (1-SQR(x))  ;0 <= x  <=1  *)

CONST
 B=0; C=1; H=1;
VAR
 K,N,ASEED  :INTEGER;
 X,Y : REAL;

FUNCTION MTH$RANDOM(VAR SEED:INTEGER):REAL;EXTERN;
 (* external FORTRAN function for generating    *)
  (*   random numbers in the range (0,1)      *)

FUNCTION FUNCTNX (X,Y:REAL):BOOLEAN;
 BEGIN  (* functnx *)
   FUNCTNX:=(Y<=SQRT(1-SQR(X))) ;
 END;    (* functnx *)

BEGIN  (* simulation *)
 WRITELN ('no.of trials N    simulated area   A ');
 WRITELN ;
 ASEED:=123457;
 N:=0;
 K:=0;
 FOR N:=1 TO 3000
  DO BEGIN
       X:=(C-B)*MTH$RANDOM(ASEED)+B;
       Y:=H*MTH$RANDOM(ASEED); (* get random values for (x,y) *)
       IF FUNCTNX(X,Y)  THEN K:=K+1;
       IF  (N MOD 500 ) =0
         THEN BEGIN
              WRITELN ('    ',N:5, '    ' ,(K*H*(C-B)/N):19:8);
              END; (* if *)
     END; (* for *)
END. (* simulation *)


no.of trials N     simulated area   A

    500              0.76800001
   1000              0.76899999
   1500              0.76933336
   2000              0.78100002
   2500              0.78560001
   3000              0.78399998
```

Figure 1.4   Pascal program for computer simulation.

$$= \tfrac{1}{2}[\theta + \tfrac{1}{2}\sin(2\theta)]_{x=0}^{x=1}$$
$$= \tfrac{1}{2}[\theta + \sin\theta\cos\theta]_{x=0}^{x=1}$$
$$= \tfrac{1}{2}[\sin^{-1}x + x\sqrt{1-x^2}]_{x=0}^{x=1}$$
$$= \tfrac{1}{2}[\Pi/2] = \frac{\Pi}{4} = 0.7853981$$

6

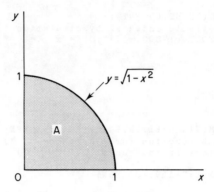

Figure 1.5 Monte Carlo evaluation of definite integral.

The solution by Monte Carlo simulation (Figures 1.3–1.5) is given by

$$A = \frac{K}{N} = 0.7856 \quad \text{when } N = 2500$$

The arrival and departure of customers, the type and number of items bought, the check-out time, and the number of check-outs open at a particular point in time in a supermarket are inherently stochastic in character. The analysis of such systems by building a stochastic model is an example of simulation.

It should be clearly understood that the solution of several problems by conventional methods is difficult, and here Monte Carlo methods are useful in finding approximate solutions fairly easily. This approach was particularly popular in the 1940s when the computing power was limited and the methods of numerical analysis were less developed.

1.4 Nature of computer modelling and simulation

A model is a simplified representation of a system, and simulation (Pritsker, 1979; Gordon, 1978) is the process of imitating (appearance, effect) important aspects of the behaviour of the system (or plans or policies) in real time, compressed time, or expanded time by constructing and experimenting with the model of the system. A model adapted for simulation on a computer (i.e. mathematical/logical relations and operational rules built into the computer program) is known as a computer simulation model or simply simulation model.

Simulation is similar to the laboratory experiments conducted by physical scientists to gain insight into the existing theories or to develop and validate new theories. Studying the behaviour of the system by this indirect method — by modelling and simulation — becomes a necessity in several situations where we have either no other alternatives (e.g. observation, analysis, experimentation, non-destructive testing, etc., not possible) or the alternatives available are not efficient. For example, the provision of traffic lights at a complex road junction is not a trivial matter. There is no simple analytical method for finding the best traffic signalling policy which will ensure smooth traffic flow through the junction. The modelling and simulation approach can help us to experiment with different policies on a computer and identify the best strategy for that particular junction without using the general public as guinea pigs. Computer modelling and simulation is the only way of evaluating various designs of a new city or a new computer which is still on the drawing board. Very often solvable analytic models are of no use for practical applications because some of the conditions assumed (e.g. queuing systems) in the derivation of the analytic model do not hold in the real world. Here simulation can be used to suggest aproximate model and determine the validity of the analytic model (Walker *et al.*, 1978).

1.4.1 Continuous versus discrete approach

We see around us two distinct types of systems—*continuous systems* where variables (attributes of system elements or entities) undergo smooth changes (e.g. electric current) and *discrete systems* where changes in variables take place instantaneously in discrete steps (e.g. number of customers in a bank). There are two basic approaches (or perceptions of the real system) in simulation—the continuous approach and the discrete approach. In the discrete approach we use a discrete model of the discrete system or the discrete approximation (e.g. digital computer representation of a picture) of a continuous system, and in continuous approach we use a continuous model of the continuous system or the continuous approximation (e.g. exponential population growth models) of a discrete system. The accuracy, size, range, and possible levels of aggregation of the variables involved, solution techniques, ease of solution, and the period of study are some of the factors that will influence the choice of a particular approach. The techniques used for simulating continuous systems are entirely different from those used for simulating discrete systems.

The continuous approach. The continuous simulation models are generally described by deterministic differential or algebraic equations. Earlier applications of computer simulation were in engineering by using analogue computers to study continuous systems. Analogue computers are still being used for the simulation of systems in specialized areas. However, digital computers can be programmed to mimic analogue machines, and because of their (digital computers;) accuracy, reliability, and flexibility, they have become an attractive alternative. Consequently several languages have been developed for continuous system simulation. The digital computer simulation of continuous systems boils down to the generation of one or more numerical solutions which satisfy the differential equations defining the model for given initial conditions using some standard step-by-step method.

The discrete approach. Digital computer models of physical systems are basically discrete approximations, and here continuous changes in system variables are represented by a series of discrete events which can be specified and programmed in great detail. The discrete system simulation models generally tend to be both stochastic and dynamic in nature. Here, simulation consists of the observation and analysis of the results obtained by generating random events at different points in time in a digital computer model of the system.

1.4.2 Computer modelling and simulation process

The theoretical and practical contributions over the past several years have resulted in the evolution of a methodology which, even though imperfect, has put computer modelling and simulation on a scientific footing. Problem-solving by modelling and simulation is an iterative process as depicted in Figure 1.6. Systems analysis; formulation of hypotheses; formulation of mathematical/logical models; identification of solution strategy; numerical solution of equations; simplification and validation of models; computer adaptation of models; computer programming; organization of computer runs; documentation of all the details; and collection, analysis, and interpretation of results are part and parcel of modelling and simulation process. The reformulation of the model and subsequent validation and interpretation of results are repeated until the simulation results are satisfactory for the specified application.

Unlike mathematical models, logical relations of the form 'if $A=B$ and $C=D$ then $E=F$' and statistical data from direct observations as well as data derived from probability distributions can be easily embedded into computer simulation models. The adaptation of the model for computer simulation (Innis and Rexstad, 1983) may require approximation and discretization of the model and all the mathematical/logical relationships must be expressed as a series of explicit computational steps.

One of main aims of systems study is to establish optimum parameters for the design, construction, and operation of systems. Simulation models cannot identify optimum solutions; they can only compare several alternative solutions. Oversimplification of simulation models may lead to loss of accuracy and generality while too many built in details may make the model more complex than the real system itself. In general, simulation is expensive and requires far more detailed input than analytic models. Minor structural changes in models (e.g. linear versus nonlinear) may call for an entirely different approach for solution by analytic methods, whereas the overall simulation strategy remains the same.

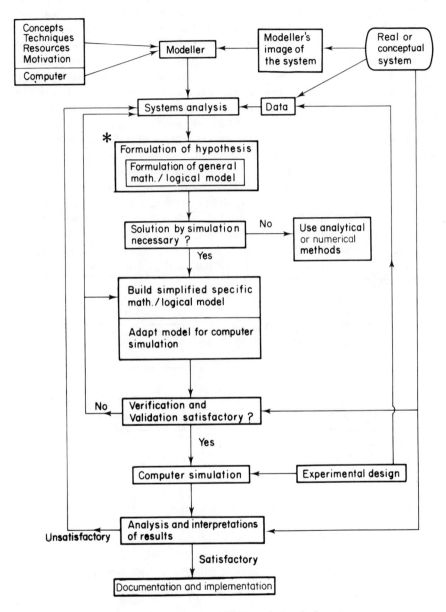

Figure 1.6 Computer modelling and simulation process.

* Starting from the outer box activities, proceed inwards and several local iterations may be necessary before a usable model is evolved.

Figure 1.6 is an aggregation of both the computer modelling and the computer simulation processes. Here, the term *validation* is concerned about proving that the model is an adequate representation of reality, whereas the term *verification* involves checking the design consistency (accuracy and correctness of modelling and solution methodologies, algorithms, numerical solutions, computer programs, etc.) of the model. The real system is never completely known and the model is never an exact representation of the real system. Therefore, validation can only be approached, but never achieved. The simplified specific model, as well as the simulation model, are subjected to verification tests followed by validation tests. For example, consider the situation when the maximum supportable number of users on the local computer have already logged on to the system at time t. A procedure to process the arrival and departure of customers (users) in a program which simulates the operation of the computing system can be implemented in two ways (Figure 1.7). If an arrival and a departure take place simultaneously at time t, then the procedure in Figure 1.7a will allow Log-in by the new customer, whereas the procedure in Figure 1.7b will block Log-in by the new customer. Such errors should be detected and eliminated during the verification stage.

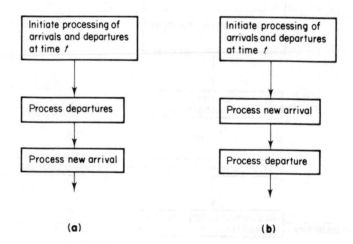

(a)   (b)

Figure 1.7 Two different ways of handling arrivals and departures.

The comparison of model output with the actual observations and/or theoretical predictions is an essential step in the validation of simulation models and results. Validation (Greig, 1979; Shannon, 1977; Van Horn, 1971) is difficult and still remains one of the least developed areas in system simulation. A model has no value until it is judged valid, except perhaps that it enhances our understanding of the system. Simple agreement between simulation results and real-world observations does not necessarily imply that the simulation model is an acceptable representation of reality, and one must be critical and very careful in drawing conclusions. Neither the computer nor the model can replace human judgement and experience, which play a significant role in determining the validity and usefulness of simulation models for practical applications.

The experimental nature of simulation should not be underestimated. Like any laboratory experiment, simulations must be designed and executed systematically so as to ensure accuracy and economy. The order in which simulation experiments are conducted, the number of replications and the accuracy of results, are some of the important points to be considered. The design of experiments, analysis and interpretation of results, and the assessment of credibility and acceptability of simulation studies (Ören, 1981) generally require a good knowledge of probability and statistics and this has, to some extent, inhibited the growth of simulation studies.

The discrete system simulation programs are usually written in general-purpose languages like Fortran, Pascal, Basic and Ada, or in high-level simulation languages (SCS, 1985) such as GPSS, SIMSCRIPT, SIMULA, GASP–IV, SLAM, etc. CSSL–III, CSSL–IV, ACSL, CSMP, and DYNAMO are some of the languages used for continuous system simulation. The development of software aids (for model description, analysis, and presentation) for simulation, the availability of cheap computing power, and colour graphics have eased the burden of programming simulation problems and hence the widespread usage of simulation for problem-solving in several disciplines.

1.4.3 The impact of microprocessors and computer graphics

The development of inexpensive microprocessors with graphics and software has added a new dimension to the practice of modelling and simulation. Micros are usually operated as *single-user* systems rather than being *time-shared*. The speed and memory size are not serious constraints today, and hardware prices are falling. A conference on 'Modelling and Simulation on Microprocessors', organized by the Society for Computer Simulation (SCS) has become an annual feature, and this shows the growing interest in the field. Several microprocessor-based models have been implemented (Ellison et al., 1982; Miller, 1982; Cutlip and Shacham, 1985), and this trend is likely to continue.

Discrete system simulation languages such as SIMSCRIPT (CACI), GPSS (Minuteman Software; Cox and Cox, 1985), SIMAN (System Modeling Corp.), SLAM (Pritsker and Associates), and continuous system simulation languages such as ACSL/PC (Rodrigues, 1985), ISIM (Crosbie et al., 1985), etc. are already available on personal computers. A catalogue of micro, mini, and mainframe simulation software can be found in SCS, 1985. It is generally accepted that humans can much more easily assimilate complex information from pictorial images. Undoubtedly, colour graphics and animation can be of great value in understanding the dynamics of system behaviour. SimAnimation and CINEMA provide interactive colour graphics and animation facilities to enhance SIMSCRIPT and SIMAN simulation models, respectively.

The use of analogue computers (Havrenak, 1983) for the simulation of continuous and hybrid (mixture of continuous and discrete) systems is also likely to be revived as a result of these developments.

1.5 When to use simulation

Simulation is a slow, iterative, experimental problem-solving technique. Sometimes it is referred to as the method of last resort. One should contemplate problem-solving by simulation only when,

(a) The real system does not exist and it is expensive, time-consuming, hazardous, or impossible to build and experiment with prototypes (new design of a computer, solar system, nuclear reactor).
(b) Experimentation with the real system is expensive, dangerous, or likely to cause serious disruptions (transport systems, nuclear reactor, manufacturing system).
(c) There is a need to study the past, present, or future behaviour of the system in real time, expanded time or compressed time (real-time control systems, slow-motion studies, population growth, side-effects of new drugs).
(d) Mathematical modelling of system is impossible (oil exploration, meteorology, world economy, international conflicts, computer networks).
(e) Mathematical models have no simple and practical analytical or numerical solutions (nonlinear differential equations, stochastic problems).
(f) Satisfactory validation of simulation models and results is possible.
(g) Expected accuracy (results cannot be better than input data) of simulation results is consistent with the requirements of the particular problem (the accuracy of radiation dosage for treating cancer patients is critical compared to the accuracy of forecasts on world tiger populations).

1.6 Limitations of simulation
(a) Neither a science nor an art, but a combination of both.
(b) Method of last resort.
(c) Iterative, experimental problem-solving technique.
(d) Expensive in terms of manpower and computer time.
(e) Generally yields suboptimum solutions.
(f) Validation difficult.
(g) Collection, analysis, and interpretation of results require a good knowledge of probability and statistics.

(h) Results can be easily misinterpreted and difficult to trace sources of errors.

(i) Difficult to convince others.

1.7 The organization of this book

The ordering of chapters in the book is based upon our experience in teaching both undergraduate and postgraduate students in computer science, engineering, management science, and economics at Trinity College, Dublin. However, the background of students and the style and preferences of the individual lecturers may demand a different approach in the presentation of various topics, and we are confident that the built-in flexibility will allow the lecturers to adapt this book for their own needs.

In this chapter we have given a general introduction and overview of computer modelling and simulation, its strengths and weaknesses, and a brief outline of various topics covered in the book. An understanding of the fundamental systems concepts and modelling methodology is essential for practical multidisciplinary applications of modelling and simulation. Chapters 2 and 3 are designed to meet this need. Validation of simulation models and results is a difficult, but essential, operation. Chapter 4 is devoted to the discussion of both philosophical and practical aspects of model validation and verification procedures, and the student is well prepared to face the problems in real-world situations. The discrete systems simulation depends heavily on statistical techniques which form the subject matter of Chapter 5. The generation of random events is at the centre of every discrete system simulation package and one may be forced to write routines for random number generation when standard library routines are not available on new mainframes or micros with different word-lengths. The generation and testing of pseudo-random numbers are explained in Chapter 6. Various approaches to the study of discrete systems and, in particular, the simulation of discrete systems including various simulation concepts, strategies, and languages for computer implementation are introduced in Chapter 7. The two popular discrete system simulation languages, GPSS and SIMSCRIPT, and their use in solving practical problems, are discussed in Chapters 8 and 9. Simulation is an experimental problem-solving technique and extreme care must be taken in the design of simulation experiments and in the collection, statistical analysis, and interpretation of simulation data. Several aspects of practical experimentation with the simulation models are dealt with in Chapter 10. The principle of analogue computing, the evolution of digital analogue and direct digital simulation languages for the simulation of continuous systems, and several examples to illustrate the application of CSMP are presented in Chapter 11. The concluding Chapter 12 is on the applications and trends in simulation, including the role of desktop computers, supercomputers, artificial intelligence, and expert systems.

1.8 Summary

The fundamental concepts of computer modelling and simulation of systems are presented. Simulation is the process of imitating the behaviour of the real system by constructing and experimenting with a model which is only a simplified representation of the system. The computer is a powerful tool and partner in problem-solving through modelling and simulation which is preferable only when analytical, numerical, or physical methods break down, or impractical or inefficient. Simulation method of problem-solving was revived during World War II. Two basic approaches, continuous and discrete, are used in simulation. Validation of models and results should be taken seriously at all stages of modelling and simulation, which is an iterative process. Like physical experiments, simulation experiments should be planned and executed in a scientific way so as to ensure accuracy and economy. There is no substitute for human judgement and experience in drawing conclusions. The availability of high-level simulation languages on micro, mini, and mainframe computers (SCS, 1985) has popularized the multidisciplinary applications of simulation. A brief outline of various chapters in the book is given in Section 1.7.

1.9 Exercises

1. Write a critical essay on the nature, applications, and limitations of simulations.
2. (a) Distinguish between simulation (discrete) and Monte Carlo simulation.
   (b) Give examples to illustrate the use of simulation and Monte Carlo simulation for problem-solving.
3. (a) Identify some of the techniques usually employed in problem-solving.
   (b) Can you think of some real-life problems which can be and cannot be solved by analytical/numerical methods.
4. Give example of
   (a) Simple systems and their models from physics, biology, engineering, economics, management science, and social sciences. Can you generalize various steps involved in the derivation of these models into a modelling methodology?
   (b) Systems which can be studied by physical experimentation (i.e. using real system or prototypes).
   (c) Systems which cannot be studied by physical experimentation.
5. (a) Write a Pascal or Fortran program to compute the area bounded by $y=f(x)$, the x axis, and the vertical lines at $x=b$ and $x=c$ by Monte Carlo method, when
   (i) $f(x) = e^{-x}$
   (ii) $f(x) = x^2$

(iii) $f(x) = \dfrac{1}{1+x^2}$

(iv) $f(x) = \dfrac{x}{1+x^2}$

Print the computed area for $N=1000$, 2000, . . . , $10{,}000$; where N is the total number of pairs of random numbers generated.

(b) If you are familiar with computer graphics, display the area bounded by $y=f(x)$ as well as all the points generated during Monte Carlo simulation, on the graphics screen.

(c) Compute the area analytically by evaluating the definite integrals and compare the results. How do you explain the errors in simulated results?

References

CACI (1986). *PC–SIMSCRIPT II.5 and SimAnimation, Users manual*. CACI, 12011 San Vicente Blvd., Los Angeles, CA 90049.

Cox, S., and Cox, A. J. (1985). GPSS/PC(tm): a user oriented simulation system. In *Modelling and Simulation on Microcomputers* (ed. R. G. Lavery). SCS Conference, San Diego, CA, pp. 48–50.

Crosbie, Hay & Associates (1985). 'ISIM'. In catalog of simulation software, *Simulation*, **45**(4), 196–209.

Cutlip, M. B., and Shacham, M. (1985). 'A microcomputer simulation package for small scale systems'. In *Modeling and Simulation on Microcomputers* (ed. R. G. Lavery), SCS Conference, San Diego, pp. 76–92.

Ellison, D., Herschdorfer, I., and Wilson, J. H. (1982). 'Interactive simulation on a microcomputer', *Simulation*, **38**(5), 161–175.

Forrester, J. W. (1961). *Industrial Dynamics*. John Wiley, New York.

Gordon, G. (1978). *Systems Simulation*. Prentice Hall, Englewood Cliffs, NJ.

Greig, I. D. (1979). 'Validation, statistical testing and decision to model', *Simulation*, **33**(2), 55–60.

Hammersley, J. M., and Handscomb, D. C. (1964). *Monte Carlo Methods*. Methuen, London.

Havrenak, W. A. (1983). 'Simulation in the 80s', *Proc. 1983 Summer Computer Simulation Conference*, vol. 1. Vancouver, Canada.

Innis, G., and Rexstad, E. (1983). 'Simulation model simplification techniques', *Simulation*, **41**(1), 7–15.

Miller, R. R. (1982). 'Simulation and graphics on microcomputer', *Simulation*, **38**(6), 215–220.

Minuteman Software (1985). *GPSS/PC Users Manual*. Minuteman Software, PO Box 171, Stow, MA 01775, USA.

Ören, T. I. (1974) 'A bibliography of bibliographies on modelling, simulation and gaming', *Simulation*, **23**(3), 90–95 and **23**(4), 115–116.

Ören, T. I. (1976) *Annotated Bibliography of Simulation*. Simulation Council, Inc., La Jolla, CA.

Ören, T. I. (1981). 'Concepts and criteria to assess acceptability of simulation studies: a framework of reference', *CACM*, **24**(4), 180–189.

Pritsker, A. A. B. (1979). 'Compilations of definitions of simulation', *Simulation*, **33**(2), 61–63.

Pritsker & Associates (1985). *SLAM II for the PC*, Pritsker & Associates, Inc., PO Box 2413, W. Lafayette, IN 47906.

Rodrigues, J. (1985). 'ACSL/PC' In catalog of simulation software, *Simulation*, **45**(4), 196–209.

SCS—Society for Computer Simulation (1985). 'Catalogue of simulation software', *Simulation*, **45**(4), 196–209.

Shannon, R. E. (1977). 'Simulation modelling and methodology', *Simuletter*, **8**(3), 33–38.

Shreider, Y. A. (1966). *Monte Carlo Methods*. Pergamon Press, London.

System Modeling Corp. (1985). *SIMAN and CINEMA Users Manual*. System Modeling Corp., Calder Sq., PO Box 10074, State College, PA 16805.

Tocher, K. D. (1963). *The Art of Simulation*. English Universities Press, London.

Van Horn, R. L. (1971). 'Validation of simulation results', *Manag. Sci.*, **17**(5), 247–258.

Walker, W. E., Ignall, E. J., and Kolesar, P. (1978). 'Using simulation to develop and validate analytic models: some case studies', *Operations Res.*, **26**(2), 237–253.

Zeigler, B. P. (1979). 'Modelling and simulation methodology: state of the art and promising directions'. In *Simulation of Systems* (ed. L. Dekker). North Holland, Amsterdam.

2

Systems

2.1 Introduction

The word *system* is no longer a privileged word accessible only to the exclusive society of academics, philosophers, and professionals. It has become a common word used by all sections of the society at work and at home. Evidently the meaning (Figure 2.1) of this word is generally understood by everybody, even though the theoretical and philosophical interpretations are likely to be unclear to many of them.

The revolutionary advances in modern communication and computing methods speeded up the interaction between seemingly different branches of studies as well as various sections of the society. Today a human being is considered to be merely a piece of a complex jigsaw puzzle which makes up the entire universe. The failure of conventional problem-solving methods in dealing with the highly interactive multidisciplinary problems of today gave momentum to systems thinking, and cleared the way for the development of new tools and techniques.

2.2 Systems concept

A system can be defined as a set or assemblage of entities (elements or components) interrelated to each other and to the whole so as to achieve a common goal.

The emphasis is on the organization of components that act together, and not on the individual elements. One of the most familiar examples is the

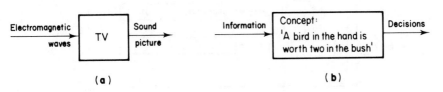

Figure 2.1 (a) Physical system; (b) conceptual system.

18

university system (Figure 2.2) where various departments are dependent on each other for service teaching, use of laboratories, and other joint activities and the individual departments are linked to the whole university system through central facilities and administration. The performance of individual departments is bound to influence the performance of some other departments as well as the overall performance of the entire university system. But one cannot draw general conclusions about the university system by looking at the individual departments in isolation, and the production of graduates is the result of combined and coordinated action of several departments together. Outsiders attending a public lecture or a rugby match in the university do not qualify to be part of the university system.

Interrelationship or interdependence is the *key word* in the above definition of *systems*, and the importance of this concept was really understood only during World War II. The effects of inflation which followed the dramatic increase in oil prices in the 1970s highlighted the ever-increasing economic interdependence of nations which constitute the world system. Symbolic systems (computer languages, mathematics), economic systems, engineering systems, computing systems, political systems, trade union systems, business systems, social systems, biological systems, and industrial systems are examples of some of the areas where systems concepts are widely used.

The interactions between various system elements are so complex that it may not be possible to predict the outcome of an action by looking at the behaviour of the subsystems in isolation. In other words, even though the system is *structurally divisible, functionally it is indivisible*, and this implies that the characteristics of the system will be lost if it is split into subsystems. Individually, the bricks in a wall are relatively weak, but a combined orderly arrangement of the bricks in the wall gives it its load-bearing characteristics. Hydrogen and oxygen molecules do not display the properties of water. The

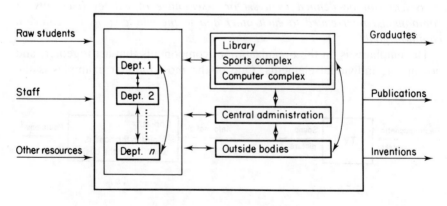

Figure 2.2   University system.

success or failure in a war depends not merely on the relative strength of the land, sea, and air forces but also on the well-coordinated deployment of all these forces together. There exists interaction as well as conflicts between various subsystems, and hence the problem must be analysed as a whole integrated system.

2.3 Systems approach to problem-solving

The problems of this century cut across several branches of study and cannot be compartmentalized into physics, chemistry, medicine, engineering, economics, mathematics, or psychology. The conventional analytical methods are not powerful enough to tackle the present-day multidisciplinary problems, and this accounts for the rise of systems theory (Lilienfeld, 1978) and the emergence of computer science, numerical analysis, simulation, operations research, control engineering, ergonomics, cybernetics, robotics, biomedical engineering, and industrial engineering.

In the nonsystems approach to studying multivariable systems, we hold some of the variables steady and then observe the changes in the remaining variables (Figure 2.3a), and here meaningful results can be expected only by carrying out a large number of experiments and subsequent analysis of massive data. In the systems approach, shown in Figure 2.3b, all variables are allowed to vary freely, thereby creating a real-world situation. The contrast between the two approaches is significant; one relies on an artificial roundabout way of looking at a problem while the other is a direct, natural, and logical procedure.

The representation of a system need not necessarily be *unique* and hence the need for systematic methods for the evaluation and grading of different designs. The criteria for the selection of a particular design depend on several factors, including the purpose for which the system is built. A cylinder with

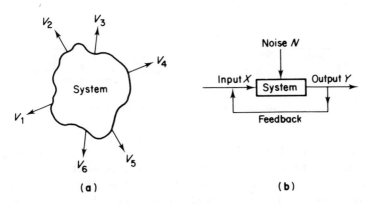

(a)   (b)

Figure 2.3   Multivariable system.

fixed volume can be constructed for different values of r and h in $\pi r^2 h$. But how do we select the best design? For this we need a precise definition of constraints as well as performance criteria; for example, the height must be less than a constant h and the surface area minimum. To some, the purpose of an education system is for the advancement of learning and fulfilment of social and cultural desires of the individual, and for others it is to meet the manpower (womanpower) requirements of the economy. Profit may be the goal of a private company, while employment and social satisfaction are likely to be the overriding criteria used in the selection of state-sponsored industries. The cost versus benefit, reliability, controllability, flexibility, mobility, maintainability, and operating costs are some other points to be considered in the selection of optimum systems.

If the behaviour of the system is clearly understood, then it is comparatively easy to predict or measure the system output for specified input (Figure 2.4). It is worth mentioning here that there are several complex systems (e.g. business, politics, medicine) whose outward behaviour (input and output) is known and yet the process which produces such behaviour is not clearly understood. That is, *prediction without explanation*.

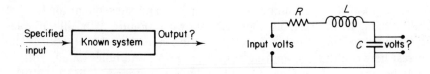

Figure 2.4   Unknown system output.

Sometimes the input to the system is known and the problem is to design a system which produces a desired output (Figure 2.5). For example, the provision of facilities in a bank (or computer centre) to cater for known arrival pattern of customers so that the waiting time (response time) will not exceed 5 minutes.

Figure 2.5   Unknown system structure.

A third situation (Figure 2.6) is where one would like to compute the input which will produce a desired output. The production of graduates according to a specified schedule by controlling the input is an example.

In modern times, mathematical models play a vital role in systems analysis. Numeric, analytic, and simulation methods are powerful tools in the study

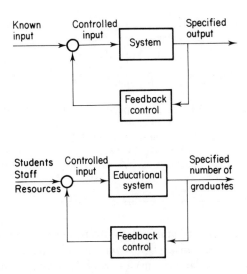

Figure 2.6   Unknown system input.

of models, and these aspects are dealt with in the following chapters. The conventional methods of systems analysis and evaluation by constructing prototypes or by direct experimentation are rapidly becoming a thing of the past.

2.4   Characteristics of systems

A *system* is composed of one or more *subsystems*, and subsystems consist of one or more sub-subsystems, and so on. We come across several systems in our daily life such as tax system, postal system, hospital system, electrical, gas, and water distribution systems. The body, engine, electrical circuits, hydraulics, steering, seating, and suspension are examples of subsystems of an automobile. Systems have several characteristics in common. *Entities*, *attributes* (parameters and variables), *interrelationships* and *activities* are associated with Systems. The CPU, I/O, memory, people, money, and building are entities of a computing system, while the number of students, number of staff, and type of courses are some of the attributes of the university entity which is a part of the national educational system. Any process that changes the attributes of an entity is called an *activity*. The arrival and departure of customers and getting a shopping basket are activities which change the attributes of '*people*' and '*basket*' entities in a supermarket. Some of the entities and attributes of a computing system are shown in Table 2.1.

The interrelationships between entities, and between entities and the system, are expressed in the form of parameters and variables. The variables

Table 2.1 Entities and attributes of computing system.

System	Entity	Attributes	Activity
Computer	Compiler	Type, cost, speed, capability, usage	Compilation
	Hardware	Type, cost, speed, capacity, usage	Hardware faults
	Job	Class, number, time, type	Execution
	Operator	Skills, salary, sex, age, busy period	Interactions wtih computer
	I/O	Tape, disc, speed, cost, usage	I/O operations

may be *independent* (free to manipulate) or *dependent*, *controllable* or *uncontrollable* (rain, sunrise, sunset) and *continuous* or *discrete*. Systems can be classified as *natural* (solar system) or *artificial* (computing system), *stable* (returns to equilibrium after a disturbance) or *unstable*, *dynamic* or *static*, *deterministic* or *stochastic*, *adaptive* (responds to environmental changes) or *nonadaptive* and *linear* or *nonlinear*. Another classification is based upon whether the system is *repeatable*, *recurrent* (repeats periodically) or *unique*.

2.5 The state of a system

The purpose of systems study is to learn, to design, to change, to preserve, and if possible control the behaviour of the systems. Some of the variables describing the behaviour of the system may not be accessible (Noton, 1972) for observation and measurement (see Figure 2.7) and such variables are to be estimated. For example, the intelligence and foresight are two of the variables, associated with the brain, which are not amenable to observation and measurement.

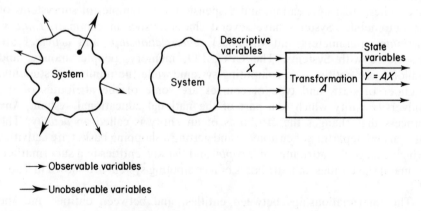

→ Observable variables

⇒ Unobservable variables

Figure 2.7 Descriptive and state variables.

The absolute minimum description of entities, attributes, and activities at a particular point in time necessary for predicting the future behaviour of the system define the *state of the system* and the corresponding variables are called *state variables*. The state variables relate the past to the future via the present. The state of the system may change as a result of the activities internal to the system (*endogenous activities*) or due to activities external to the system (*exogenous activities*). As shown in Figure 2.7, the subset of system descriptive variables which define completely the future behaviour of the system constitute (Zeigler, 1976) a state variable set. The possible permutations and combinations of state variables increase sharply as the number and domain of these variables increase. Each element of a binary system has only two states, while those of a decimal system have ten states. In other words, a small rise in the number of components or states could result in a substantial increase in the complexity of the system. Some state variables undergo changes while others remain constant over a long period of time. The resistance, capacitance, inductance, shape, colour, size, temperature, weight, and current flow describe the state of an electrical system and the values of some of the associated state variables remain constant. The type and number of jobs waiting for I/O, elapsed times, jobs waiting for core memory, jobs in progress, the disposition of operators, jobs waiting in the queue, etc., describe the state of a computer system.

The transition probabilities of the system from one state to another in response to a specified activity determine the stochastic or deterministic nature of the system. In Figure 2.8 the probability of the system in state A changing to state B is 100%, which is the property of *deterministic systems*. For *stochastic systems* the probability p of changing state from C to D or E is less than 100%, as shown in Figure 2.9. The atmospheric turbulence, the waves in the sea, the job mix in a computer, and the customers in a supermarket are elements which make those systems stochastic, while an automated production system—and electricity, gas, and water distribution systems—are examples of deterministic systems.

The state of the system describes the dynamic and static properties as well. In Figure 2.10 the system in state A moves to states B, C, D and finally stabilizes in state D which is the *static steady state* of the system. The *dynamic steady state* $A{\rightarrow}B{\rightarrow}C{\rightarrow}D{\rightarrow}A$ of the system is illustrated in Figure 2.11.

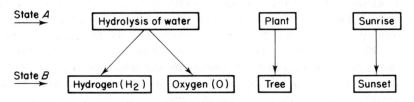

Figure 2.8   Deterministic systems.

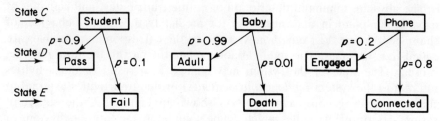

Figure 2.9   Stochastic systems.

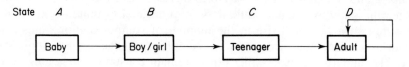

Figure 2.10   Static steady state.

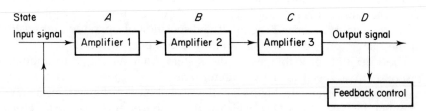

Figure 2.11   Dynamic steady state.

In mathematical terms, differential or difference equations generally characterize the dynamic states of the system, while algebraic equations describe non-dynamic aspects.

2.6   Systems boundary and environment

Systems operate in an environment, and the changes in the environment are likely to affect the behaviour of the systems. Therefore it is essential to clearly identify the *systems boundary* and the *systems environment* which is a subset of the total environment. The systems boundary encloses all the components and their interrelationships which describe the problem under study. Those elements of the environment which lie outside the systems boundary (may be conceptual or physical) and capable of exerting significant influence on the system's behaviour, but cannot be controlled from within the system, constitute the systems environment. It should be noted that the same entity may belong to several systems at the same time. A human being is basically a member of a family, a political party, a trade union, a race, a religion, and a social class. Similarly, IBM and DEC are two of the firms belonging to the three sets defined by: American companies, multinational companies, and computer companies.

In Figure 2.12, elements of E have some influence on the behaviour of S, the elements of S have no influence on E and the elements of W have no influence on S. If the set E is empty (i.e. no interaction between S and the outside world) then S is said to be a *closed system* and the system's behaviour is purely due to internal interactions (endogenous activities) of its sub-systems. In practice. E is unlikely to be empty and almost all systems we come across are *open systems* which interact with the outside environment and the state changes are effected by both exogenous and endogenous activities. The identification of the boundaries between the subsets S, E, and W is a delicate operation and one must take extra care to retain all the significant features of these sets but at the same time restrict their size to manageable proportions.

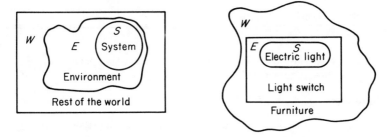

Figure 2.12   System and system environment.

2.7   Different views of systems

We are all familiar with the old fable of the elephant and the blind men who all had different perceptions about the anatomy of the elephant. Depending on the objectives, methods of study, and the expertise, different observers are likely to see the same object in different forms (Figure 2.13). A department is the whole system for the head of a university department, all the departments in a faculty form the whole system for the dean of a faculty, and all the faculties and central facilities together form the university system for the head of a university. The definitions of various system elements and their attributes vary considerably from analyst to analyst depending upon their interests, expertise, and motivation, and this may lead to different definitions of systems environment and systems boundary, as shown in Figure 2.14. In general the analyst's view of the system tends to be biased, and therefore it is essential that systems analysts should develop an aptitude for detecting this bias in system descriptions.

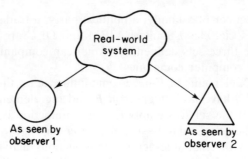

Figure 2.13   Different views of system.

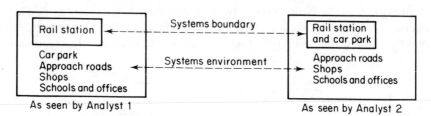

Figure 2.14   Non-unique definitions of a system.

2.8   Summary

Systems are composed of components which act together in an organized way. Properties of individual components may not reveal the overall characteristics of the total system. Systems may be structurally divisible but functionally indivisible. Representation of systems need not be unique. Entities, attributes, activities, and interrelationships are associated with all systems. The description of entities, attributes, and activities at a point in time describes the state of the system. The definition of system, systems boundary, and systems environment is a delicate but essential first step in a system's study. Different people are likely to look at the same system from different angles and one must be vigilant in detecting bias in a system's description. Systems approach is essential for solving modern multidisciplinary problems.

2.9   Exercises

1. Describe a system you are familiar with and identify entities, attributes, events, and activities.
2. Give examples of large-scale systems which cut across several disciplines and name some of the elements common to several systems. What decides whether an element is part of the system or not?
3. (a) What are state variables and how do they influence the complexity of the system?

    (b) Distinguish between state variables and systems variables (or descriptive variables).

      Note: read Noton, 1972; Zeigler, 1976.

4. Give an example for each of the following systems and point out system elements, systems boundary and systems environment:

    Man–machine system
    Traffic control system
    Biological system
    Ecosystem
    Engineering system
    Socioeconomic system
    Management system
    Political system

5. Describe the components of the following systems and identify systems boundary and systems environment:

    Motor car
    Domestic central heating unit
    Hospital
    Restaurant
    Human being

6. Write a philosophical essay on
    (a) systems view of man.
    (b) systems view of nature.

      Note: read Laszlo, 1972.

7. What are the general characteristics of systems? How do you classify them?

8. Write an essay on 'The rise of systems theory'.
   Note: read Lilienfeld, 1978.

9. 'A system may be structurally divisible, but functionally indivisible'. Discuss this concept in the context of a national or international system.

10. Write notes on
    (a) different views of systems.
    (b) non-unique representation of systems.

References

Laszlo, E. (1972). *The Systems View of the World*. Blackwell, Oxford.
Lilienfeld, R. (1978). *The Rise of Systems Theory*. John Wiley, New York.
Noton, M. (1972) *Modern Control Engineering*. Pergamon Press, Oxford.
Zeigler, B. P. (1976) *Theory of Modeling and Simulation*. John Wiley, New York.

Bibliography

Ackoff, R. L. (1972). *On Purposeful Systems*. Aldine-Atherton, Chicago, IL.
Basar, E. (1976). *Biophysical and Physiological Systems Analysis*. Addison-Wesley, New York.

28

Bayraktar, B. A. (1979). *Education in Systems Sciences, NATO Advance Study Report*. Taylor & Francis, London.
Emshoff, J. R. (1971). *Analysis of Behavioural Systems*. Macmillan, New York.
Forrester, J. W. (1976). *Principles of Systems*. Wright-Allen Press, Cambridge, MA.
Gordon, G. (1978). Systems Simulation. Prentice Hall, Englewood Cliffs, NJ.
Popper, K. R. (1972). *The Logic of Scientific Discovery*. Hutchinson, London.
Wiener, N. (1948). *Cybernetics: Control and Communication in the Animal and the Machine*. MIT Press, New York.

3

Models

3.1 Introduction

In Chapter 2, I mentioned that the representation of systems is not unique. Depending upon the object of the study, the same systems can be represented in a variety of ways giving different types and amounts of information. Clearly, some representations are more informative than others, but referring to Figure 3.1 one can confidently say that none of the representations give us the same pleasure as having a real TV set in our living room. Systems can be studied in many ways. The physical construction of the real system may be impossible, expensive, or time-consuming and experimentation with many of the systems so constructed could be dangerous and destructive. Some systems may not exist while others may not be available for experimentation. One would not wish to construct and experiment with a nuclear reactor for the purpose of simply gaining insight into its behaviour. It is not a practical proposition to experiment with existing systems like solar systems, economic systems, and human systems. In modern times the emphasis is on building models of systems (new or existing) and studying these models with the help of high-speed computers.

Modelling is an iterative process which derives its power from computational efficiency and feedback of results from the model to aid human judgement. Modern computers are about a billion times faster than human beings in computational work, and this quantitative change has brought about a qualitative change in human activities. The high-speed, high-capacity computer of today with real-time data processing capabilities (i.e. as events are actually taking place) has become a powerful tool and partner in the

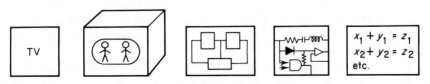

Figure 3.1   Representations of TV.

29

total modelling process. The computers act as hosts for models and they provide an environment in which models can be created, tested, and manipulated. They are basically an extension of our effective memory and the computer programs are the building blocks for modelling and simulation.

3.2 What is a model?

A model is a simplified representation of a system (or process or theory) intended to enhance our ability to understand, predict, and possibly control the behaviour of the system.

Understanding is necessary to change, to preserve, or just to know and explain the behaviour of the system. An understanding of the system may lead to prediction and control while the reverse need not be true. The aim of those involved in fundamental research is to understand the ultimate reality, while others including some modellers are quite satisfied with the prediction and control of the external behaviour of the system even if they cannot explain the underlying principles.

The term *model* may mean different things to different people. The clay models for children, fashion models for an advertising agency, *mathematical models* for control engineers, and *physical models* for architects are some examples. The model representation of a system may take different forms. It may be mental, physical, or symbolic. For example:

Mental:
personal decision-making process,
personal view of an object or an event,
personal view of a foreign country or ideology.

Physical:
model of a house,
model of a bridge,
wax model of a person.

Symbolic:
$H_2 + O \rightarrow$ water (hydrogen + oxygen $\rightarrow$ water)
$F = ma$ (force = mass $\times$ acceleration)
electric circuit diagram.

The quality and quantity of information content in the above models vary considerably, but they all have one major characteristic in common: they help us to evaluate the outcome of an action in a real-world situation without actually taking that action. That is, one can evaluate alternatives without actually conducting live experiments.

A model is only a representation of a system and not the system itself; models cannot have all the attributes of the real system; they are artificial and do not exist freely in nature; they tend to be abstract, general, and very often details are collapsed many to one. The road map is only a man-made model of the road networks of a region. An ordinary photograph is simply an analogue representation of a scene or an object and not the real thing itself. Surely one should not expect to receive picture and sound by fiddling with the circuit diagram of a television set.

3.3 Why study models?

Mental modelling is a basic human activity that simplifies planning and decision-making processes. Frequently we find solutions to problems by building mental models based upon experience, intuition, imagination, and judgement. Mental models of road map and traffic regulations guide us from one location to another, possibly along the shortest or fastest route. We use mental models to express personal opinions; to operate within the law of the land; to recognize each other; to develop attitudes towards others, and for strategic and tactical planning.

The pictures, the equations, and written descriptions of something in a book or a paper are in fact models of an event, activity, experience, experiment, observation, perception, or investigation. The clear and concise language of models enhances the power of communication, and one can easily convey developments in a field of study without actually revealing the surrounding circumstances. The CPM (critical path method) or PERT (program evaluation and review techniques) network gives at a glance the initiation and termination of various phases of a project and the implications of delays. A flowchart explains in a nutshell the logical sequence of execution of various segments in a computer program.

Models aid learning, design, prediction, and evaluation of alternatives quickly, cheaply, and harmlessly. The experiments with models often lead to generation of new hypotheses and formalization of knowledge about systems. With the help of mathematical models it is possible to determine optimal solutions which would not be obvious otherwise. *A bird in the hand is worth two in the bush* is a model of a concept which we all use in decision-making. The controlled experiment with the model of an oil rig in a water tank helps us to understand and predict its likely behaviour in the open sea under changing weather conditions, and alternative designs and control policies can be evaluated. Dangerous experiments with reactor systems, biological systems, and economic systems have now been replaced by experiments with their models. Studies on models of computers have led to improved design, maintenance, operation, and utilization of computing systems.

Models are useful in training personnel. Management games for training managers; aircraft/spacecraft mockups for training pilots/astronauts; and models of bridges, machines, reactors, and buildings used for teaching in the classroom are examples. Models facilitate concentration, stimulate human imagination, and they are aesthetically pleasing. We all use them in some form or the other to amuse ourselves.

Models are helpful in expressing ideas clearly. The formula $F = ma$ has only one interpretation, whereas statements like '*social and cultural societies*' can be interpreted as either '*social societies* and *cultural societies*' or '*societies* which are both *social* and *cultural* in character'.

3.4 Types of models

Models can be classified in many ways and one of the classifications is shown in Figure 3.2.

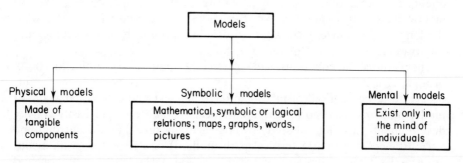

Figure 3.2 Types of models.

3.4.1 *Physical models*

Physical models are representations of physical systems like electrical, mechanical, fluid, and thermal systems and they are made of tangible components. These models are described by measurable variables such as voltages, current, temperature, heat, length, weight, pressure, flow, force, velocity, etc. The construction of physical models could be expensive, time-consuming, impractical, and even impossible. Physical models can be further subdivided into static and dynamic models (Figure 3.3).

Scale models:
wax statues, models of cars, bridges, aircraft, ships.

Imitation models:
puppets, dolls, shop window models, molecular structure, cartoons, geological or political divisions in a map, dummy used in car crash experiments.

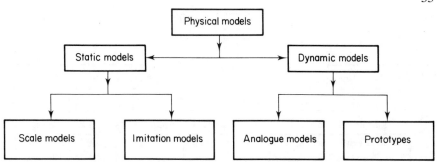

Figure 3.3 Physical models.

Analogue models:
LCR (inductance, capacitance, resistance) circuit to study car suspension system; mercury or alcohol to measure temperature; water flow to study traffic flow, blood flow, or money flow; rats and monkeys to test new medicines.

Prototypes:
LCR circuit to study electrical oscillations; mass, spring, and damper assembly to test car suspension system; prototypes of chemical reactors; experimental management information system; functional railway engine.

As the name implies, the variables associated with static models remain constant and those of dynamic models may undergo changes in time. The static scaled (up or down) models are non-operational replicas of the actual system, and the simplified imitations which look like the real system are called imitation or iconic models. Imitation models are not very accurate, but they are easily understood. Scale models are accurate to scale, difficult to build, and some of the features (e.g. stress, strain) may not be easily understood. In analogue modelling we use one type of physical model to represent another type of physical model. An LCR electrical circuit is often used to study the oscillatory characteristics of a car suspension system; but it must be clearly understood that the electrical analogue does not reveal anything about the chemical, structural, or other properties of the car suspension system. The prototypes are, of course, the functional replica of the real system.

3.4.2 Symbolic models

Symbolic models are built easily and economically compared to physical models. A classification of symbolic models is shown in Figures 3.4 and 3.5. The mathematical models need further explanation as it is the most important

34

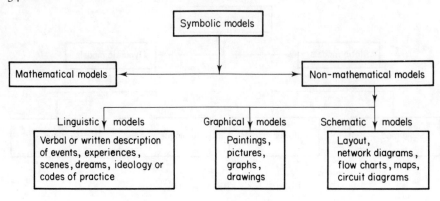

Figure 3.4 Symbolic models.

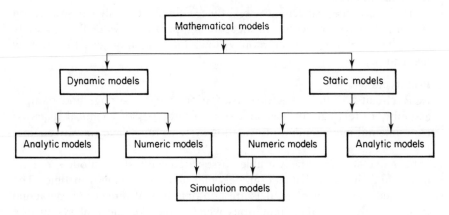

Figure 3.5 Mathematical models.

and widely used category of model. A mathematical model is a set of mathematical and logical relations between various system elements. A theory expressed in mathematical form is a mathematical model. Unquantifiable elements like attitudes, values, etc., cannot be included in mathematical models. The data derived from social and behavioural sciences tend to be *qualitative* rather than *quantitative*. Mathematical models expedite analysis; they are unambiguous and less expensive in evaluating alternatives. Some analytic models are mathematically intractable, and such models are expressed in terms of their approximate numerical equivalents which form the core of simulation models. The dynamic models are generally described by *differential* or *difference* equations, while *algebraic* equations characterize static mathematical models. The mathematical model of a simple car suspension system (see Figure 3.19) is given by

$$M\ddot{x} + Dx + Kx = F(t)$$

where M = mass
            D = damping factor
            K = stiffness of spring
            x = displacement
            F = applied force.

The solution of this differential equation displays (Figure 3.20) the operation of the system in time (i.e changes in the value of the variable x with respect to time) and this is the fundamental property of dynamic models. On the other hand, the solution ($x=5$; $y=6$) of the algebraic equations

$$3x + 4y = 39$$
$$6x + 5y = 60$$

which describe a static mathematical model, remains constant with respect to time. A simple *linear programming* problem (Dantzig, 1963), a company balance sheet, syntax of a language, library classification scheme, and biological taxonomies are examples of static models. The quadratic equation

$$ax^2 + bx + c = 0$$

has the solution

$$x = \frac{-b \pm \sqrt{b^2 - 4ac}}{2a}$$

The beauty of this *analytic solution* is that we have solved the whole class of problems once and for ever, and x can be easily computed for any combination of values of a, b, and c. The numerical approximation of analytic functions is illustrated by the following examples.

(a) Exponential function

$$y = e^x = 1 + x + \frac{x^2}{2!} + \frac{x^3}{3!} + \frac{x^4}{4!} + \ldots + \frac{x^k}{k!}$$

where k is finite and $0 \leqslant x < 1$

(b) Integration (trapezoidal rule: see Figure 3.6)

$$\int_a^b f(x)dx \approx \frac{h}{2}(y_0 + 2y_1 + 2y_2 + \ldots 2y_{n-1} + y_n)$$

where P_i denotes the point (x,y) and $h = (b-a)/n$.

3.4.3   Mental models

These are heuristic or intuitive models which exist only in our minds. They are fuzzy, imprecise, and difficult to communicate. Unlike animals, we are

36

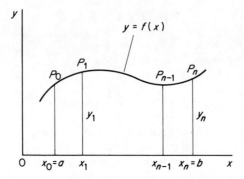

Figure 3.6 Trapezoidal rule.

good in accumulating experience and this stored experience serves as a mental model. The skill in painting or writing poetry or fiction, the ability to perform mental arithmetic, the ability to understand the operation of various loops in a computer program, and the process of decision-making in complex situations are examples of mental models in action.

3.4.4 Other models

A broader classification of models based upon the characteristics of the original system is also worth looking at. A model may be (Figure 3.7c) *continuous*, *discrete*, *hybrid*, *linear*, or *nonlinear* and *deterministic* (Figure 3.7a) or *stochastic* (Figure 3.7b). The variables describing continuous models undergo continuous change while those of discrete models take values only in discrete steps or jumps. In other words, the change of state in discrete systems takes place at discrete points in time separated by periods of inactivity. Models of chemical plants, steel mills, oil refineries, and electricity (gas, water) networks are continuous, whereas the models of teleprocessing networks connecting several computers, and models of supermarkets and telephone exchanges are discrete in nature. Many systems around us (e.g. manufacturing systems) are in fact hybrid (both continuous and discrete properties), but for simplicity we tend to treat them as either continuous or discrete depending upon their dominating characteristics. Hybrid (analogue plus digital) computers are sometimes used for solving hybrid problems.

Linear relationships exist between input and output of linear models, and nonlinear relationships bind the input and output of nonlinear models. The price versus quantity of petrol at a filling station and the applied weight versus extension of the spring of a balance are linearly related. The fare versus distance travelled (by air, land or sea) and length of attention span versus age of a person, are nonlinearly related. Deterministic models have predictable relationships between input and output variables, while stochastic

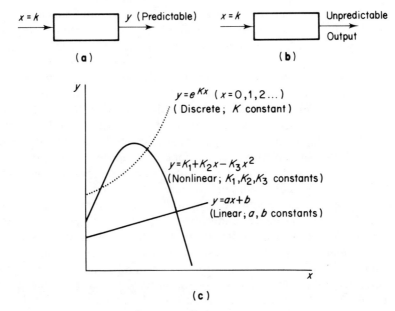

Figure 3.7 (a) Deterministic model; (b) stochastic model; (c) linear, nonlinear, continuous and discrete models.

systems do not have such reliable relationships. For the same input stimulus, the output of a stochastic system is unpredictable and the interaction between the variables in stochastic models is expressed in terms of statistical probabilities. The model of a radar system receiving signals corrupted by noise, and a model of several species of insects in a region are both stochastic. Modern electricity and gas supply networks can be considered to be deterministic systems.

Some models are amenable to a *black box* approach to analysis, and such models predict the system response without actually explaining the properties of individual system components. The output is expressed in terms of inputs and this approach is likely to be satisfactory only if the system is reasonably stable. The growth and shift in student population can be predicted by examining the trends. Similarly, one can confidently predict that an indoor plant will bend towards the window without knowing anything about botany. A black box approach gives answers to specific questions; it *predicts without explaining* or gaining insight into the internal structure of the system and therefore its applications are limited.

3.5 Modelling methodology

Here, methodology means a set of systematic procedures based upon knowledge accumulated over a number of years, for tackling a class of problems.

The modelling methodology is well developed and effective in those areas where mature theory is available. For example, the application of modelling methodology is much more successful in science and engineering than sociology and psychology (Ward, 1984) where the theory is comparatively weak.

Modelling is the process of establishing interrelationships between important entities of a system, and models are expressed in terms of goals, performance criteria, and constraints. For each modeller there exists a base model (i.e. modeller's view or image of the real system) from which a simplified (Neelamkavil, 1971; Wang and Sterman, 1985) specific model is built. By experimenting with this simplified model we hope to enhance our understanding of the base model as well as the real system characterized by the base model.

The first step in model-building is to state the problem *clearly*, *logically*, and *unambiguously*. There may be several ill-defined, complex, interacting, and possibly conflicting interrelationships between system elements; hence the need for formulating a modelling methodology setting out a series of well-defined logical steps. It is almost impossible to understand and isolate all the interrelationships in a real-world system, and one is forced to trade off reality, generality, and accuracy for simplicity. Therefore the models we build usually include only a *subset* of the variables and interrelationships of the original system. Obviously the ability to build models by selecting the *smallest subset* of variables which adequately describe the real system is a very important and highly desirable quality of a good modeller. The skill in modelling depends also on experience, expertise, intuition, judgement, foresight, and imagination.

Simplicity is an essential criterion of a good model. Very often there may not exist a one-to-one correspondence between system variables and model variables (e.g. automobiles to represent cars, buses, trucks, etc., in a traffic model) and details are collapsed many to one at different levels of abstraction (i.e. a lumped parameter model) depending upon the purpose for which the model is built. The accuracy of a human respiratory model is crucial if the results are to be used for practical implementation; on the other hand, minor errors due to flat-earth assumptions in a traffic network model will not make it unsuitable for practical use. Simple models are easier to build (less data and few variables), developed faster, easily understood, mathematically tractable, and very likely to be used for practical applications. Analytic models, once solved, give a family of solutions for various parameter values and these models can be easily grafted on to other models. The question of numerical models arises only if the problem cannot be formulated in analytical form, or if it is not possible to find analytical solutions at reasonable speed and cost.

Modelling is an interactive process. The translation of the base model into a specific model is generally accompanied by a transformation of qualitative information into quantitative data. A general view of the *modelling process* is shown in Figure 3.8, which also highlights the evolutionary nature of models from speculation, to hypothesis, to general models, and finally to a simplified specific model.

Computers are used at every stage of the modelling process including data collection, data reduction, systems analysis, experimental design, hypothesis testing, verification, and validation. Standard software packages are provided by most computer installations for optimization, matrix operations, solution of algebraic and differential equations (Spriet and Vansteenkiste, 1982) and statistical computations. Interactive computing facilities and colour graphics have made computer-aided modelling more effective, reliable, and accurate. The appeal for computer-aided modelling is further enhanced by the availability of cheap microprocessors.

Important stages in the development of models are illustrated through the following simple examples. It should be noted that the general philosophy behind the development of more complex models remains the same.

3.5.1 Example 1

Let us consider the problem of a farmer who owns 100 acres of land which is suitable only for growing cereals and sugar-beet, and the problem is to determine the best farming policy. That is, what to grow and how much to grow by using the available resources.

Referring to Figure 3.8, the modeller here is the farmer or his consultant who is conversant with the concepts and techniques used for studying problems of this type. A *concept* is a hypothesis or theory (e.g. *linear programming*) which has wide applications, and it is important that the users of concepts understand the underlying principles. A *technique* is a programmed concept or a set of operational rules (e.g. *simplex algorithm* for solving *linear programming* problem) which can be practised by a user without actually understanding the principles behind the concept. Meanings of concepts are sometimes obscured by techniques, and blind application of techniques without understanding the concepts is a recipe for eventual disaster.

Armed with concepts and techniques of optimization, and motivated by the desire to maximize return on investments, the consultant takes a close look at the real-world system defined by the farm and its surroundings.

(a) Systems analysis. First of all the problem must be restated clearly and accurately. Then, the system entities, their attributes (parameters and variables), the system's boundary and system's environment are isolated and recorded as in Table 3.1 and Figure 3.9. Relevant data are collected and analysed for general patterns, correlations, and other statistical properties by using graphs, histograms, and regression analysis. There are two possible approaches to analysis: if the system is not in existence one could use physical, chemical, and theoretical characteristics of the system; otherwise physical, chemical, theoretical, and historical data may be used. The analysis of systems which do not obey well-known physical laws (e.g. Kirchhoff's laws) is comparatively difficult and here statistical analysis (regression) should be helpful in deriving empirical relations. The modeller analyses the farm system very carefully and identifies potential candidates for selection as

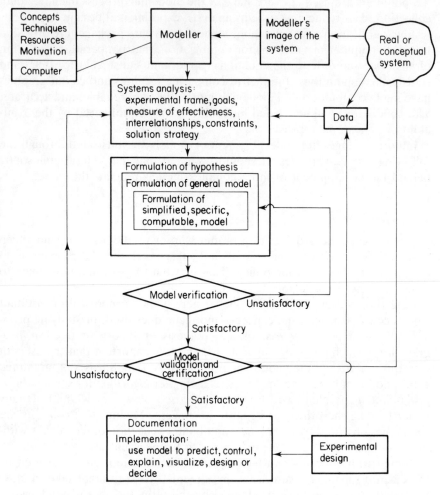

Figure 3.8 Modelling process.

Table 3.1 Farm system—entities and attributes.

Entities	Attributes
Acreage	No. of acres, costs, yields, profits, prices
Money	Amount, interest rate
Labour	Men, women, wages, productivity
Time	Days, starting date
Machines	Type, cost, speed, repair cost, resale value, flexibility
Fertilizer	Type, cost, composition

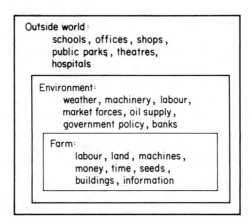

Figure 3.9 Farm and its environment.

variables, parameters, interrelationships, constraints, goals, measures of effectiveness, and methods of solutions. Possible candidates are:

Goals:
maximize profit this year; maximize profit over a number of years; maximize profit and good will; minimize costs; maximize land usage; maximize tax benefits and government subsidies.

Measures of effectiveness:
optimum of a cost or profit function expressed in terms of farm variables; maximum of a function which describes the utilization of land; optimum of a function which incorporates both tangible and intangible benefits expressed in terms of farm variables.

Interrelationships, constraints, and experimental frame:
important versus unimportant, continuous versus discrete, input versus output, controllable versus uncontrollable variables; static and dynamic relationships between variables and the derivation of associated constants; availability of men, money, machines, and time; restrictions on the usage of land, machines, and fertilizers; pricing mechanism; range of the variables and their probability distributions; integer versus noninteger solutions; period of study; limitations of data; assumptions.

Solution strategy:
methods for the collection and analysis of data and estimation of parameters; linear versus nonlinear model; computational methods and facilities to be used; generality, applicability, and flexibility of solutions; possible extensions.

The experimental frame sets out the limited conditions under which the system or its model is to be observed and experimented with, and how the resultant model should be tested, validated, and implemented. We use the terms *goals* and *objectives* synonymously even though there is a subtle difference in their meanings. The specification of a purpose converts a goal into an objective. For example, maximization of profit is a goal and maximization of profit from a particular section of a factory during the current year subject to constraints is an objective. A clear definition of goals or objectives which act as a frame of reference for decision-making by narrowing down a specific aspect of reality is crucial for the success of the modelling project. So, too, are the measures of effectiveness or performance criteria which provide a means of evaluating alternative solutions by measuring the convergence towards the goals. It is well worth examining several possible measures of effectiveness, their meaning, and computational feasibility before selecting a particular one.

If happiness or satisfaction of a community is defined as a goal, one can possibly use either (a) number of cars, number of four-bedroom houses, number of graduate students, annual income, number of social and cultural events, or (b) number of patients, number of prisoners, number of unemployed, and number of crimes committed, as measures of effectiveness. The increase in profits from a factory can be measured in terms of the reduction in costs or increase in the volume of sales. Similarly, the efficiency of a computer centre may be measured in terms of its throughput or response time. It will be clear later on that in our farmer's problem, maximum utilization of land need not necessarily lead to maximum profits because of the constraints on resources.

The relationship between costs versus type of machine, yield versus type of fertilizer, price versus time of harvest, etc. are complex and difficult to establish. At the end of systems analysis the modeller should have a fair idea about what is available and what is not available, and the constraints within which he has to operate. He must have a good estimate of time, funds and manpower needed for the study.

(b) Formulation of model. A simple flowchart of the proposed model could be used as a starting point. Detailed descriptions of the behaviour of the banking system and the market place could lead to nonlinear and highly complex models which may be too expensive to build and operate. The emphasis should be on simplicity, ease of formulation and understanding, computational efficiency, and reasonable degree of accuracy. Only the minimum necessary subset of variables which adequately describe the farm system should be included in the model. Oversimplification makes the model useless, while the inclusion of trivial details makes it unnecessarily large, complex, and possibly intractable.

The average number of days available for farming is computed from weather records and the amount of money that can be borrowed, and its

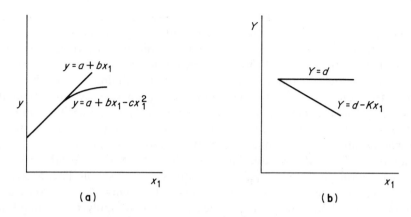

Figure 3.10 Acreage, cost and yields. (a) x_1 = acreage for cereal; a = fixed costs; b,c are constants; y = farming cost (£); (b) d,K are constants; Y = yield/acre (tons).

costs are estimated. Relationships between farm variables and the average expected profit per acre are established by formulating and testing various hypotheses. For example, one could test linear or nonlinear relationships (see Figure 3.10) between farming costs, acreage and yields and then translate these into a profit function P = Revenue − cost, remembering that the solution of nonlinear problems is comparatively difficult. Finally a simplified model which displays the significant features of the farm system is constructed as follows.

Data (see Table 3.2)
Model:
maximize $40x_1 + 120x_2$
subject to the constraints
$$x_1 + x_2 \leqslant 100$$
$$10x_1 + 20x_2 \leqslant 1100$$
$$x_1 + 4x_2 \leqslant 160$$
$$x_1, x_2 \geqslant 0$$

Table 3.2   Farm system—data and problem.

	Produce		Total availability
	Cereal	Sugar-beet	
Farming cost per acre (£)	10	20	£1100
Days required per acre	1	4	160 days
Net profit per acre (£)	40	120	
Land used (acres)	x_1 = ?	x_2 = ?	100 acres

Here, maximization of profit for the current season is the *goal* and the linear function $40x_1 + 120x_2$ is used as the *measure of effectiveness*.

Note that the use of different types of fertilizers, the effect of variable interest rates, the choice of different types of machines, changes in weather and wages, price fluctuations in the market, the timing of ploughing and harvesting, etc., are ignored. The model does not say anything about the cost of overheads, lands, and buildings, the value of farmer's experience, intuition, and judgement. Similarly the question of rotation of crops, storage problems, and the nutritional value of the crops are not taken into consideration. The model excludes all other goals except the allocation of land, so as to optimize the profit which is expressed by a simple linear function of acreage assigned for cereal and sugar-beet farming. All the constraints are defined as linear inequalities which enable us to apply well-defined and well-tested *linear programming* (LP) methods for the solution of the problem. Even though the methodology can be easily extended for solving similar problems, one should be aware of the weakness of the assumptions made in the construction of the model and the results should be evaluated and interpreted accordingly.

The standard *linear programming* (Dantzig, 1963) solution to the above problem is found to be $x_1 = 60$ and $x_2 = 25$, and a family of other *suboptimum* solutions (which may be of practical significance) can be extracted from Figure 3.11. The impact of the constraints on the solution is evident from the fact that the optimum profit is derived by utilizing only 85 acres out of a total of 100 acres of land.

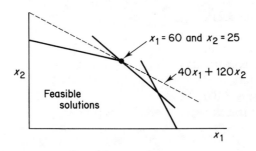

Figure 3.11   Graphical solution of LP problem.

(c) Model verification, validation, and certification. We examine very briefly the question of model verification and validation and a more detailed discussion of the subject is left to Chapter 4.

Verification is a procedure to ensure the design consistency in the structure of the model. That is, to confirm that the model is a faithful representation of what was intended. In our farmer's problem, constraints and the objective function are re-examined to make sure that there are no clerical, structural, and programming errors.

Validation is the process of confirming that the model is an adequate representation of the original system and is capable of imitating its behaviour reasonably accurately within the domain of its intended applications. The response of the verified model is compared with the actual (past and present) observations and theoretical predictions, and if the degree of fit is unacceptable then one has to go back to the systems analysis stage as shown in Figure 3.8. Feasible and optimum solutions, together with the results from *sensitivity studies* on the model, should also be useful in validating the model.

Certification of models by independent national and international bodies (e.g. Standards Institutions) is a step in the right direction to ensure credibility and acceptability of models. This is a difficult area to implement, and still remains to be a long-term future aspiration.

(d) Implementation and documentation. A validated model is ready for practical implementation. It can be used to predict, control, or explain the behaviour of the farm system. The model should be a valuable aid in deciding what to grow and how much to grow. There are several ways of generating and evaluating alternative solutions, but one should be very careful in designing experiments so as to extract the maximum amount of useful information from the model. The availability of additional resources such as land, money, time, and the price variations in the market place, affect the overall profitability and stability of the farm operations, and these can be investigated by performing sensitivity studies on the farm model.

Documentation (Gass, 1981) must be an integral part of the modelling process. This topic has not in the past been given the importance it deserves. Without documentation a model is practically useless; hence the importance of recording not only the details of the final model but also the experience gained during the construction of the model. Documentation should include full description of the model together with the details of assumptions, mathematical and computing methods, experiments conducted, validity of the model, costs, conclusions, and recommendations for further work.

3.5.2 Example 2

Let us examine the development of *population dynamics models* or exponential models which are useful in studying the growth and decay characteristics of different types of populations. These models are widely used in forecasting the growth pattern of human beings, insects, bacteria, and plants. The growth of investments, healing of wounds, decay of radioactivity, speed of chemical reactions, cooling of bodies, etc., are also studied by this method. The human population growth models, together with census data, are required to plan for future needs such as roads, schools, hospitals, houses, shops, parks, and other facilities at regional and national level.

The prediction of future population is our *goal* and the degree of fit between observations and predictions will be used as the *measure of effectiveness*. Suppose for a particular region, we have,

$N(t)$: size of the population at time t,
b: birth rate,
d: death rate due to disease and old age.

Extensive data analysis leads to the following assumptions and hypothesis.

Assumptions
(a) size of the future population is a function of its present size,
(b) ratio between the two sexes and the fertility rates remains constant,
(c) ratio between different age groups of the population remains constant,
(d) no immigration and emigration,
(e) no dramatic changes in living conditions,
(f) N is a continuous variable.

Hypothesis
The rate of change of population =

a constant × present size of the population

or

$$\frac{\mathrm{d}N(t)}{\mathrm{d}t} = (b-d)N(t)$$
$$= \lambda N(t) \qquad (3.1)$$

where λ is the net growth rate per person at time t or the biotic potential and the unit of time is left undefined (could be a year, 5 years, a decade, etc.).

The availability of data and funds, together with the assumptions, form constraints on the model. The degree of fit between the model output and the actual data is our choice for a measure of effectiveness; generality and applicability could also be used as measures of effectiveness. The proposed model defined by the differential equation (3.1), has a simple analytical solution (Figure 3.12):

$$N(t) = N(t_0)\, e^{\lambda(t-t_0)}$$
$$= N(0)\, e^{\lambda t}, \quad \text{when } t_0 = 0 \qquad (3.2)$$

and

$$t = \frac{1}{\lambda} \log\left(\frac{N(t)}{N(t_0)}\right)$$

Another possible solution (numeric approximation) to the model is obtained by expressing (3.1) as a difference equation

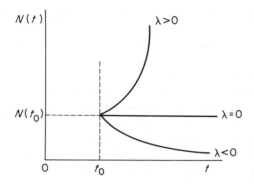

Figure 3.12   Population growth/decay model.

$$\frac{dN(t)}{dt} \approx \frac{N(t+\Delta t) - N(t)}{\Delta t} = \lambda N(t) \tag{3.3}$$

or

$$N(t+\Delta t) = N(t)\,(1+\lambda \Delta t)$$
$$N(\Delta t) = N(0)\,(1+\lambda \Delta t)$$
$$N(t) = N(0)\,(1+T)^n \tag{3.4}$$

where $t = n\Delta t$ and $T = \lambda \Delta t$.

We have translated the original model into two different simplified models (3.2) and (3.4). In this particular case the analytical solution (3.2) is easily available; hence it is far superior to the numerical solution (3.4), but this need not always be true. For a moment let us assume that computationally both the models are equally attractive.

Verfication of the model is the next stage in the modelling process. From the definition of the hypothesis it is clear that we can anticipate a very large smooth increase (or decrease) in the value of $N(t)$ in a short period of time. That is, an exponential growth (decay) model. Close examination of the models(3.2) and (3.4) reveals that both models live up to our expectations, as long as $\lambda \geqslant 0$. But, when $\lambda < 0$ and in particular when $T < -2$, the solution of model (3.4) undergoes undamped oscillations about $N(0)$ with increasing amplitude and bears no resemblance to the anticipated exponential response. The numerical model (3.4) is unstable and inaccurate; therefore it is not an adequate representation of what was intended by equation (3.1) and fails the verification test.

The model (3.2) which passed the verification test is now subjected to the *validation* procedures. From Figure 3.12 we can conclude that: (a) when $\lambda > 0$ the population will keep on growing at an alarming rate and finally fill up the whole world; (b) when $\lambda = 0$ the population remains static; and (c) when $\lambda < 0$ the population declines rapidly and eventually dies out.

Common sense suggests that none of these is likely to happen and we can confidently say that the model (3.2) is invalid and certainly useless for long-term forecasts. However, the model is found to be useful for short-term projections as can be seen from Table 3.3 (columns 1, 2, and 3), which gives the growth of the US population.

The model *failed the validation tests* and therefore we go back to the systems analysis phase and reformulate and test other hypotheses. Since the supply of resources (say, food) and space are limited, it is reasonable to assume that λ is not a constant, but a function of $N(t)$. Similarly we can inject more realism into the model by making the birth rate $b = 0$ for a specified age group (say, age $< q$). For example,

$$\frac{dN(t)}{dt} = b(N)N(t-q) - d(N)N(t)$$

is a possible modification to (3.1) but, we are begining to lose the simplicity of the original model and moreover it may not be possible to compute $b(N)$ and $d(N)$.

Long-term population growth is never likely to be strictly exponential due to various reasons such as environmental resistance, balance between species, lack of resources, and natural and man-made calamities. Therefore our first priority should be to stop the uncontrolled exponential growth forecast by the model (3.1) and make it more realistic. Introducing a *self-inhibition factor* μN into (3.1), we get

$$\frac{dN}{dt} = (\lambda - \mu N)N; \quad \lambda, \mu > 0 \tag{3.5}$$

Table 3.3   Observed and predicted US population.

| | | Population in millions | |
| | | Predicted by model | |
Year	Observed	Exponential $\lambda = 0.0314$	Logistic $\lambda = 0.0314$; $\mu = 1.586 \times 10^{-10}$
1800	5.3	5.3	5.3
1820	9.6	9.9	9.7
1840	17.1	18.6	17.4
1860	31.4	34.8	30.3
1880	50.2	65.3	50.1
1900	76.0	122.4	76.9
1920	106.5	229.4	107.6
1940	132.0	429.9	136.7

where μ is a constant and μN is the reduction in net growth rate per person due to environmental resistance. When $N = N_{max}$ (maximum supportable population, a constant), $dN/dt = 0$ and $N_{max} = \lambda/\mu$. Substituting for μ in equation (3.5),

$$\frac{dN}{dt} = [\lambda - (\lambda/N_{max})N]N$$
$$= \lambda N[1 - N/N_{max}]$$

Solving this differential equation for $0 < N < N_{max}$, we get

$$N(t) = [N(0) N_{max}]/[N(0) + (N_{max} - N(0))e^{-\lambda t}] \qquad (3.6)$$

where $N(t) = N(0)$ when $t = 0$ and $N(t) = N_{max}$ when

$$t \to \infty \text{ as } e^{-\lambda t} \to 0.$$

The graph of equation (3.6) shown in Figure 3.13 displays the desired characteristics, and this model is generally known as the *logistic growth model*, which is found to be in agreement (see Table 3.3, columns 1, 2, and 4) with the data obtained from biological and sociological studies (Lotka, 1957; Kemeny and Snell, 1962). Of course the exact nature of the logistic curve depends on the values of λ, μ, and $N(0)$.

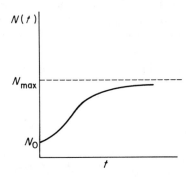

Figure 3.13   Logistic growth model.

If $N(0)$ is very small compared to N_{max} then for small values of t (say, $t < 1/\lambda$), equation (3.6) reduces to

$$N(t) \simeq [N(0) N_{max}]/[N_{max} e^{-\lambda t}]$$
$$= N(0) e^{\lambda t}$$

which is the same as equation (3.2). As t incrreases, the inhibition factor becomes more dominant, the rate of increase diminishes, and $N \to N_{max}$ as $t \to \infty$ as in Figure 3.13. The model is simple enough for several practical applications, and the degree of fit between the model output and the actual data is found to be particularly good in biology. The extension of the model (Burghes and Wood, 1980; Patten, 1971) to include several species of populations is straightforward; but the addition makes the problem and its solution more complex and difficult.

Having completed the validation of the model satisfactorily, as before, one can proceed with the documentation and implementation phases.

3.6 Models from various disciplines

The purpose of this section is to take the magic out of modelling by examining the formulation of models from various disciplines. The exercises at the end of the chapter are designed to help the reader gain experience and insight into the mechanics of modelling, and students are strongly urged to spend some time in working out the solutions.

3.6.1 Biological model

In section 3.5.2 we derived the logistic growth model

$$\frac{dN}{dt} = \lambda N(1 - N/K); K = N_{max}$$

This model can be extended to include two species of populations by treating N as a vector with two components N_1, N_2 and adding an extra term to account for the interaction between the two species. Then

$$\frac{dN}{dt} = \lambda N(1 - \text{self inhibition factor} - \text{mutual inhibition factor})$$

or

$$\frac{dN_1}{dt} = \lambda_1 N_1 (1 - (1/K_1)N_1 - \alpha N_2)$$

$$\frac{dN_2}{dt} = \lambda_2 N_2 (1 - (1/K_2)N_2 - \beta N_1)$$

(3.7)

where we have assumed that the mutual inhibition is proportional to the size of the other population and α, β are constants. If N_1, N_2 represent hosts and parasites and assuming that

(a) self-inhibition is absent,
(b) in the absence of hosts, parasite population declines,

equation (3.7) reduces to

$$\frac{dN_1}{dt} = \lambda_1 N_1 (1 - \alpha N_2)$$

$$\frac{dN_2}{dt} = -\lambda_2 N_2 \,(1 - \beta N_1) \tag{3.8}$$

These equations are generally known as *Lotka–Volterra* equations or *predator–prey* equations. Note that the presence of hosts (human beings, animals) slows down the decline of parasites (bacteria, insects) and the presence of parasites decreases the growth of hosts.

If the two populations are in equilibrium at $\bar{N}_1 = N_1$ and $\bar{N}_2 = N_2$ or if N_1 and N_2 are constants, then

$$\frac{dN_1}{dt} = \frac{dN_2}{dt} = 0; \quad \alpha = 1/\bar{N}_2, \quad \beta = 1/\bar{N}_1$$

and the equations (3.8) can be rewritten as

$$\frac{dN_1}{dt} = \lambda_1 N_1 \,(1 - N_2/\bar{N}_2)$$

$$\frac{dN_2}{dt} = -\lambda_2 N_2 \,(1 - N_1/\bar{N}_1) \tag{3.9}$$

Clearly, dN_1/dt is positive when $N_2 < \bar{N}_2$ and negative when $N_2 > \bar{N}_2$. The variations of N_2 about $\bar{N}_2$ bring about changes in the sign of dN_1/dt, which in turn changes the sign of dN_2/dt and the net result is oscillations about the equilibrium. Unfortunately, equations (3.9) have no closed-form analytic solution in terms of N_1 and N_2; therefore we look for approximate solutions.

If n_1 and n_2 are small perturbations about $\bar{N}_1$ and $\bar{N}_2$, then

$$n_1 = N_1 - \bar{N}_1; \, n_2 = N_2 - \bar{N}_2$$

and from (3.9), we have

$$\frac{dn_1}{dt} = -\lambda_1 n_2 \left(\frac{\bar{N}_1}{\bar{N}_2}\right)\left(1 + \frac{n_1}{\bar{N}_1}\right) \approx -\lambda_1 n_2 \left(\frac{\bar{N}_1}{\bar{N}_2}\right) \tag{3.10}$$

$$\frac{dn_2}{dt} = \lambda_2 n_1 \left(\frac{\bar{N}_2}{\bar{N}_1}\right)\left(1 + \frac{n_2}{\bar{N}_2}\right) \approx \lambda_2 n_1 \left(\frac{\bar{N}_2}{\bar{N}_1}\right) \tag{3.11}$$

Combining (3.10) and (3.11) and solving the second-order differential equation,

$$n_1(t) = c \left(\frac{\lambda_1}{\lambda_2}\right)^{1/2}\left(\frac{\bar{N}_1}{\bar{N}_2}\right)\sin(\lambda_1\lambda_2)^{1/2}t$$

$$n_2(t) = c\cos(\lambda_1\lambda_2)^{1/2}t$$

where c is a constant fixed by the initial conditions.

We have deduced information about the relationship between N_1 and N_2, and in particular the approximate analysis has clearly revealed the oscillatory

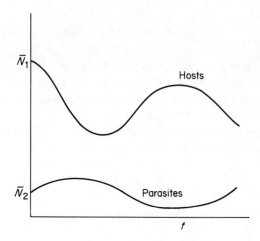

Figure 3.14   Parasite–host model.

(see Figure 3.14) behaviour of the predator–prey populations. It is evident that at no stage does either of the populations die out completely, and the oscillations take place about the initial population levels.

Note: Read Lotka, 1957; Hall and Day, 1977.

3.6.2   Optimum timing problem

Anti-nuclear and pro-nuclear groups are seeking public suport for their rival rallies to be held at the city centre on the same date. The publicity programme of each group is unknown to the other and it is generally believed that newspaper advertisements have some effect on the public only during the last 15 days prior to the actual rally. Opinion polls are used to determine whether an advertisement was effective or not. The probability of an advertisement being effective increases as the date of the rally approaches and is maximum (one) on the day before the rally. If one group advertises earlier and if it is effective, then the other group cancels their advertisement and resorts to other forms of publicity; if ineffective the other group will certainly place an advertisement on the day before the rally.

The opinion of strong supporters in both groups cannot be changed; but the lukewarm supporters in both groups can be influenced by advertisements. Each group has one unit (one unit = x thousands) of lukewarm supporters. If both advertisements (which can appear on the same day) are effective or ineffective, then there will not be any change in the public (lukewarm supporters) opinion. On the other hand, if the advertisement of one group is effective, then that group not only retains all its supporters but also gains the support of all the lukewarm supporters of the other group.

The problem facing the two groups is to determine the date of their advertisement so as to maximize their expected gain of support.

Here the rival groups do not know each other's plans and have to operate on the basis of expected gains.

Let

$t = 0$ be the date of the rally;

$P_p(t)$ be the probability that an advertisement by pro-nuclear group, t days before the rally, will be effective;

$P_a(t)$ be the probability that an advertisement by anti-nuclear group, t days before the rally, will be effective;

$0 \leqslant P_a, P_p \leqslant 1$;

$P_p(t) = P_a(t) = 1$ when $t = -1$;

$P_p(t) = P_a(t) = 0$ when $t < -15$.

Let $t_p = -1, -2, \ldots -15$ and $t_a = t = -1, -2, \ldots -15$ be the expected time of advertisements by the two rival groups. Then we can write the expected gain E_p of the pro-group as a function of t_a and t_p:

$$E_p(t_p, t_a) = -1 + 2P_p(t_p); \quad t_p < t_a \qquad \text{(a)}$$
$$= P_p(t_p) - P_a(t_a); \quad t_p = t_a \qquad \text{(b)} \quad (3.12)$$
$$= 1 - 2P_a(t_a); \quad t_p > t_a \qquad \text{(c)}$$

If the advertisement of the anti-group appears earlier (i.e. $t_p > t_a$), and is ineffective, then the pro-group will advertise on the day before the rally, when $P_p(-1) = 1$ and gains one unit of lukewarm supporters of the anti-group. But we do not know for sure how effective the anti-group advertisement is likely to be, and therefore all we can do is to express it in terms of its probability of occurrence. Since $P_a(t_a)$ is the probability that the advertisement by the anti-group will be effective, their gain in support is $(P_a(t_a)) \cdot (1)$. Similarly, the gain of support by the pro-group is given by $(1 - P_a(t_a)) \cdot (1)$ where $(1 - P_a)$ is the probability of occurrence of an advertisement by the pro-group on the day before the rally. The net gain in support by the pro-group when $t_p > t_a$ is given by

$$(1 - P_a(t_a)) - P_a(t_a) = 1 - 2P_a(t_a)$$

which is equation (3.12c)

The computation of E_p involves the evaluation of P_p and P_a which we define as follows:

$$P_p(t_p) = \frac{16 + t_p}{15}; \quad t_p = -1, -2, \ldots -15$$

$$P_a(t_a) = \frac{(16+t_a)^2}{225}; \quad t_a = -1, -2, \ldots -15$$

The probability P_p is a linear function which is maximum on the day before the rally and the nonlinear function P_a is designed to display the characteristics of the anti-group support which grows slowly in the initial stages, but rises rapidly as the day of the rally approaches. Substituting the values of P_p and P_a into equations (3.12),

$$E_p(t_p,t_a) = \frac{17 + 2t_p}{15}; \quad t_p < t_a \qquad \text{(a)}$$

$$= \frac{-16 - 17t_p - t_p^2}{225}; \quad t_p = t_a \qquad \text{(b)} \quad (3.13)$$

$$= \frac{-287 - 64t_a - 2t_a^2}{225}; \quad t_p > t_a \qquad \text{(c)}$$

The objective of the pro-group is to select t_p such that E_p is maximized while the aim of the anti-group is to choose t_a so as to minimize E_p.

The pro-group would argue that for any given t_p the antigroup will select $t_a = \bar{t}_a$ such that

$$E_p(t_p,t_a) = \min_{1 \leq \bar{t}_a \leq -15} [E_p(t_p,\bar{t}_a)]$$

and therefore the pro-group must choose $t_p = \bar{t}_p$ so that

$$E_p(t_p,t_a) = \max_{1 \leq \bar{t}_p \leq -15} \left[\min_{-1 \leq \bar{t}_a \leq -15} \{E_p(\bar{t}_p,\bar{t}_a)\} \right] \qquad (3.14)$$

Since t_p, t_a are integers and $-1 \geq t_p \geq t_a$, it follows that $-15 \leq t_a \leq -2$ and the right-hand side of equation (3.13c) is minimum when

$$t_a = t_p - 1 \qquad (3.15)$$

Substituting (3.15) into (3.13c), equation (3.14) can be written as

$$E_p(t_p,t_a) = \max_{-1 \leq \bar{t}_p \leq -15} [\min\{f_1(\bar{t}_p), f_2(\bar{t}_p), f_3(\bar{t}_p)\}] \qquad (3.16)$$

$$\text{where} \quad f_1 = \frac{17 + 2\bar{t}_p}{15}$$

$$f_2 = \frac{-16 - 17\bar{t}_p - \bar{t}_p^2}{225}$$

$$f_3 = \frac{-225 - 60\bar{t}_p - 2\bar{t}_p^2}{225}$$

The solution of (3.16) gives t_p (the day of the pro-group advertisement) and E_p, the expected gain of support by the pro-group even if the anti-group follows its best strategy.

Note: Read Buchler and Nutini, 1969; Maki and Thompson, 1973.

3.6.3 Economic system

The level of economic activity in capitalist countries undergoes oscillations, usually known as trade cycles. One of the best-known models describing the national income $Y(t)$ for any year t is given by

$$Y(t) = C(t) + I(t) + G(t) \tag{3.17}$$

where $C(t)$ = consumer expenditure on goods and services;
$I(t)$ = induced private investment in industry;
$G(t)$ = government expenditure;
and $t = -1, 0, 1, 2, 3, \ldots$

The consumption can be expressed as

$$C(t) = \alpha Y(t-1) \tag{3.18}$$

where $0 \leqslant \alpha < 1$. Similarly, the investment is related to consumption as follows

$$I(t) = \beta[C(t)-(t-1)] \tag{3.19}$$

where β is a positive constant called the accelerator. Combining (3.18) and (3.19),

$$I(t) = \beta[\alpha Y(t-1) - \alpha Y(t-2)] \tag{3.20}$$

Substituting (3.20) and (3.18) into (3.17), we get the second-order difference equation

$$Y(t) = \alpha(1+\beta)Y(t-1) - \beta\alpha Y(t-2) + G(t) \tag{3.21}$$

The graph of Y undergoes oscillations (Figure 3.15) and the nature of these oscillations is of great importance to economic planners who are particularly interested in the stabilizing characteristics of the national income. For a

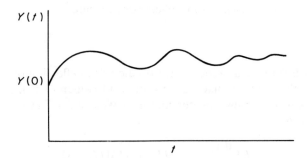

Figure 3.15 Damped oscillations.

56

given G, different values of α and β can be examined with a view to reducing the undesirable oscillatory movements of the national income. It can be shown that $Y(t)$ undergoes damped oscillations when $\alpha \simeq 0.5$ and $0.5 \leqslant \beta \leqslant 2$.

Note: Read Stiglitz, 1966; Burghes and Wood, 1980.

3.6.4 Bending of beams

It is well known in mechanics that the moment M of all external forces acting on either of the two segments of a beam is given by

$$M = \frac{EI}{R}$$

where E is the modulus of elasticity, I is the moment of inertia of the cross-section, and R is the radius of curvature of the elastic curve of the beam (Figure 3.16). For small deflections of the beam the curvature $(1/R)$ at a given point on the elastic curve is

$$\frac{1}{R} = \frac{d^2y}{dx^2} \Big/ \left[1 + \left(\frac{dy}{dx}\right)^2\right]^{3/2}$$

$$\simeq \frac{d^2y}{dx^2}$$

and therefore

$$\frac{M}{EI} = \frac{d^2y}{dx^2}$$

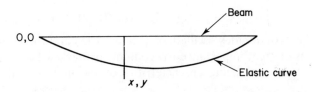

Figure 3.16   Radius of curvature.

We will now formulate a model which predicts the deflection of a horizontal beam of length L metres, fixed at the origin O (Figure 3.17), and carrying a uniform load of W newtons per metre of its length. The moment about $P(x,y)$, is given by

$$EI \frac{d^2y}{dx^2} = -\left(\tfrac{1}{2}(L-x)\right)\left(W(L-x)\right) \tag{3.22}$$

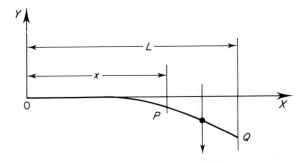

Figure 3.17 Bending of beams.

where $W(L-x)$ is the weight of the segment PQ acting at a point $(L-x)/2$ metres away from P. Integrating the equation (3.22) and applying the initial conditions $dy/dx=0$ at $x=0$, we get

$$EI\frac{dy}{dx} = \frac{1}{6}W(L-x)^3 - \frac{1}{6}WL^3 \qquad (3.23)$$

Integrating (3.23) and using the relation $y = 0$ at $x=0$,

$$Y = \frac{W}{24EI}(4Lx^3 - 6L^2x^2 - x^4)$$

It is obvious from equation (3.22) that the deflection is maximum when $L=x$ and we have

$$Y_{max} = -WL^4/8EI$$

Thus, for any given values of W, L, x, E, and I we can compute the deflection Y at any point on the beam.

Note: Read Au Tung, 1963.

3.6.5 Mechanical system

A mass, spring, and dashpot (damper) assembly is generally used as an idealization of several mechanical vibrating systems. Here the mass M which is restricted to move only in the vertical direction is connected to a fixed frame through a spring and dashpot (Figure 3.18). We assume that the mass is rigid and the spring and dashpot are massless. If x is the displacement (compression or expansion) of the system at any time t, the forces acting on the system are given by (Figure 3.18b),

$M\ddot{x}$ = reactive force due to M,
Kx = reactive force due to the stiffness K of the spring,

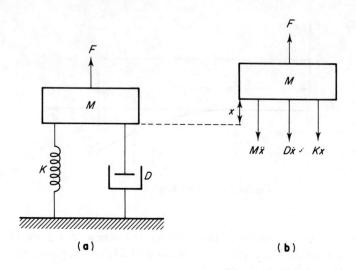

Figure 3.18 Spring, mass, damper assembly.

$\dot{Dx}$ = reactive force due to the damping factor D of the dashpot,

$F(t)$ = applied external force,

and
$$F(t) = M\ddot{x} + D\dot{x} + Kx \tag{3.24}$$

In control engineering it is customary (Doebelin, 1980) to write equation (3.24) in the form

$$\ddot{x} + 2\xi w\dot{x} + w^2x = w^2F^*(t)$$

where $F^* = \dfrac{F}{K}$; $2\xi w = D/M$; $w^2 = K/M$; $w = 2\pi f$

and f = frequency of oscillations

A real-life example of this type of mass–spring–damper system is the suspension of automobiles (Figure 3.19) where the displacement x is brought about by the movement of the wheels on a bumpy road. It can be shown that the solution of (3.24) is given by (see Figure 3.20):

$$x(t) = c_1e^{s_1t} + c_2e^{s_2t} + e^{s_1t}\int e^{(s_2-s_1)\tau_2}\int e^{-s_2\tau_1}F(\tau)d\tau_1 d\tau_2 \tag{3.25}$$

where $s_1 = \dfrac{-D}{2M} + \dfrac{(D^2 - 4MK)^{1/2}}{2M}$

$s_2 = \dfrac{-D}{2M} - \dfrac{(D^2 - 4MK)^{1/2}}{2M}$

and c_1, c_2 are constants to be determined from initial conditions.

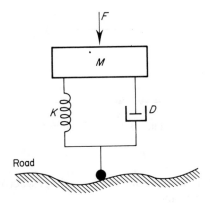

Figure 3.19   Car suspension system.

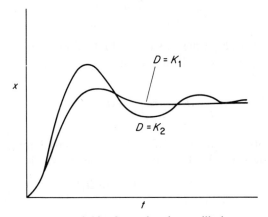

Figure 3.20   Second order oscillations.

The values of the parameters in equation (3.25) are adjusted so as to minimize the oscillations and the optimum values of D, K, and M are selected for practical implementation.

In this particular case (linear second-order differential equation) it is possible to compute analytically the conditions $D^2 \geq 4MK$ under which the oscillations are minimum, but the addition of nonlinear properties of the spring and dashpot make the problem analytically intractable.

Note: Read Shigley, 1967.

3.6.6   Electrical system

An electrical circuit consisting of capacitance C, resistance R, inductance L, and battery with voltage V is shown in Figure 3.21. From basic electricity,

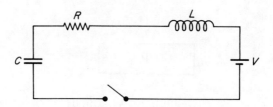

Figure 3.21 LCR circuit.

the applied voltage V is the sum of the voltages across the capacitance, inductance and the resistance

$$V = V_C + V_R + V_L$$

$$V(t) = \frac{q}{c} + \frac{R dq}{dt} + \frac{L dq^2}{dt^2} \tag{3.26}$$

where $q(t)$ is the charge on the capacitor, dq/dt is the current i in the circuit at time t, $i(0) = q(0) = 0$ and the switch S is closed at time $t = 0$.
Rewriting (3.26),

$$\ddot{q} + \frac{R\dot{q}}{L} + \frac{q}{LC} = \frac{V(t)}{L} \tag{3.27}$$

which is analogous to equation (3.24). When $L=0.05$ henry, $R=20$ ohms, $C=100$ micro-farads and $V=100$ volts, it can be shown that

$q(t) = 0.01 + e^{-t_1}(-0.01 \cos 2t_1 - 0.005 \sin 2t_1)$
$dq/dt = i(t) = 5e^{-t_1} \sin 2t_1$, and
$\quad t_1 = 200t$

It is evident that the solution is oscillatory and the values of L, C, and R can be adjusted so as to generate the desired solution.

3.6.7 Thermal system

Thermal capacity, thermal resistance, and temperature are analogous to electrical capacitance, electrical resistance, and voltage. Assuming that the temperature is uniformly distributed, the heat flow through a body with boundary temperatures θ_1 and θ_2 can be expressed as,

$$q = \frac{\theta_1 - \theta_2}{R} \text{ Btu/min}$$

(Note: 1 Btu = 778 ft-lbf; 1 ft-lbf = 1.3549 joules)
where R is the thermal resistance (degree/Btu/min). The additional heat stored in a body whose temperature is raised from θ_3 to θ_4 is given by

$$h = C(\theta_4 - \theta_3) \text{ Btu}$$

$$\text{and } q = C\frac{d}{dt}(\theta_4 - \theta_3) \text{ Btu/min}$$

where C is the thermal capacity (Btu/degree).

We will now examine the formulation of a model of an ordinary mercury thermometer whose network representation is shown in Figure 3.22.

where θ_0 = temperature of the bath

$\quad\quad \theta_s$ = temperature at the inner surface between glass and mercury

$\quad\quad \theta_m$ = temperature of mercury

$\quad\quad R_j$ = resistance of glass to heat flow

$\quad\quad R_m$ = resistance of mercury to heat flow

$\quad\quad C_g$ = capacity of glass

$\quad\quad C_m$ = capacitance of mercury

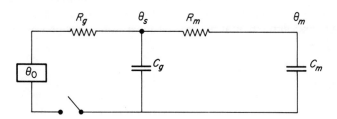

Figure 3.22   Electrical equivalent of a thermometer.

Analysis of heat flow at nodes s and m gives

$$\frac{\theta_0 - \theta_s}{R_g} = \frac{\theta_s - \theta_m}{R_m} + C_g\frac{d\theta_s}{dt}$$

and

$$\frac{\theta_s - \theta_m}{R_m} = C_m\frac{d\theta_m}{dt}$$

Combining the above two equations and eliminating θ_s, we get

$$C_g C_m \frac{d^2\theta_m}{dt^2} + \left(\frac{C_g}{R_m} + \frac{C_m}{R_g} + \frac{C_m}{R_m}\right)\frac{d\theta_m}{dt} + \frac{\theta_m}{R_g R_m} = \frac{1}{R_g R_m}\theta_0$$

or

$$K_1\frac{d^2\theta_m}{dt^2} + K_2\frac{d\theta_m}{dt} + K_3\theta_m = K_3\theta.$$

which is similar to equation (3.24). Proper selection of K_1, K_2, K_3 in the construction of the thermometer ensures that the temperature of mercury settles down to its final value rapidly, thereby minimizing the possible errors in temperature readings.

Note: Read Hornfeck, 1949.

3.7 Summary

A model is a simplified representation of a system. It can take different forms: mental, physical, or symbolic. Models help us evaluate alternatives without actually conducting live experiments. Models aid learning, design, prediction, and evaluation of alternatives quickly, cheaply, and harmlessly and serve as a powerful and concise medium of communication. Models are attractive for training personnel, computer implementation of problems, and expressing ideas clearly and unambiguously. A model may be linear or nonlinear, discrete or continuous, and stochastic or deterministic. Modelling is an iterative process and hence the need for a modelling methodology. The definition of the problem, systems analysis, formulation of hypothesis, formulation of a simple specific model, verification, validation, documentation, and implementation are the most important phases in the modelling process.

3.8 Exercises

1. Write Pascal program to graph the following functions and explain their characteristics;
   (a) $y = ax + b$; $b = \pm 12$ and $-8 \leqslant a \leqslant 8$
   (b) $y = k_1 + k_2 x - k_3 x^2$; $k_1 = 50$, $k_3 = 16$ and $75 \leqslant k_2 \leqslant 125$
   (c) $y = ce^{kx}$; $-0.3 \leqslant k \leqslant 0.3$; $c = 10,20$
   (d) $N(t) = N(0)(1 + \lambda \Delta t)^n$; $t = n \Delta t$, $\lambda = -5,0,5$; $N(0) = 3$
   (e) $y = a + bx \pm cx^2$; $a = 500$, $b = \pm 0.4$, $c = \pm 0.001$
   (f) $y = f(d)$; $f = 15$ for $0 \leqslant d \leqslant 1$; $f = 25$ for $1 < d \leqslant 2$; $f = 30$ for $2 \leqslant d \leqslant 5$
2. Give examples of models from each of the following areas:
   engineering
   science
   business studies
   chemistry
   psychology

   and comment on the

   (a) goals,
   (b) characteristics of the model,
   (c) assumptions in the models,
   (d) strengths and weaknesses of the model,
   (e) possible improvements.

3. Specify the goals, measures of effectiveness, and experimental frame in the study of the following systems:

motor car
hospital
library
freezer
computer program to solve quadratic equations.

4. Why study modelling? Explain the modelling process by formulating a simple exponential population growth model.

5. What is a model? Describe various types of models and their general characteristics.

6. You are asked by the admissions officer of your university to build a model of the university admission system. Familiarize yourself with the admissions procedures and then, with the help of a flowchart, describe the admissions process. What sort of data do you need and how do you collect them? Give an outline of the proposed model by working through the modelling methodology described in Section 3.5.

7. The director of the local university computer centre has asked you to build a model to forecast the growth in the usage of the computing facilities. Given that

$Y(t)$ = number of computer users at time t
C = potential number of computer users, a constant,
$X(t)$ = number of computer plotter users at time t
$Y(0)$ = 1000
$X(0)$ = 250

formulate a simple model which predicts the number of computer and plotter iusers at any time t. Justify the assumptions, if any, and interpret the results.

8. The data on the growth of an insect population given in Table 3.4. Draw a graph showing the net growth rate versus time. Using the models developed in Section 3.5.2:

(a) compute the expected growth rate at $t = 25$,
(b) compute the expected population at $t = 30$,
(c) what was the population at $t = 0$,
(d) compute the date when the population will be 1 million.

Table 3.4

Time t (months)	3	6	9	12	15	18
Population (thousands)	56	207	509	614	658	689

9. The data on Irish (north and south) population from 1790 to 1950 are shown in Table 3.5. Formulate a model or models to fit the data. Graph the observed and predicted populations and explain the effect of the potato famine around 1845–48.

Table 3.5

Year	1790	1800	1810	1820	1830	1840	1845
Population (thousands)	4.6	5.2	5.9	6.7	7.6	8.2	8.3
	1850	1860	1870	1890	1910	1930	1950
	6.9	5.8	5.4	4.7	4.4	4.2	4.3

10. (a) For a logistic growth model, show that the rate of population growth is maximum when $N(t) = N_{max}/2$.

(b) Collect statistics on population growth (e.g. flies, deer, penguins, whales, yeast, etc.) from relevant books, and test the validity of the logistic growth models.

(c) Write a Pascal programme to plot the solution to the predator–prey model, when

$$\lambda_1 = 0.004, \lambda_2 = 0.04; \quad \bar{k}_1 = 10^{-6}, \bar{k}_2 = 10^{-5}$$

where

$$\bar{k}_1 = \lambda_1/\bar{N}_2 \text{ and } \bar{k}_2 = \lambda_2/\bar{N}_1.$$

11. (a) Solve the farmer's problem of Section 3.5.1 by graphing the constraints and the objective function.

(b) Solve the same problem by the simplex method (read Dantzig, 1963).

12. (a) Prove that the solution to the second-order system

$$M\ddot{X} + D\dot{X} + KX = F(t)$$

is given by equation (3.25).

(b) Find the solution, when $M = 2.5$, $K = 450$, $F = 1.5$, and $D = 0.5$, 28.0, 55.0 and $\dot{x} = x = 0$.

(c) Verify that the oscillations are minimum when $D^2 \geq 4 MK$.

(d) Assuming that you have access to a software package for solving differential equations, write Pascal program to graph the solutions $x, \dot{x}$ and $\ddot{x}$ for nonlier values of spring and damper forces given in Table 3.6, Table 3.7 and $M = 1$ kg, $F = 900$ newtons, $x(0) = 0$, and $\dot{x}(0) = 0.02$.

Table 3.6

x	−3.5	−1.5	−0.9	0	0.9	1.5	−3.5
kx	−750	−300	−150	0	145	400	1700

Table 3.7

$\dot{x}$	−100	−45	0	45	100
$D\dot{x}$	−600	−300	0	400	1780

13. For an electric circuit with inductance L henries; capacitance C farads, and a variable e.m.f. of $E = 10 \cos 50t$, show that the current i is given by

$$i(t) = 5\left(\frac{1}{50} \sin 50t + t \cos 50t\right) - \frac{1}{2} \sin 50t$$

where $q(\text{o}) = 0.01$ coulomb and $i(0) = 0$.

14. Write a Pascal program to tabulate and graph the functions $Y(t)$, $C(t)$, and $I(t)$ of Section 3.6.3 for $t = 1, 2, 3, \ldots 10$, when
    (a) $G = 1$, $Y(0) = 1$, $Y(-1) = 1.8$; $\alpha = 0.58$ and $\beta = 1.8$
    (b) $G = 1.5$, $Y(0) = 1$, $Y(-1) = 5$; $\alpha = 0.75$ and $\beta = 3.9$
    (c) $G = 1$, $Y(0) = 2$, $Y(1) = 3$; $\alpha = 0.5$ and $\beta = 1$.

15. (a) Compute E_p and t_p of equation (3.16) by
        (i) plotting graphs of functions f_1, f_2, and f_3
        (ii) computing f_1, f_2, and f_3
        (iii) solving $f_1 = f_2$ and $f_2 = f_3$, and interpreting results.
    (b) Plot the functions P_a and P_p and interpret the significance of these graphs. Can you suggest some other forms for P_a and P_p and compute their effects on the final solution?

References

Au Tung (1963). *Elementary Structural Mechanics*. Prentice Hall, Englewood Cliffs, NJ.

Buchler, I. R., and Nutini, H. G. (1969). *Game Theory in the Behavioural Sciences*. University of Pittsburgh Press, Pittsburgh.

Burghes, D. N:, and Wood, A. D. (1980). *Mathemaical Models in the Social, Management and Life Sciences*. Ellis Horwood, Chichester.

Dantzig, G. (1963). *Linear Programming and Extensions*. Princeton University Press, NJ.

Doebelin, E. O. (1980). *System Modelling and Response*. John Wiley, New York.

Gass, S. I. (1981). 'Documentation for a model: a hierarchical approach', *CACM*, **24**(11), 728–733.

Hall, C. A. S., and Day, J. W. (1977). *Ecosystem Modelling in Theory and Practice*. John Wiley, New York.

Hornfeck, A. J. (1949). 'Response characteristics of thermometer elements', *Trans. ASME.*, **71**, 121–133.

Kemeny, J. G., and Snell, J. L. (1962). *Mathematical Models in the Social Sciences*. MIT Press, Cambridge, MA.

Lotka, A. J. (1957). *Elements of Mathematical Biology*. Dover, New York.

Maki, D. P., and Thompson, M. (1973,. *Mathematical Models and Applications*. Prentice Hall, NJ.

Neelamkavil, F. (1971). *Computable Models in National Educational Planning*. Research Report, Dept. of Computer Science, Trinity College, Dublin.

Patten, B. C. (1971). *Systems Analysis and Simulation in Ecology*. Academic Press, New York.

Shigley, J. E. (1967). *Simulation of Mechanical Systems*. McGraw-Hill. New York.

Spriet J. A., and Vansteenkiste, G. C. (1982). *Computer-aided Modelling and Simulation*. Academic Press, London.

Stiglitz, J. E. (1966). *The Collected Scientific Papers of P. A. Samuelson*, Vol. 2, MIT Press, Cambridge, MA.
Wang, Q., and Sterman, J. D. (1985). 'A disaggregate population model of China', *Simulation*, **45**(1), 7–14.
Ward, W. D. (1984) 'Modelling the USA–USSR arms race', *Simulation*, **43**(4), 196–202.

Bibliography

Bartlett, M. S. (1960). *Stochastic Population Models in Ecology and Epidemiology*. John Wiley, New York.
Bender, E. A. (1978). *An Introduction to Mathematical Modelling*. John Wiley, New York.
Cellier, F. E. (1980). *Progress in Modelling and Simulation*. Academic Press, London.
Cross, M. (1979). *Modelling and Simulation in Practice*. John Wiley, New York.
Feller, W. (1968). *An Introduction to Probability Theory and its Applications*. John Wiley, New York.
Forrester, J. W. (1971). *World Dynamics*. Wright-Allen, Cambridge, MA.
Freudenthal, H. (1961). *The Concept and the Role of the Model in Mathematics and Natural and Social Sciences*. Gordon & Breach, New York.
Greig, I. D. (1979). 'Validation, statistical testing and decision to model', *Simulation*, **33**(2), 55–60.
Gross, D., and Harris, C. (1974). *Fundamentals of Queuing Theory*. John Wiley, New York.
Haberman, R. (1977). *Mathematical Models: mechanical vibrations, population dynamics and traffic flow*. Prentice Hall, Englewood Cliffs, NJ.
Innis, G., and Rexstad, E. (1983). 'Simulation model simplification techniques', *Simulation*, **41**(1), 7–15.
Jacoby, S. L. S. (1980). *Mathematical Modelling with Computers*. Prentice Hall, Englewood Cliffs, NJ.
Jacquez, J. A. (1972). *Compartmental Analysis in Biology and Medicine*. Elsevier, New York.
Packer, A. H. (1972;. *Models of Economic Systems: a theory for their development and use*. MIT Press, Cambridge, MA.
Rivett, P. (1972). *Principles of Model Building: the construction of models for decision analysis*. John Wiley, New York.
Wymore, A. W. (1976). *Systems Engineering Methodology for Interdisciplinary Teams*. John Wiley, New York.
Zeigler, B. P. (1976). *Theory of Modelling and Simulation*. John Wiley, New York.
Zeigler, B. P. (1976). *Methodolgy in Systems Modelling and Simulation*. North Holland, New York.

4

Model Validation

4.1 Introduction

To *validate* means to prove that the model is true or an exact replica of reality. We know that a model is basically a specific expression of a *hypothesis* or *theory* about the behaviour of a system and the progression from the formulation of a hypothesis to a valid simplified specific model (see Figure 3.8) is propelled by a combination of *deductive* and *inductive* processes. Before examining the question of model validation in practice, I would like to explore some of the philosophical concepts which are fundamental to the discussion.

4.1.1 Hypotheses, theories, and laws

Our knowledge is transmitted to the future in the form of generalizations rather than a list of specific observations (medical science is not defined as a collection of symptoms, drugs, and possible cures). These tentative generalizations are called *hypotheses* (not good theses). A *theory* is a hypothesis about why systems behave in a certain way. It usually summarizes those aspects of *reality* which are not obvious to us and provides testable predictions. The strength of a theory depends upon its precision, simplicity, domain of applicability, ease of use, disprovability, degree of surprise, and the depth of our understanding. A robust and well-tested theory is usually kionwn as a *law*, particularly in physical sciences (Newton's laws, Ohm' law, etc.). The truth remains unchanged but our knowledge about the truth keeps on changing (e.g. atomic structure), and therefore always there exists a finite probability that the present theories will be placed by better ones some time in the future.

4.1.2 Inductivism

The method of drawing conclusions by observing, collecting evidence, and detecting patterns is generally known as *inductive reasoning*. It is based on extrapolation of trends derived from known data. It was predicted in 1950 that there will be about 300,000 vehicles in Ireland by the year 1970. Figure 4.1 shows the actual and predicted number of vehicles in Ireland. The errors in extrapolation are obvious.

The *inductivist theory* assumes that the ultimate reality can be accessed by amassing data from observations and then formulating a hypothesis to fit all the data. That is arguing from the *particular* to the *general*. Unfortunately, it is impossible to collect and examine all the data produced by the phenomenon and one has to be satisfied with the tests on samples. The weakness of this approach is immediately apparent; one can not make an assertion that 'all animals eat grass', simply by observing the eating habits of cows, horses, donkeys, and sheep. Additonal evidence may well prove our conclusions wrong. This implies that even though we have never seen a flying horse in the past, we are not certain that we will never encounter a flying horse in the future. Similarly, we cannot be 100% sure that a widely used computer programme will be error-free in the future because no bugs showed up in the past. Further complications arise because of our inability to repeat the same experiment at the same place, at the same time, and under the same conditions. Naturally we cannot logically validate a model by this method. In inductive reasoning the emphasis is on the formulation of a hypothesis and comparatively less attention is given to its testing. *Inductivism* heavily depends upon facts, objectivity, judgement, and reliability of observations (e.g. a flying object was seen as a horse). It does not say much about the consequences of errors and possible refutations of existing theories (e.g. implications of a new atomic structure).

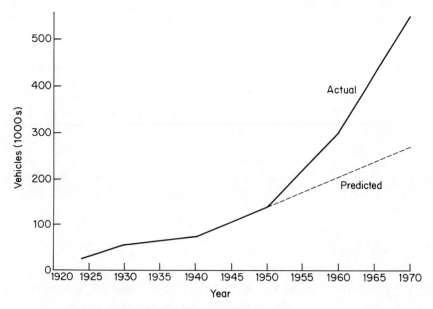

Figure 4.1   Errors in extrapolation.

4.1.3   Deductivism

The method of drawing conclusions by logically combining new ideas with facts that we accept as true is referred to as *deductive reasoning*. That is, arguing from the *general* to the *particular* or reasoning from known principles to deduce an unknown. In modern times a scientific method is considered to be a *deductive process*. The starting point is an educated guess about the internal structure that explains the behaviour of the system, and this is followed by the formulation of a *hypothesis*. In practice, inductive reasoning acts as a catalyst in the crystallization of ideas which led to the educated guess or inspiration and a set of tentative statements or generalizations which we call a *hypothesis*. The logical implications of the hypothesis are then empirically tested, and if the results are satisfactory, then we will have confidence in the hypothesis. If unsatisfactory, the hypothesis is reformulated, tested, and the iterative process is repeated. In Section 3.5.2, deductive reasoning suggested that the rate of the population growth must be a function of the current size of the population, the birth rate, and death rate, and this resulted in the formulation of equation (3.1)

$$\frac{dN}{dt} = \lambda N(t)$$

A hypothesis or theory can never be *proved* (Popper, 1969), only *disproved* or *failed to disprove*. There is always a chance that the existing theory may be replaced by a better one (e.g. Einsteins theory versus Newton's theory) some time in the future. Note that the theories or models may change but the facts remain unchanged.

Deductivist theory emphasizes the importance of the relative rather than the absolute nature of truth. It introduces the notion of *falsifiability* as opposed to *provability* of a theory. Even though a theory can never be proved, its robustness can be judged in terms of its ability to withstand detailed persistent and severe tests aimed at disproving them. Deductivist theory concentrates on testing hypotheses and comparatively very little attention is given to the question of formulation of hypotheses. Furthermore, it relies on the accuracy of falsifying observations which may be biased, corrupted, abnormal, or wrongly interpreted. It is quite possible that a red rose appeared to be pink to a colour-blind person or the experimenter happened to see a diseased rose or observed the rose in poor lighting conditions, or simply recorded a pink flower which resembled a rose as a pink rose.

4.1.4   Scientific method

Validation is at the heart of all scientific research which is centred around the truth and nothing but the truth. The important features of *scientific methods* can be summarized as follows:

1. Accurate recording of observations and definition of the problem.
2. Formulation of a hypothesis with the aid of imagination and creative ability.
3. Testing the hypothesis by experimentation, and if necessary reformulating the hypothesis.
4. Confirming that the hypothesis is equally valid for all reasonable people.
5. Defining methods capable of disproving the hypothesis by others.

Scientific theories or models must give positive answers to all the above tests, and only those theories which survive prolonged falsifiability tests are accepted. There is no question of accepting compromise solutions under any circumstances.

4.2 Modelling as a scientific process

Without *validation*, a model is of very little practical use. *Inductivism* and *deductivism* are the classical and modern versions of scientific method and we have already seen that neither of them can guarantee perfect validation of theories or their models. Therefore, true validation is a philosophical impossibility and all we can do is either *invalidate* or '*fail to invalidate*'. The sighting of a suspected green rose in a million observations should not immediately discredit the generally held belief that roses are never green. In practice those theories which survive prolonged falsifiability tests are accepted as valid.

The extension of the criteria used for validating scientific theories to model validation is not simple and straightforward process unless we are absolutely certain that modelling is in fact a scientific process. Unlike fundamental researchers the vast majority of modellers are engaged in building and validating practical models at reasonable cost within reasonable time, and not in understanding the ultimate reality at any cost. Modelling is a comparatively new area of activity involving the marriage of ideas from various disciplines, whereas scientific research is a long-established area which deals with the natural world. Scientific theories are formulated such that they can be tested in ideal laboratory conditions while models may not be amenable to controlled experiments under ideal conditions. The contrast between modelling and scientific activities is significant, and it is obvious that, in general, models are unlikely to be robust enough to withstand the same rigorous validation tests usually applied to scientific theories.

4.3 Possible approach to validation

In the past, several models have been built and implemented with reasonable degree of success, particularly in engineering and physical sciences. Each model should be judged on its own merits, and our objective should be to establish the degree of confidence by examining how accurately the model represents the system rather than testing for absolute validity of the model. This can be done by collecting evidence to support the validity of (a) *concepts*, (b) *methodogy*, (c) *data*, (d) *results*, and (e) *inference*.

4.3.1 Validity of concepts

There are two basic approaches—the rationalist approach and the empiricist approach. One can test the assumptions or axioms (a statement that is assumed to be true) directly or test the predictions or theorems (statements that are proved by other statements) directly and thereby test the underlying assumptions indirectly. There is no point in testing the validity of theorems internally in the model; they are to be tested in the real world and of course there is no guarantee that the predictions of model will match exactly with reality.

Rationalist approach. We blindly accept that the model is basically a set of logical deductions from a series of premises whose truth is obvious and unquestionable, and here validation reduces to the quetion of tracing the fundamental assumptions on which the model is based. In deriving equation (3.24) of Section 3.6.5, we started off by accepting $M\ddot{x}$, Kx, and $D\dot{x}$ as the reactive forces due to mass M, stiffness K, and damping factor D respectively.

Empirical approach. Here we refuse to accept any axioms, theorems, or other assumptions including obvious ones without positive evidence, and validation involves the collection of empirical evidence to support the postulates or assumptions.

Example

For the electrical circuit shown in Figure 4.2,

$$E(t) = V_R + V_L = R_i + L\frac{di}{dt}$$

$$i = \frac{E_0}{R}(1 - e^{\frac{-Rt}{L}}) + i_0\, e^{\frac{-Rt}{L}} \tag{4.1}$$

where $E(0) = E_0$ and $i(0) = i_0$

There are several assumptions in the derivations of equation (4.1). For example, we replace V_R and V_L by Ri and $L\,(di/dt)$ and assume that the resistance R and inductance L do not change with temperature. One can design experiments to test these assumptions or accept these assumptions and test the relationship between i and E in an experiment, thereby testing the assumptions indirectly.

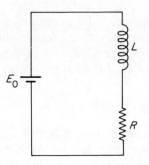

Figure 4.2   Simple electric circuit.

4.3.2   *Validity of methodology*

The methodology used in the formulation of the model and subsequent solution of the problem is examined here. The approximation of nonlinear problems by linear methods, the use of inaccurate numerical and computational methods (e.g. divergence or oscillations instead of convergence), the classification of a phenomenon as a random process and the use of pseudorandom numbers, the representation of continuous system elements by their discrete equivalents etc., are to be analysed with great care.

The use of continuous functions to represent discrete systems is obviously incorrect (Figure 4.3). Similarly, the use of wrong methodology could lead to absurd solutions. Figure 4.4 shows two methods for computing the optimum

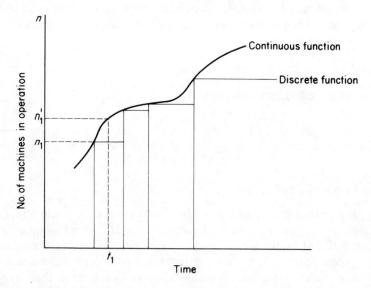

Figure 4.3   Errors in the use of continuous function to approximate a discrete phenomenon.

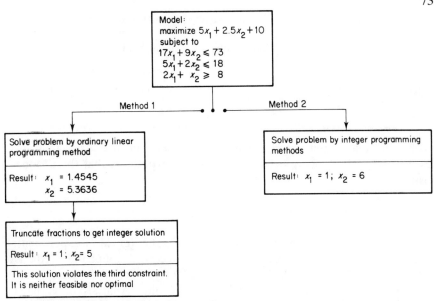

Figure 4.4   Possible errors due to wrong solution methodology.

number of aircraft needed for successful completion of a secret military mission. Method 2 gives a correct solution to the problem, whereas the solution given by method 1 is neither feasible nor optimum.

4.3.3   Validity of data

The data may be defective due to several reasons, and the integrity of the data must be established before jumping to conclusions. The data may be defective as a result of observational errors, calibration errors, interpolation/extrapolation of data, and inaccurate estimation of parameters. The available data may fit the model, but may not be sufficient for long-term projections as in Section 3.5.2, where an exponential population growth model was found to be satisfactory for short-term projections.

Example

The simulation model of a computing system assumes that 25% of the jobs processed are small jobs, 50% are medium-sized jobs, and 25% are large-scale jobs. On an average 96 jobs are processed per day. Table 4.1 shows the actual frequencies observed per day. The chi-square statistic (see Chapter 5) gives

$$\chi_1^2 = \frac{(25-24)^2}{24} + \frac{(52-48)^2}{48} + \frac{(19-24)^2}{24} = 1.4165$$

Table 4.1 Observed and expected frequency of jobs.

	Small jobs	Medium jobs	Large jobs
Observed frequency	25	52	19
Expected frequency	24	48	24

From chi-square tables, for two degrees of freedom and 5% significance level $\chi^2 = 5.991$. Since $\chi_1^2 < \chi^2$ we accept the hypothesis that the assumed distribution of jobs is valid.

4.3.4 Validity of results

The degree of fit between the model output and theoretical or experimental results is the key issue here. We are only concerned about the predictive validity of the model and do not worry about the validity of the assumptions, some of which may well be known to be wrong. Analysis of variance, regression, factor analysis, spectral analysis, chi-square tests, etc. are useful in interpreting the results.

Table 4.2 Growth of bacteria.

Time $t \times 10$ hours	1	2	3	4	5	6	7	8	9	10
Number of bacteria	80	190	240	350	400	460	520	540	580	650

Example 1

The following three models have been proposed to represent the growth of bacteria in a confined space:

Model 1: $y = t^2$
Model 2: $y = (5/7)t$
Model 3: $y = 1 - e^{-t}$

where $0 \leqslant t \leqslant 1$, time t is in hours, and y is the number of bacteria in thousands. The results observed in an actual experiment are shown in Table 4.2. The model predictions and the experimental results are plotted in Figure 4.5. The degree of fit between model 3 and the actual observations is good.

Example 2

Table 4.3 shows the results obtained from the study of queuing phenomenon (see sections 5.16 and 7.4) in a post office. The degree of fit between experimental results (observed), theoretical predictions (using queuing theory) and model output (simulation) is very good.

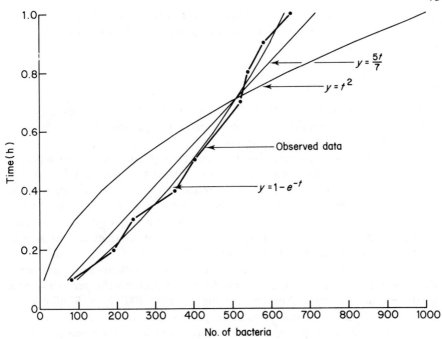

Figure 4.5 Degree of fit between model and experimental results.

Table 4.3 Observed, simulated, and predicted queue statistics.

	Observed	Theoretical predictions	Simulated in Pascal
Average waiting time in queue (minutes)	4	4.08	3.94
Average number of customers in queue	0.79	0.84	0.793

Arrival rate = 0.208/minute; service rate = 0.352/minute (interarrival and service times are negative exponentially distributed.

4.3.5 Validity of inference

After an in-depth study, if the conclusions drawn by all reasonable people are the same, then the inference is treated as valid.

Since we operate with imperfect information, we cannot achieve ultimate reality and therefore models should be judged in terms of their relative rather than absolute contributions in improving our understanding of the universe. The best strategy seems to be to test models to increase or decrease our confidence in them by exploring their limitations in comparison with the other known alternatives. The positive versus negative results from experiments with the models, and the strength and weakness of assumptions in the models, together with empirical evidence to support them, should serve this purpose.

4.4 Validation in practice

Model validation can be defined (Schlesinger, 1979) as the process of substantiating that the model within its domain of applicability is sufficiently accurate for the intended applications.

The above definition emphasises the need for a pragmatic approach (Ören, 1981; Friedman and Friedman, 1985; Törn, 1985) to model validation. The procedures of Section 4.3 should be applied with caution, and there is no question of attempting to prove that the model is an exact replica of the real system. Both users and builders of models should be prepared to accept those models which produce results within a given range of accuracy consistent with the specific applications of the model. The accuracy of a model which predicts the dosage of radiation treatment in cancer patients is of paramount importance compared to that of a model which predicts the growth of blue whale population in the Antarctic during the next 100 years. Similarly, for short-term applications the population growth model defined by equation (3.2) is more than adequate, and there is no need to go for a more complex logistic growth model given in equation (3.6). In other words, validation should be with respect to a specific experimental frame.

Even though it is beyond the scope of our current knowledge, one should not underestimate the need for demonstrating *retrospective* (model results agree with past data), *predictive* (model results should agree with future data), and *structural* (model faithfully mimics the internal behaviour of the real system) validity of *repeatable systems*, *recurrent systems*, and *unique systems*. Validation by statistical hypothesis testing may lead to two types of errors (Balci and Sargent, 1981; Greig, 1979). Rejecting the validity of the model when it is actually valid is referred to as *type 1 error* (model builder's risk) and this may lead to model revision and associated costs. Similarly, accepting validity of a model when it is actually invalid is usually known as *type 2 error* (model user's risk) and obviously the implementation of such models would be disastrous. The trade-off between various parameters by model builders, model users, and model-sponsors plays a very important role during the validation phase.

4.5 Validation versus verification

Verification is a procedure to ensure that the model is built according to specifications and to eliminate errors in the structure, algorithm, and computer implementation of the model. Proving programmes correct, walk-through methods (i.e. consulting other experts) and checking for ill-conditioning, convergence, accuracy, robustness (erroneous data should not give

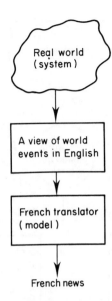

Figure 4.6 Verification versus validation: example 1.

meaningless results) and clerical errors are the main features of this phase. On the other hand, validation concentrates on the degree of fit between reality and its model representation. It examines the question of whether the model provides an accurate description of a real-world situation or whether model predictions are consistent with observations.

Figure 4.6 shows the reporting of a news item by an English-speaking journalist and its translation by a bilingual secretary. The purpose of verification is to confirm that the news in French (output of model) is an accurate (adequate) translation of the original source of English. The validation process ensures that the French news is an accurate (adequate) description of what actually happened in the real world. If there is any discrepancy between what actually happened and its French reporting, then we conclude that the English version of the news is wrong provided that the French translator model has already passed severe and detailed verification tests (see Figure 3.8).

Another example to illustrate verification and validation processes is shown in Figure 4.7, where the real world is viewed as a circle and for the particular application the user is quite happy to accept a reasonably smooth version of the circle to represent reality. The output of model 1 is a crude representation (generated by unequally spaced straight lines) of the original circle, and this is not what was intended and therefore fails verification. The model 2 output, on the other hand, gives a reasonably smooth circle and thus satisfies the verification test. Consistency between output 2 and the real world itself

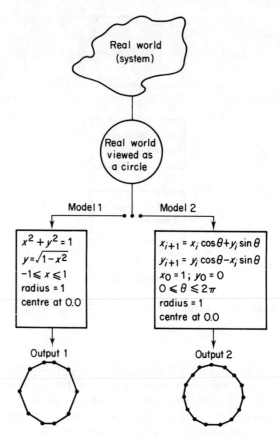

Figure 4.7 Verification versus validation: example 2.

ensures validity of model 2 subject to the comments made in Sections 4.3 and 4.4.

4.6 Summary

Without *validation* a model is of very little use. The concepts of *inductive* and *deductive* reasoning are introduced, and it is shown that it is impossible to validate models in the strictest sense of the word. Modelling is not a precise science; hence the criteria used for testing the robustness of scientific theories should not be strictly applied to models at the present time. Here, 'validation' means substantiating that the model within its domain of applicability is sufficiently accurate for the intended applications. The emphasis is on establishing the degree of confidence in the model rather than testing for its absolute validity, and this is achieved by collecting evidence to support the validity of concepts, methodology, data, experimental results, and inference. Model sponsors, model builders and model users must be prepared to accept compromise solutions. *Verification* refers to the correctness, consistency, and completeness of model implementation with respect to the design specifications, whereas validaton is concerned with the correctness and consistency of a model with respect to the real-world system under study. Verification and validation must be part and parcel of every modelling project right from the start, remembering that the later an error is discovered the more expensive it is to fix it.

4.7 Exercises

1. Distinguish between hypothesis, theory, and law.
2. What is meant by inductive and deductive reasoning? Give examples to illustrate the two approaches.
3. What are the major characteristics of scientific methods?
4. 'A theory can never be proved'—Popper; why not? How do you establish confidence in a theory?
5. Explain what is meant by model validation. How do you validate models in practice? What are the major sources of errors in validation.
6. Distinguish between verification and validation; construct a simple example to illustrate verification and validation. How do you go about validating a large-scale linear/integer programming model?
7. Write notes on
   (a) Type 1 and type 2 errors
   (b) Model-builder's, model-user's and model-sponsors risks
   (c) Validity of concepts
   (d) Model robutness
   (e) Retrospective and predictive validity
   (f) Recurrent, repeatable, and unique systems.

References

Balci, O., and Sargent, R. G. (1981). 'A methodology for cost–risk analysis in the statistical validation of simulation models', *CACM*, **24**(4), 190–197.

Friedman, L. W., and Friedman, H. H. (1985). 'Validating the simulation metamodel: some practical approaches', *Simulation*, **45**(3), 144–146.

Greig, I. D. (1979). 'Validation, statistical testing and decision to model', *Simulation*, **33**(2), 55–60.

Ören, T. I. (1981). 'Concepts and criteria to assess acceptability of simulation studies: a framework for reference', *CACM*, **24**(4), 180–189.

Popper, K. R. (1969). *Conjectures and Refutations: the growth of scientific knowledge*. Routledge & Kegan Paul, London.

Schlesinger, S. (1979). 'Terminology for model credibility', *Simulation*, **32**(3), 103–104.

Törn, A. A. (1985) 'Simulation nets, a simulation modelling and validation tool', *Simulation*, **45**(2), 71–75.

Bibliography

Ackoff, R. L., Gupta, S. K., and Minas, J. S. (1962). *Scientific Method*. John Wiley, New York.

Adrian, W. R., Branstad, M. A., and Cherniavsky, J. C. (1982). 'Validation, verification and testing of computer software', *Comp. Surveys*, **14**(2), 159–192.

Borger, R., and Cioffi, F. (1975). *Explanation in the Behavioural Sciences*. Cambridge University Press, Cambridge.

Nagel, E. (1961). *The Structure of Science: problems in the logic of scientific explanation*. Routledge & Kegan Paul, London.

Naylor, T. H., and Finger, J. M. (1967). 'Verification of computer simulation models', *Manag. Sci.*, **14**(2), 92–101.

Parducci, A. (1968). 'The relativism of absolute judgements', *Scientific American*, **219**(6), 84–90.

Pearson, K. (1911). *The Grammar of Science*. A & C Black, London.

Sargent, R. G. (1980). 'Verification and validation of simulation models'. In *Progress in Modelling and Simulation* (ed. E. E. Cellier), pp. 159–169. Academic Press, London.

Schruben, L. W. (1980). 'Establishing the credibility of simulations', *Simulation*, **34**(3), 101–105.

5

Basic Probability and Statistics

5.1 Introduction

The concept of probability, or the likelihood that some specific event will occur, is expressed in some form or other by almost everybody in our daily lives. We use terms such as *'very likely'*, *'probable'*, or *'chances are good'*, etc., to assign the probability of occurrence of an event. In general, simulation models are stochastic in nature and an understanding of stochastic variables is essential for our study. The representation of model input by probability distributions, the generation and testing of random numbers corresponding to the input data, validation of simulation models, design of simulation experiments, and the collection and analysis of simulation output are some of the major steps in systems simulation. We want to develop methods to extract information about the entire population by using data which describe only a subset of the population. Important concepts in probability and statistics usually encountered in modelling and simulation are introduced here. Our discussion will be confined to basic results in probability, statistics and queuing theory and readers should consult (Blum, 1972; Lee, 1966; Mihram, 1972) for further details.

5.2 Permutations and combinations

The number of permutations of n elements taken k at a time is given by

$$P_{n,k} = n(n - 1) \ldots (n - k + 1)$$

$$= \frac{n!}{(n - k)!}$$

The number of combinations of *n elements taken k* at a time is given by

$$C_{n,k} = \binom{n}{k} = \frac{P_{n,k}}{k!}$$

The two permutations (a,b) and (b,a) can be generated from a set containing two elements a,b whereas we can obtain only one combination (a,b) or (b,a) from the same set.

5.3 Sets

The set (collection) of all possible outcomes $s_1, s_2, \ldots s_n$ of an experiment is called *sample space S* of the experiment. The relation $s \in S$ is used to denote that s is a member or element from the set S. Suppose a coin is tossed twice, then the set S contains

s_1: HH
s_2: TH
s_3: HT
s_4: TT

where H = head and T = tail.

Now, let E be an event that at least one tail is obtained in two tosses and D be an event that a tail is obtained on the second toss. Then,

$E = \{s_2, s_3, s_4\}$
$D = \{s_3, s_4\}$

The following notations are generally used in set theory (Figure 5.1),

$A \subset B$: A is a subset of B (i.e. event A is contained in event B
$B \supset A$: B contains A
$A \cup B$ or $A + B$: A union B (i.e. event containing all outcomes that belong to A, B, or both A and B)
$A \cap B$ or AB: intersection of A and B (i.e. event containing all outcomes that belong both to A and to B)
A^c: complement of an event A (i.e. event containing all outcomes in S that do not belong to A.

5.4 Definition of probability

For each event A in the sample space S of an experiment, a number $P_r(A)$ or $p(A)$, *which indicates the probability that A will occur, is defined as the probability* of occurrence of the event A.

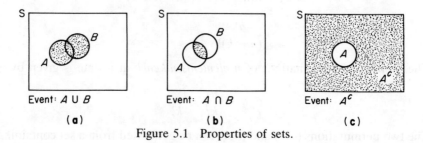

Event: $A \cup B$ Event: $A \cap B$ Event: A^c

(a)   (b)   (c)

Figure 5.1 Properties of sets.

A probability or a probability distribution on a sample space S of an experiment is a specification of the number $p(A)$ which satisfies the following relations:

(a) For any event A, $p(A) \geqslant 0$
(b) $p(A) = 1$ if the event A is certain to occur
(c) $p(A_1 \cup A_2 \cup A_3 \ldots \cup A_\infty) = \sum p(A_i)$ for an infinite sequence of disjoint events $A_1, A_2, \ldots A_\infty$.

It follows that, for any two events A and B:

(a) $0 \leqslant p(A) \leqslant 1$
(b) $p(A^c) = 1 - p(A)$
(c) $p(A \cup B) = p(A) + p(B) - p(AB)$
(d) $p(A) \leqslant p(B)$, if $B \supset A$

Example

Let A be an event that student A will complete the project on time, and B be the event that student B will complete the project on time. If $p(A) = 1/4$ and $p(B) = 1/5$, determine the probability that at least one of the students will complete the project on time.

$$p(A \cup B) = p(A) + p(B) - p(AB)$$

But $p(AB) = p(A) \cdot p(B)$, if events A and B are independent.

Therefore $p(A \cup B) = (1/4) + (1/5) - ((1/4) \cdot (1/5)) = 8/20$.

5.5 Conditional probability

Given that the event E_1 has occurred, the probability of event E_2 occurring is denoted by the conditional probability function $(p(E_2/E_1)$. If the two events E_1 and E_2 are statistically independent (i.e. the occurrence of either event has no effect on the probability of occurrence of the other event), then $p(E_2/E_1) = p(E_2)$. Similarly, for joint events $E_1 E_2$ and $E_1 E_2 E_3$, the joint probability functions are given by

$$p(E_1 E_2) = p(E_1) \cdot p(E_2/E_1)$$
$$p(E_1 E_2 E_3) = p(E_1) \cdot p(E_2 E_3/E_1)$$
$$= p(E_1) \cdot p(E_2/E_1) \cdot p(E_3/E_1 E_2)$$
$$= p(E_1) \cdot p(E_2) \cdot p(E_3) \text{ for independent events}$$

Examples

A box contains two yellow balls, three red balls, and five black balls. Let events E_1, E_2, E_3 represent the drawing of yellow, red, and black balls. The balls are drawn one at a time; black and red balls are replaced, while the yellow balls are not replaced. Then the conditional probabilities can be computed as follows.

The probability that the first two balls drawn are red followed by black is

$$p(E_2\ E_3) = p(E_2) \cdot p(E_3/E_2)$$
$$= p(E_2) \cdot p(E_3) = (3/10) \cdot (5/10)$$

The probability that the first two balls drawn are yellow followed by red is

$$p(E_1\ E_2) = p(E_1) \cdot p(E_2/E_1)$$
$$= (2/10) \cdot (3/9)$$

The probability that the first two balls drawn are red followed by yellow is

$$p(E_2\ E_1) = p(E_2) \cdot p(E_1/E_2)$$
$$= (3/10) \cdot (2/10)$$

5.6 Bayes' theorem

Let $E_1, E_2, \ldots E_k$ be k different events, and let any of these events cause the occurrence of another event A. Then

$$p(E_i/A) = \frac{p(E_i) \cdot p(A/E_i)}{\sum\limits_{j=1}^{k} p(E_j) \cdot p(A/E_j)}$$

where $i, j = 1, 2 \ldots k$; $p(E_j) > 0$ and $p(A) > 0$

Bayes theorem is very useful in computing the conditional probability of event E_i when A is given, from the unconditional probability of E_i and the conditional probability of A when each event E_i is given.

Example

Wine glasses of the same type were bought from three suppliers, (25% from supplier 1, 40% from supplier 2, and 35% from supplier 3) mixed and sold in the open market. It was found that one-fifth of the glasses bought from supplier 1, one-tenth of the glasses bought from supplier 2, and one-twentieth of the glasses bought from supplier 3 were slightly imperfect. Determine the probability that a defective glass picked up at random from the batch was bought from supplier 2.

Let E_i be the event that the selected glass was bought from supplier E_i

Let A be the event that the selected glass is defective

From the definition of the problem, we have

$$p(A/E_1) = 0.2; p(A/E_2) = 0.1; p(A/E_3) = 0.05$$
$$p(E_1) = 0.25; p(E_2) = 0.4; p(E_3) = 0.35$$

From Bayes theorem

$$p(E_2/A) = \frac{p(E_2) \cdot p(A/E_2)}{\sum\limits_{j=1}^{3} p(E_j) \cdot p(A/E_j)}$$

$$= \frac{(0.4) \cdot (0.1)}{(0.25) \cdot (0.2) + (0.4) \cdot (0.1) + (0.35) \cdot (0.05)}$$

$$= 0.372$$

5.7 Discrete distributions

If a discrete stochastic variable X_i can take a set of values in the range $X_1 \leqslant X_i \leqslant X_k$ with probability $p(X_i)$ such that

$$\sum_{i=1}^{k} p(X_i) = 1; \quad p(X_i) \geqslant 0$$

then the set of numbers $p(X_i)$ is called a discrete probability function or distribution (Figure 5.2).

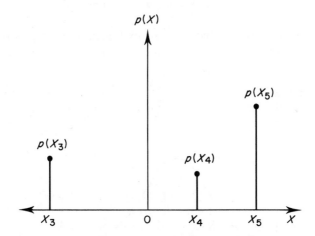

Figure 5.2   Discrete probability function.

By cumulating probabilities we get the cumulative probability function

$$C(X_j) = \sum_{i=1}^{j} p(X_i)$$

which gives the probability of a variable attaining a value less than or equal to X_j.

Example

A coin was tossed five times and the total number of heads obtained and the corresponding probabilities are shown in Table 5.1.

Table 5.1 Probability distribution for the number of heads in five tosses.

H	0	1	2	3	4	5
$p(H)$	1/32	5/32	10/32	10/32	5/32	1/32
$C(H)$	1/32	6/32	16/32	26/32	31/32	1

5.8 Continuous distributions—probability density and distribution functions

When the value of k in section 5.7 tends to infinity the distribution becomes continuous and we get $f(X) = p(X)$ and define

$$\int_{-\infty}^{\infty} f(X)dX = 1; \quad f(X) \geq 0$$

where $f(X)$ is called the probability density function (p.d.f.). A typical p.d.f. is shown in Figure 5.3 where the value of $p(a \leq X \leq b)$ is given by the

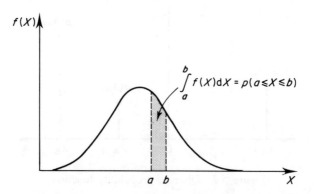

Figure 5.3   Probability density function.

shaded area and the total area under the curve is one. The probability of a stochastic variable assuming a particular value is defined by the p.d.f., which is widely used in describing the input to simulation models.

The continuous cumulative distribution function $F(y)$ which gives the probability of the stochastic variable assuming a value $\leq y$ is defined by

$$F(y) = \int_{-\infty}^{y} f(X)dx$$

$$= p(X \leqslant y) \text{ for } -\infty < y < \infty$$

Sometimes $F(y)$ is called the distribution function or probability distribution function (Figure 5.4). Note that $0 \leqslant F(y) \leqslant 1$, $F(\infty) = 1$ and $F(-\infty) = 0$.

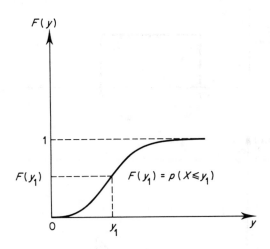

Figure 5.4   Cumulative distribution function.

5.9   Uniform distributions

Uniform distributions are used for a variety of applications because of the simplicity and ease of implementation. The uniform or rectangular probability density function is a constant wherever the probability is non-zero. That is, there is an equal likelihood of any value occurring in the given range. For a variable in the range $a < X \leqslant b$ the probability density function and the distribution function for a rectangular distribution are as follows (Figure 5.5):

$$f(X) = \begin{cases} \dfrac{1}{b-a} & \text{for } a < X \leqslant b \\ 0 & \text{elsewhere} \end{cases}$$

$$\int_{-\infty}^{\infty} f(X)dX = \int_{a}^{b} \frac{1}{(b-a)} dX = 1$$

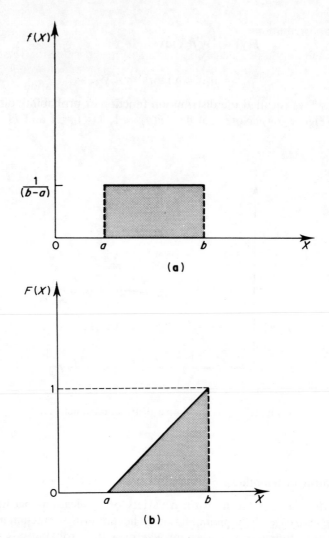

Figure 5.5 (a) Uniform probability density function; (b) cumulative uniform distribution function.

and

$$F(X) = \int \frac{1}{(b-a)} \, dX = \frac{X}{(b-a)} + \text{constant } C$$

when $X = a$, $F(X) = 0$ and $C = -a/(b-a)$

$$\therefore \quad F(X) = \frac{X}{(b-a)} - \frac{a}{(b-a)}$$
$$= 0 \text{ when } X = a$$
$$= 1 \text{ when } X = b$$

5.10   Joint distributions

In some simulation experiments it is necessary to consider the relationship among two or more variables simultaneously. The joint probability distribution of stochastic variables is called bivariate distribution. The joint probability fnction of X and Y is defined as a function f such that for any point (x,y) in the x,y plane

$$f(x,y) = p(X=x \text{ and } Y=y)$$

The discrete joint distribution is given by

$$\sum_{i=1}^{x} \sum_{j=1}^{x} p(x_i,y_i) = 1$$

$$p(x_i,y_i) \geqslant 0$$

and the joint probability density function is

$$\int_{-\infty}^{\infty} \int_{-\infty}^{\infty} f(x,y) \, dxdy = 1$$

$$f(x_i,y_i) \geqslant 0$$

Example

The stochastic variable X which represents the number of users on a small computing system can take values 1, 2, 3, or 4. Another variable Y which respresents the use of different compilers can take values 1 (Pascal), 2 (Fortran) or 3 (Cobol). Determine $p(X=2)$ and $p(X \geqslant 2 \text{ and } Y \geqslant 2)$, given the following joint probability function of X and Y (Table 5.2).

$$p(X=2) = \sum_{i=1}^{3} p(2,Y_i) = 0.1$$

$$p(X \geqslant 2 \text{ and } Y \geqslant 2) = \sum_{i=2}^{4} \sum_{j=2}^{3} p(X_i, Y_j)$$

$$= p(2,2) + p(2,3) + p(3,2) + p(3,3) + p(4,2) + p(4,3)$$

$$= 0.3$$

Table 5.2.   Discrete bivariate distribution.

Y	1	2	3	4
1	0.2	0	0.1	0.1
2	0.3	0.1	0	0
3	0	0	0.1	0.1

X

5.11 Expectation—discrete distributions

The expectation $E(X)$ of a discrete stochastic variable X is defined as

$$E(X) = \sum_{i=1}^{k} X_i p(X_i)$$

The number $E(X)$ is also known as expected values of X or mean of X or mean of the distribution of X. The mean is the most likely value of a sample taken from probability density function. It can also be regarded as the centre of gravity of the distribution.

Example

Suppose, in an experiment, the stochastic variable X can take any of the five discrete values -3, -2, 0, 4, 5 such that $p(X=-3) = 0.1$; $p(x=-2) = 0.2$; $p(X=0) = 0.3$; $p(X=4) = 0.25$ and $p(X=5) = 0.15$. Then,

$$E(X) = (-3) \cdot (0.1) + (-2) \cdot (0.2) + (0) \cdot (0.3) + (4) \cdot (0.25) + (5) \cdot (0.15)$$
$$= 1.25$$

5.12 Expectation—continuous distributions

The *expectation* (mean) of a continuous distribution is given by

$$E(X) = \int_{-\infty}^{\infty} Xf(X)dX$$

Example

For the uniform distribution of Section 5.9,

$$E(X) = \mu = \int_{a}^{b} \frac{X}{(b-a)} dX$$

$$= \frac{1}{(b-a)} \left[\frac{X^2}{2} \right]_{a}^{b} = \frac{(b+a)}{2}$$

when $f(X) = 1; 0 \leq X \leq 1$

$$\mu = \int_{0}^{1} XdX = 0.5$$

5.13 Variance, standard deviation, and moments

The *variance* of the distribution of a stochastic variable X denoted by var(X) is defined as

$$\sigma^2 = \text{var}(X) = E[(X-\mu)^2] = E(X^2) - \mu^2$$

$$= \int_{-\infty}^{\infty} (X-\mu)^2 f(X) dX \text{ for continuous variable } X$$

For discrete variable X,

$$\sigma^2 = \frac{1}{(k-1)} \sum_{i=1}^{k} (x_i - \mu)^2 \qquad (5.1)$$

In equation (5.1) the term $1/(k-1)$ is used instead of $1/k$ because of the difference in the interpretation of sample mean and population mean.

Since $(X-\mu)^2$ is positive, $\text{var}(X) \geq 0$. The variance of a distribution gives a measure of the dispersion or spread of the distribution around its mean μ.

The non-negative square root σ of the variance is known as the *standard deviation* of the stochastic variable.

Example

For the uniform distribution of Sections (5.9) and 5.12,

$$\text{var}(X) = \int_{a}^{b} \left(X - \frac{b+a}{2} \right)^2 \cdot \left(\frac{1}{b-a} \right) dX$$

$$= \frac{1}{(b-a)} \left[\frac{X_3}{3} - \frac{X^2(b+a)}{2} + \frac{X(b+a)^2}{4} \right]_{a}^{b}$$

$$= \frac{(b-a)^2}{12}$$

For any stochastic variable X, the expectation $E(X^k)$ where k is a positive integer is defined as the kth moment of X. Evidently, the mean of X is the first moment of X.

5.14 Correlation and covariance

The variance and the mean provide useful information about the dispersion in the distribution of a single variable. A measure of the association between two variables is very important in determining the dependence or independence of various events on each other in simulation modelling. These measures help us quantify the degree of relationship between two variables or their tendency to vary independently rather than together.

Let X and Y be two stochastic variables with a specified joint distribution, then the *covariance* of X and Y is defined as

$$\text{cov}(Y,X) = \text{cov}(X,Y) = E[X-\mu_X)(Y-\mu_Y)] = E(XY) - \mu_X \mu_Y$$

where $E(X) = \mu_X$, $E(Y) = \mu_Y$ and it is assumed that $\text{var}(X) = \sigma_X^2 < \infty$ and $\text{var}(Y) = \sigma_Y^2 < \infty$. The *covariance* $\text{cov}(X,Y)$ can be positive or negative.

When $X = Y$

$$\text{cov}(X,Y) = \text{cov}(X,X) = \sigma_X^2$$

When X and Y are independent

$$\text{cov}(X,Y) = 0$$

The dependence between X and Y is usually measured by the correlation $\rho(X,Y)$ of X and Y which is defined as

$$\rho(X,Y) = \frac{\text{cov}(X,Y)}{\sqrt{\sigma_X^2 \sigma_Y^2}}$$

Notice that $\rho(X,Y)$ and $\text{cov}(X,Y)$ have the same sign, and ρ is independent of the choice of units of X and Y. It can be shown (Fishman, 1973) that $-1 \leq \rho(X,Y) \leq 1$. The variables X and Y are positively correlated if $\rho(X,Y) > 0$ and here if X increases (decreases), Y also tends to increase (decrease). When $\rho(X,Y) < 0$, X and Y are negatively correlated and in this case if one variable increases (decreases), the other variable is likely to decrease (increase). The variables X and Y are uncorrelated when $\rho(X,Y) = 0$. In general, independence implies zero correlation, but the reverse need not be true. It can be shown that $\rho(X,Y) = 0$ for two mutually exclusive events even though they are not independent.

Example

The number of jobs processed (variable X) and the daily average load (variable Y) on the university computing system is shown in Table 5.3. Determine the covariance and correlation coefficient of the stochastic variables X and Y.

Table 5.3   Correlation and covariance.

Day	X	Y	$x = X - \mu_X$	$y = Y - \mu_Y$	x^2	y^2	xy
1	8	5	1	0	1	0	0
2	4	4	-3	-1	9	1	3
3	14	9	7	4	49	16	28
4	1	1	-6	-4	36	16	24
5	11	8	4	3	16	9	12
6	3	2	-4	-3	16	9	12
7	6	4	-1	-1	1	1	1
8	9	7	2	2	4	4	4

We have

$$k = 8; \quad \mu_X = \frac{56}{8} = 7; \quad \mu_Y = \frac{40}{8} = 5, \quad \sum x^2 = 132;$$

$$\sum y^2 = 56; \quad \sum xy = 84$$

$$\text{cov}(X,Y) = \frac{1}{(k-1)} \sum_{i=1}^{k} (X_i - \mu_X)(Y_i - \mu_Y) = \frac{84}{(8-1)} = 12$$

$$\text{var}(X) = \sigma_X^2 = \frac{1}{k-1} \sum_{i=1}^{k} (X_i - \mu_X)^2 = \frac{132}{(8-1)} = \frac{132}{7}$$

$$\text{var}(Y) = \sigma_Y^2 = \frac{1}{(k-1)} \sum_{i=1}^{k} (Y_i - \mu_Y)^2 = \frac{56}{(8-1)} = 8$$

Standard deviation of $X = \sigma_X = \sqrt{132/7}$
Standard deviation of $Y = \sigma_Y = \sqrt{8}$

$$\text{Correlation } \rho(X,Y) = \frac{\text{cov}(X,Y)}{\sigma_X \sigma_Y} = \frac{12}{\sqrt{\left(\frac{132}{7}\right) \cdot (8)}} = 0.9355$$

There is a strong positive correlation between the variables X and Y, and this is shown in Figure 5.6.

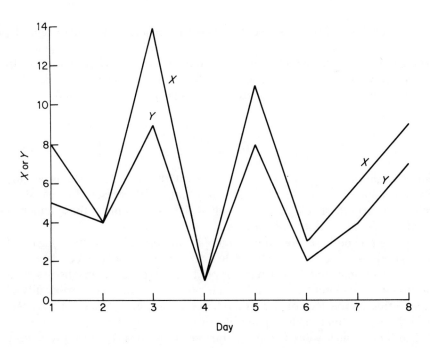

Figure 5.6   Example of positive correlation.

5.15 Hypothesis testing, significance levels, and confidence intervals

The process of choosing between two alternative outcomes of an experiment by using probability theory so as to minimize he risk of wrong decisions is known as *hypothesis testing*. The hypothesis being tested is denoted by H_0 (null hypothesis) and any hypothesis different from H_0 is alternative hypothesis and denoted by H_1. It will always be assumed that H_0 is true unless the data convince us otherwise. If H_0 is $p = 0.6$, then $p > 0.6$ or $p < 0.6$ are examples of H_1. In practice, we use a sample of a population in testing the truth or falsity of a hypothesis, as it is impossible to examine the entire population.

Consider the hypothesis H_0: the coin is honest (i.e. the theoretical probability of getting head is 1/2). Suppose 18 tosses of the coin produced 11 heads . We are inclined to doubt the honesty of the coin and reject the hypothesis that the coin is fair. But it is quite possible that the coin is in fact fair, but a rare event has occurred. For a fair coin the probability of getting 11 or more heads in 18 tosses (see definition of binomial distribution in Section 6.13.2) is given by

$$p(\geqslant 11) = \sum_{i=11}^{18} \left[\binom{18}{i} \cdot (\tfrac{1}{2})^i \cdot (q)^{18-i} \right] = 0.239 \tag{5.2}$$

The stated hypothesis is accepted or rejected according to the following rule.

If $p < \alpha$, the hypothesis is rejected.
·   If $p > \alpha$, the hypothesis is accepted (even though a rare event has occured).

where α is called the significance level, confidence level, or critical level. In statistical work, significance level is usually set at $\alpha = 0.05$, or 5% level of significance. An example of hypothesis testing is givn in Section 6.8.2. Now, let

$$\alpha = 0.05 = p(\geqslant j) = \sum_{i=j}^{18} \left[\binom{18}{i} \cdot (\tfrac{1}{2})^i \cdot (q)^{18-i} \right] \tag{5.3}$$

From equations (5.2) and (5.3) it is evident that $j > 11$. That is, as the starting value of i increases, the value of p in (5.2) decreases. Therefore we reject the hypothesis H_0 (i.e. the result is significant) only if the number of heads observed in 18 tosses exceeds j.

Testing a hypothesis does not mathematically prove the truth or falsity of the hypothesis. The conclusions reached are purely on the basis of data used and may or may not be correct. Type 1 and type 2 errors discussed in Section 4.4 are closely associated with hypothesis testing. The probability of committing a type 1 error (i.e. the relative frequency of rejecting a correct hypothesis) is equal to the significance level.

The limits which will contain a parameter (e.g. mean) with a probability of 95% are called the 95% confidence limits for the parameter and the interval between the confidence limits is called the confidence interval.

5.16 Simple queuing models

The theory of *queues* or waiting lines is concerned with the study of causes and remedies for cogestion in systems. Queues of people in banks or super-markets, queues of ships waiting for loading or unloading, queues of jobs in a computing system, and queues of machines waiting for repair are all familiar sights (Figure 5.7). The question of queues does not arise if there are sufficient number of servers to satisfy all customers at the same time. The three main parties involved in a queuing system are customers, servers, and the management. It is the function of the management to strike a balance between customer waiting time and service charges so as to make the system economically or otherwise viable. Several simulation models describe queuing situations and the analytical models presented in this section are useful in checking the validity of simulation models.

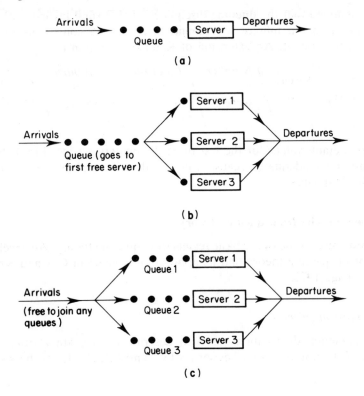

Figure 5.7 (a) Single queue, single server; (b) single queue, multiple servers; (c) multiple independent queues, multiple servers.

In a deterministic system, queues are formed whenever the arrival rate (i.e. number of arrivals per unit time) is greater than the service rate (i.e. number of customers served in unit time). If the *interarrival times* and *service times* vary randomly, then queues may be formed even if the average service rate is greater than the average arrival rate simply because arrivals need not be equally spaced. The service time and interarrival time distributions give a measure of random variations or uncertainties in queuing systems. Two other important parameters which determine the performance of the queuing system are the organization of the service system (number of servers) and the queuing discipline (method of selecting which customer is to be served next).

Queuing systems are classified according to the following notations due to D. G. Kendall (1953).

$X/Y/n$: arrival process/service process/number of servers

where $X, Y = M$ for negative exponential distributions (see Section 6.12.2)

$ = E_k$ for Erlang-k distributions

$ n$ = number of servers

and it is assumed that the queuing discipline is FIFO (first in–first out), the arrivals are from an infinite source and there are no constraints on the number in the system. An extension of Kendall's notation is

$$\left.\begin{array}{c}\textit{Arrival}\\\textit{process}\end{array}\right/\left.\begin{array}{c}\textit{Service}\\\textit{process}\end{array}\right/\left.\begin{array}{c}\textit{Number}\\\textit{of}\\\textit{servers}\end{array}\right/\left.\begin{array}{c}\textit{Limit on}\\\textit{number in}\\\textit{system}\end{array}\right/\left.\begin{array}{c}\textit{Number}\\\textit{in the}\\\textit{source}\end{array}\right/\left.\begin{array}{c}\textit{Queuing}\\\textit{discipline}\end{array}\right/$$

where the default values for the last three parameters are ∞/∞ FIFO. Even this notation is inadequate because it fails to describe multiple service rates and multiple queues.

5.17 Basic results from queuing theory

This section gives some of the basic results from queuing theory. An excellent treatment of queuing theory and its application is given in Cox and Smith, 1961 and Page 1972.

5.17.1 Poisson process

Two fundamental distributions used to describe queues are *Poisson* and *exponential* distributions (see Sections 6.13.1 and 6.12.2). It can be shown that

1. If the chance of an event occurring at any instant of time is constant, then the probability of X successes (arrivals, departures, changes, etc.) in time t' is given by the Poisson distribution

$$p(X) = \frac{m^X e^{-m}}{X!} = \frac{(\lambda t')^X e^{-(\lambda t')}}{X!}$$

where m = $\lambda t'$ = average number (mean) of successes in a time interval of length t'

λ = constant.

2a. If the chance of an event occurring at any instant of time is constant, then the probability of an interval t between successes is given by the exponential distribution

$$p(t) = \frac{1}{T} e^{\frac{-t}{T}}$$

where T = average time interval between successes.

2b.
$$p(>t) = \int_t^\infty \frac{1}{T} e^{\frac{-t}{T}} \, dt = e^{\frac{-t}{T}}$$

Both Poisson and exponential distributions give different descriptions of the same random process. A queuing system which can be described by a Poisson distribution is called a Poisson process.

Example

Students arrive at the university health centre randomly at an average rate of 15 per hour. Determine the probability of (a) exactly 15 students arriving in 1 hour, (b) more than 16 students arriving in 1 hour, and (c) probability of 30 or more arrivals per hour.

(a) $p(15) = \dfrac{15^{15} e^{-15}}{15!} = 0.1024$

(b) $p(>16) = \displaystyle\sum_{j=17}^{\infty} \dfrac{15^j \, e^{-15}}{j!} = 0.3359$

(c) Average interarrival time = 4 minutes.
Probability of 30 or more arrivals/hour = probability of one or more arrivals in 2 minutes.
Probability of an arrival in less than or equal to 2 minutes
= 1 − probability of an arrival in over 2 minutes
= $1 - e^{\frac{-2}{4}}$
= 0.3935

5.17.2 Single-server queues

Here we consider $M/M/1/\infty$ type queues where customers arrive randomly (Poisson) from an infinite source, service times are negative exponentially distributed, single server, single queue, and there are no constraints on the queue size. The standard results for this queuing system (Figure 5.8) are:

1. Average interarrival time = $1/\lambda$
2. Average service time = $1/\mu$
3. Service factor or utilization of facility $\rho = \lambda/\mu < 1$
4. Probability of j customers in system = $P_j = p(j) = \rho^j(1-\rho)$
5. Average number of customers in system = $\rho/(1-\rho)$
6. Average queue length = $\rho^2/(1-\rho)$
7. $p(>j) = \rho^{j+1}$

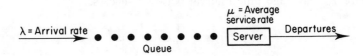

Figure 5.8   Single server, single queue.

8. Average waiting time in queue = $\dfrac{\rho}{(1-\rho)\mu}$

9. Average waiting time for those who must wait = $\dfrac{1}{(1-\rho)\mu}$

10. Average time spent in the system = $1/(\mu-\lambda)$
11. Probability density function for waiting time = $\rho(\mu-\lambda)e^{-t(\mu-\lambda)}$
12. Probability of waiting time greater than t = $\rho e^{-t(\mu-\lambda)}$
13. Probability density function for the total time spent in the system = $(\mu-\lambda)e^{-t(\mu-\lambda)}$
14. Probability of spending longer than t in the system = $e^{-t(\mu-\lambda)}$

Example

On an average 20 passengers arrive every hour at the airport check-in facility. The check-in time was found to be negative exponentially distributed with a mean of 2.5 minutes. Compute

(a) Probability that the check-in clerk is busy
(b) Average passenger waiting time for check-in
(c) Probability that the passenger queue length will be greater than 4
(d) Probability that passengers have to wait for more than 15 minutes for check-in
(e) Proportion of time the check-in clerk is idle
(f) What must be the average check-in time in order to reduce the average waiting time to 10 minutes.

Solution

(a) Probability of one or more $\}$ $= 1 -$ Probability of zero
     customers in system $\}$ customers in system
                              $= 1 - (1 - \rho) = \rho$
                              $= 5/6$

(b) $\dfrac{\rho}{(1-\rho)\mu} = \dfrac{(1/3)}{(2/5 - 1/3) \cdot (2/5)} = 12.5$ minutes

(c) Probability of more than j $\}$ $= \displaystyle\sum_{i=j+1}^{\infty} P_{i+1} = \rho^{j+2}$
     passengers queuing $\}$

                                $= (5/6)^6$ when $j=4$

(d) Probability of waiting time $\}$ $= \displaystyle\int_{15}^{\infty} \rho(\mu - \lambda)e^{-t(\mu - \lambda)}\, dt$
     longer than 15 minutes $\}$

                                $= \rho e^{-15(\mu - \lambda)}$

                                $= (5/6) \cdot (e^{-1})$
                                $= 0.307$

(e) $1 - \rho$ $= 1 - (5/6)$
              $= 1/6$

(f) $\dfrac{\rho}{(1-\rho)\mu}$ $=$ 10 minutes

     i.e. $10\mu^2 - 10\mu\lambda - \lambda = 0$
Substituting for $\lambda = 1/3$,

$$30\mu^2 - 10\mu - 1 = 0$$

Positive $\mu = \dfrac{10 + \sqrt{220}}{60}$

     $= 0.4139$

Therefore average check-in time should be $= 1/\mu = 1/0.4139 = 2.416$ minutes.

5.17.3   *Multiple-server queues*

This is the $M/M/s/\infty$ type queue which is similar to $M/M/1/\infty$ except that there are s servers. For stability $\rho < s$. The basic results for this type of queuing systems are:

1. Utilization of facility: $\dfrac{\lambda}{\mu s} = \rho/s$

2. Probability of zero customers in the system

$$P_0 = \left[\left(\sum_{k=0}^{s-1} \frac{\rho^k}{k!} \right) + \frac{\rho^s}{(s-1)!(s-\rho)} \right]^{-1}$$

similarly, $P_N = \dfrac{1}{N!} \rho^N P_0$ if $N < s$

$$= \frac{1}{s!\, s^{N-s}} \rho^N P_0 \text{ if } N \geq s$$

$P_{N \geq s}$ (i.e. all servers busy) $= B = \dfrac{P_0 s \rho^s}{s!(s-\rho)}$

3. Average waiting time in the queue:
$$W_q = \frac{P_0}{\mu}\, \frac{\rho^s}{\mu(s-1)!(s-\rho)^2}$$

4. Average time spent in the system (system response):
$$W = W_q + \frac{1}{\mu}$$

5. Standard deviation of system response time:
$$= \left(\sqrt{B(2-B) + (s-\rho)^2} \right) \left(\frac{W_q}{B} \right)$$

6. Probability of customer waiting longer than time t in queue:
$$p(W_q > t) = D = B e^{-\mu(s-\rho)t}$$

7. Average number of customers in the queue: $L_q = \lambda W_q$
8. Average number of customers in the system: $L = \lambda W$

A Pascal programme (VAX-11/780) for evaluating the queue statistics for multi-server queues is given in Figure 5.9.

5.18 Summary

Modelling and simulation involve the processing of stochastic variables. Since it is not possible to draw conclusions by examining the entire population, one has to develop methods to derive useful information by sampling a subset of the population. Important concepts in probability and statistics

```
PROGRAM MULTISERVER_QUEUE(INPUT,OUTPUT);
 (* single queue multiserver system..M/M/S/infinity.. *)

VAR     COUNT,n,t,S : INTEGER;
        LAMBDA,MU,U,RHO,PO,Pn,SUM,B,D,Wq,W,SD,Lq,L : REAL;

FUNCTION FACTORIAL(VALUE:INTEGER):INTEGER;
BEGIN
 IF VALUE <=1
  THEN FACTORIAL := 1
  ELSE FACTORIAL := VALUE * FACTORIAL(VALUE-1);
END;

BEGIN (* mainine *)

WRITELN('enter arrival rate LAMBDA : ');
READLN(LAMBDA);
WRITELN('enter service rate  MU : ');
READLN(MU);
WRITELN('number of servers  S : ' );
READLN(S);
WRITELN (' enter value for n of Pn : ');
READLN (n);
WRITELN (' enter value for time t of pr(Wq>t) ');
READLN (t);
RHO := LAMBDA/MU;
U := RHO/S ;
SUM := O;
FOR COUNT := O TO (S-1)  DO
         SUM := SUM + (RHO**COUNT)/FACTORIAL(COUNT);
PO := 1/(SUM+(RHO**S)/((FACTORIAL(S-1))*(S-RHO)));
IF N < S
  THEN  Pn := ( 1/FACTORIAL (n)) * (RHO ** n) * PO
  ELSE  Pn := (1/(FACTORIAL(S)*(S**(n-S))))*(RHO**n)*PO ;
B := (PO*S*(RHO**S))/(FACTORIAL(S)*(S-RHO));
D := B*EXP(-MU * (S-RHO)*t);
Wq := (PO/MU)*((RHO**S)/(FACTORIAL(S-1)*SQR(S-RHO)));
W := Wq + (1/MU);
SD := (SQRT((B*(2-B))+(SQR(S-RHO))))*(Wq/B);
Lq := LAMBDA * Wq;
L := LAMBDA * W;

WRITELN;
WRITE('LAMBDA =',LAMBDA:7:4,'  MU =',MU:7:4);
WRITELN('   S =',S:2,'    n =',n:2,'   t =',t:2);
WRITELN;
WRITELN('utilisation of facility: ',U:25:6);
WRITELN('prob. of O customers in system : ',PO:17:6);
WRITELN('prob.of ',n:2,' customers in system:',Pn:19:6 );
WRITELN('prob. that all servers busy : ',B:20:6);
WRITELN('prob.of queuing time longer than',t:2,' is',D:13:6)
WRITELN('average queuing time : ',Wq:27:6);
WRITELN('average  time spent in system : ',W:18:6);
WRITELN('std.-dev of system response time : ',SD:15:6);
WRITELN('average number of customers in queue:',Lq:13:6);
WRITELN('average number of customers in system : ',L:10:6);

END.(* mainline *)
```

Figure 5.9   Pascal program for multi-server queues.

```
LAMBDA =15.9000   MU = 5.4000   S = 3   n = 4   t = 8

utilisation of facility:                     0.981481
prob. of 0 customers in system :             0.004201
prob.of  4 customers in system:              0.017543
prob. that all servers busy :                0.965217
prob.of queuing time longer than 8 is        0.087562
average queuing time :                       3.217388
average  time spent in system :              3.402573
std.-dev of system response time :           3.336457
average number of customers in queue:       51.156467
average number of customers in system :     54.100910
```

Fig. 5.9 *continues*

generally used in modelling and simulation are presented. The results from queuing theory given in Section 5.17 are useful in validating some of the simulation models developed later on in this book. Several numerical examples are given to illustrate the practical applications of theoretical results.

5.19   Exercises

1. There are 20 yellow bricks, 15 grey bricks, 10 red bricks, and 15 black bricks, and these are to be arranged in a row. How many different arrangements can be formed.

2. In how many ways can a four-letter word be constructed out of the English alphabet.

3. (a) For any three events D, E, F show that

$$(DE) \cup (DF) = D(E \cup F)$$

(b)

For any two events C and D show that

$$p(C \cup D) = p(C)+p(D)-p(CD)$$

4. Assuming equal probabilities for left-handed and right-handed children, find the probability of left-handed and right-handed children in families with three children.

5. At the university computer centre it was observed that on an average 35% of the students use Fortran, 45% use Pascal, and 20% use Cobol for their programming exercises. On a particular day, 70% of the Fortran, 85% of the Pascal, and 60% of the Cobol programs were compiled successfully. If a student at the computer centre was selected at random and it was found that his program was aborted during compilation on that day, what is the probability that his program was written in Pascal.

6. (a) The cumulative distribution function of a stochastic variable is given by

$$F(X) = \begin{cases} e^{X-2} & \text{for } X \leq 4 \\ 1 & \text{for } X > 4 \end{cases}$$

find $f(X)$ and graph $f(X)$.

(b) *The probability density function of a stochastic variable is given by*

$$f(X) = \begin{cases} (1/4)(8-X^2) & \text{for } -2 \leq X \leq 2 \\ 0 & \text{elsewhere} \end{cases}$$

compute the probability $p(-1 \leq X \leq 1)$ and $p(x > 1.5)$.

7. The average service time and the average number of customers in the checkout queue of a supermarket were observed on an hourly basis for 8 hours as shown in the following table.

Hour	1	2	3	4	5	6	7	8
Average service time in minutes	3	5	6	9	2	8	6	4
Average number in queue	3	4	7	11	12	7	5	8

Determine the standard deviation, variance, covariance, and correlation coefficient of the stochastic variables. Plot the variables and interpret the behaviour of the graph.

8. Generate the parasite–host populations described in Section 3.6.1 at discrete points in time for 20 time units. Compute the covariance and correlation coefficients of the two populations and interpret the results.

9. For any stochastic variables X and Y, show that

$$\text{cov}(X,Y) = E(XY) - E(X)\,E(Y)$$

where $0 < \sigma_X^2 < \infty$ and $0 < \sigma_Y^2 < \infty$

10. A random sample of 100 variates taken from a normal population is found to have a mean of 50 and standard deviation 12. Show that the 95% confidence limits is given by 50 ± 2.35.

    Hint: area under normal curve can be obtained from statistical tables.

11. In a factory it is known that on an average only 25% of the components produced by a machine passed inspection. In an experiment, 70 out of 500 components produced passed inspection. Is this considered a significantly poor result on the basis of the 1% level of significance?

12. Request for processing simulation jobs arrive at an average rate of 5 per hour from remote computer terminals. The CPU (central processing unit) can process only one job at a time and the processing

time was found to be negative exponentially distributed with a mean of 6 minutes/job. Jobs are queued whenever the CPU is busy. Compute:
- (a) probability of having more than 6 jobs waiting in the queue;
- (b) average queue length,
- (c) average waiting time in the queue;
- (d) idle time of CPU;
- (e) if the arrival rate goes up to 9 jobs/hour, what must be the service time so that the probability of any job queuing for more than 15 minutes is not more than 0.15.

13. On an average 40 students require the assistance of a university programming adviser who works continuously for 10 hours per day. Students arrive at random and require, on an average, 10 minutes of individual advice at a cost of £10 to the university. Compute various system statistics using the formulae given in Section 5.17.

   It was found that the students wasted a lot of time by waiting in the queue. How much will it cost to reduce the average queue length from the present value to 1/2, if it costs an additional £1 for every minute of reduction in service time?

References

Blum, J. R., and Rosenblatt, J. I. (1972). *Probability and Statistics*. W. B. Saunders, Philadelphia, PA.

Cox, D. R., and Smith, W. L. (1961). *Queues*. John Wiley, New York,

Fishman, G. S. (1973). *Concepts and Methods in Discrete Event Digital Simulation*. Wiley-Interscience, New York.

Kendall, D. G. (1953). 'Stochastic processes occurring in the theory of queues and their analysis', *Ann. Math. Stat*, **24**(3), 338–345.

Lee, A. M. (1966). *Applied Queuing Theory*. St Martin's Press, New York.

Mihram, G. A. (1972). *Simulation: Statistical Foundations and Methodology*. Academic Press, New York.

Page, E. (1972). *Queuing Theory in OR*. Butterworth, London.

6

Random Numbers and Random Variates

6.1 Introduction

Random numbers are widely used in physics, computer science, operations research, numerical analysis, management science, social sciences, statistics, and other areas where chance variables are introduced in the analysis and solution of problems. The majority of systems we see around us are stochastic in nature and random numbers are extensively used in the simulation of such systems. For example, the arrival of customers in a supermarket, computer centre, or bank; the errors in computer programs; the processing time for simulation jobs; the failure of machines in a factory, etc., can be generated by means of random numbers.

Random numbers were studied thoroughly by several authors almost 20 years ago. However, the availability of new machines with different word sizes, and the increasing trend in the implementation of simulation models on microprocessors where random number generators are not provided as standard routines, justify the inclusion of a chapter on random numbers and random variates.

If a variable (chance variable or stochastic variable) X can take any value in the range (a,b) with equal probability, then X is said to be a *random variable*. A random variable is not influenced by its past values. When we discuss random variables we are concerned not only about the *distribution* of variables, but also the *sequence of occurrence* of these variables. A set of random numbers may be *uniformly* or *nonuniformly* distributed (Figure 6.1), *positive* or *negative* and *continuous* or *discrete*. Some readers may find it difficult to grasp the concept of nonuniformly distributed random numbers and they should read additional material (Knuth, 1969; Naylor, 1971) before proceeding further. In Figure 6.1 the $X = 1$, 2, 3 or 4 could be visualized as the outcome of a random experiment and $p(X)$ is the probability.

6.2 Generation of random numbers

The random numbers can be provided in many ways. For example, tables of random numbers (Table 6.1), pack of cards, numbered tokens, spinning

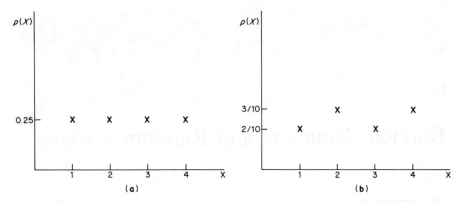

Figure 6.1 (a) Uniformly distributed discrete random numbers; (b) non-uniformly distributed discrete random numbers.

wheels, and electronic counters are some of the *physical methods* of generation of random numbers. Physical methods (Rand Corp., 1955) are generally slow, inconvenient, or expensive to build and maintain, and the sequence of numbers is not *reproducible* for program testing. In modern times, *algebraic methods* are used to generate random numbers because of their *simplicity*, *speed*, and *reproducibility*. They start off with a number X_0 called the *seed* and produce sequences of the form

$$X_1 = f(X_0)$$
$$X_2 = f(X_1)$$
$$\cdot$$
$$\cdot$$
$$\cdot$$
$$X_i = f(X_{i-1})$$

However, since the number of digits on a computer is finite, one can generate only a finite number of distinct numbers; therefore the machine-produced numbers which appear to be random and satisfy most of the tests for randomness are known as *pseudo-random* or *quasi-random* numbers.

A good pseudo-random generator must be capable of producing different sequences of numbers which are
1. Uniformly distributed between 0 and 1 (nonuniform distributions can be generated from uniform distributions).
2. Statistically independent (future random numbers are not influenced by past values).
3. Reproducible (repeat the same sequence for testing different versions of a program).
4. Non-repeating for any desired length (i.e. long period. The number of

Table 6.1 Example of random numbers *r*.

(a) $0 \leqslant r \leqslant 0.99999999$

0.00204229	0.06206775	0.95782053	0.70911676	0.98829061
0.24708664	0.03053004	0.68130517	0.06973368	0.43774658
0.71930534	0.70121771	0.40792847	0.21165913	0.08560377
0.56970781	0.15263301	0.21106845	0.28720772	0.15357375
0.18613034	0.83849074	0.62674737	0.81713784	0.89391923
0.10822773	0.18127841	0.72003728	0.25864726	0.51102787
0.18478930	0.21560067	0.32416141	0.50477183	0.08551353
0.33418500	0.82655007	0.98705566	0.94992083	0.08584946
0.53905308	0.86114800	0.63526422	0.06673944	0.62771362
0.55399531	0.90255547	0.60355675	0.06464684	0.09575045
0.39184612	0.42049104	0.89580154	0.12020051	0.13168806
0.56298643	0.91008836	0.89546686	0.00464839	0.06271994
0.00675040	0.24435478	0.34075457	0.57816541	0.30785102
0.96372551	0.56074351	0.99511808	0.81275392	0.10226786
0.54099119	0.72155583	0.14147019	0.20604205	0.12199622
0.16121072	0.66374767	0.39117301	0.93229377	0.60022670
0.06077766	0.85306644	0.44967335	0.49127847	0.11639333
0.17152369	0.97157723	0.86952585	0.28463590	0.52112979
0.91655278	0.38477939	0.33056283	0.64629030	0.62863487
0.18425184	0.09117270	0.21029121	0.60653299	0.63027048

(b) $0 \leqslant r \leqslant 9999$

8811	5719	3721	2534	1670	2640	5165	8231	1394	7947
8256	6531	7783	2751	0513	7259	9111	2931	6993	1281
8963	0723	8617	7889	1084	4926	1667	7018	4551	6381
2412	7238	4667	8585	4587	9613	2145	5431	2212	1942
7528	2547	1823	1484	5528	7268	2739	9368	2467	6979
4009	7673	4579	8794	0587	9629	4229	9691	5246	3302
5701	0900	0723	7097	7785	2713	3807	6639	7650	4819
2155	2970	0466	1642	8829	9143	4891	0796	6590	2946
7479	5339	9735	7911	2968	7058	1055	8199	2964	8271
4125	6761	8302	0568	2345	7706	2983	0894	4310	0506
8749	3476	6745	8133	3041	3816	6713	8835	3455	3597
8327	3375	1515	0432	9315	3713	7775	0861	9174	2297
9202	2090	2936	6842	2122	3067	8599	0810	3574	1514
1126	7909	4713	5254	3759	1658	7955	5553	5490	9605
6033	7592	0109	7260	0070	5436	4766	7997	1727	5993
1961	4358	2856	8625	0523	1492	4293	1039	3804	4889
7229	9206	0019	3212	4213	6753	6936	1230	3762	5998
3769	9813	2771	3258	7641	7915	5334	1362	8960	6124
8826	4717	5896	4418	1158	8232	9373	5665	4859	0358
5346	5377	2348	8950	9428	7695	6968	1741	0685	8143

distinct numbers in the sequence must be sufficiently large compared to the number of random numbers needed for an experiment).

5. Generated fast and should not use large amounts of computer memory.

6.3 Von Neumann's midsquare method

This method, which is simple and easy to implement, was proposed in the 1940s, but did not produce good random sequences and had a tendency to degenerate rapidly to zero. Figure 6.2 illustrates the operation of this method, which comes to a halt when $X_{n+1} = 0$.

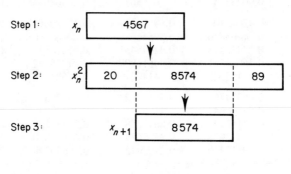

Figure 6.2   Midsquare method.

Notes:
1. X_n is any K-digits long number.
2. X_n^2 is $2K$ digits long.
3. X_{n+1} is K digits long.

6.4 Linear congruential generators

The most popular method in use today for the generation of pseudo-random numbers is the congruential method. It is built on the mathematical concept of *congruence* or *residues* in number theory and was originally introduced by D. H. Lehmer in 1951. Since then several variations of this method have been implemented on various computers. It is based on the formula (Knuth, 1969; Fishman, 1973; Marsaglia and Maclaren, 1965):

$$X_{n+1} = (CX_n + C_0) \text{ modulo } M \tag{6.1}$$
$$= \text{remainder of } [(CX_n + C_0)/M]$$

Where C_0, C, and M are all non-negative constants. This recursive relationship, which is known as the *linear congruential method*, is initiated by setting $X_n = X_0$, where X_0 is called the *seed* (Kleijnen, 1986).

Example

For $X_0 = 2$, $C = 8$, $C_0 = 3$ and $M = 10$, we get

$$X_1 = 9; \quad X_2 = 5; \quad X_3 = 3; \quad X_4 = 7; \quad X_5 = 9 = X_1$$

and therefore the same sequence is repeated.

The random numbers r_1, r_2, . . . generated by (6.1) satisfy the relations

$$0 \leqslant X_{n+1} \leqslant (M-1) \text{ and } 0 \leqslant r_{n+1} = \frac{X_{n+1}}{M} < 1$$

When $C_0 > 0$ the method is known as the mixed (multiplication + addition) linear congruential method, and when $C_0 = 0$ it is called the *multiplicative linear congruential method*. Whenever X_{n+1} takes on a value it has had before, exactly the same sequence of numbers is repeated. The length of this cycle is usually known as the *period P* of the generator. If $P = M$, then the generator has the full period, and obviously it is desirable to have a very large value for M.

6.4.1 Selection of constants

Accomplishment of full period is one of the major criteria used in the selection of the constants C_0, C, M and X_0. This is achieved when (Knuth, 1969; Naylor, 1971; Hull and Dobell, 1962):

1. C_0 is odd and relatively prime to M (i.e. both M and C_0 are exactly divisible only by 1)
2. $(C-1)$ s a multiple of every prime (i.e. divisible only by itself and one) dividing M
3. $(C-1)$ is a multiple of 4 if M is a multiple of 4

For a machine with b bit word size (excluding sign), $M = 2^b - 1$, and Knuth shows that the serial correlation between successive numbers is minimized when $C_0 = 0.21 M$ and $C = 8K + 5$ for $K = 0, 1, 2, ...$ When $P = M$ the sequence will contain all possible distinct numbers exactly once, and therefore the choice of X_0 is not critical.

6.5 Multiplicative congruential generators

This is a special case of linear congruential generators where $C_0 = 0$.

$$X_{n+1} = (CX_n) \bmod M \tag{6.2}$$

The equation (6.2) does not satisfy the condition (1) of Section (6.4.1) and therefore cannot have full period $P = M$. The maximum period 2^{b-2} is obtained when

$M = 2^b; \quad b \geqslant 4$
$C = 8K + 5; \quad K = 0, 1, 2, \ldots .$
X_0 is odd.

The multiplicative generators are faster, simple and easy to implement. When $M = 2^b$, the operation on the right-hand side of (6.2) can be achieved by simply discarding the overflow (i.e. b higher-order bits of the $2b$ bits long product) during the computations in integers and then shifting the decimal point to the left by b bits. Thus, explicit division is avoided. Hutchinson (1966) found that the statistical behaviour of the generator is better when M is equal to the largest prime number which is less than 2^b and here $P = M - 1$.

For 32-bit (31 + sign bit) machine IBM use (Lewis *et al.*, 1969; Payne *et al.*, 1969):

$C = 7^5 = 16,807$ or $C = 630,360,016$
$M = 2^{31} - 1 = 2,147,483,647$
$2^{-31} = 0.46566613 \ E - 9$

For a 36-bit machine (Hutchinson, 1966), the recommended values are

$M = 2^{35} - 31$ (largest prime number $< 2^{35}$) $= 34,359,738,337$
$C = 5^5 = 3125$ or $C = 5^{13} = 1,220,703,125$ (primitive roots of M)
$2^{-35} = 0.29103805 \ E - 10$
Period $P = (M - 1) = 2^{35} - 32$.

The *algorithm* for machine implementation of the multiplicative congruential generators is summarized below and the general format of the computer program is given in Figure 6.3.

We have $\hspace{3cm} X_{i+1} = C \, X_i \ (\text{mod } 2^b)$

Step 1:
Set $i = 0$; choose any odd integer $X_i = X_0 \leqslant 2^b$ (b = number of bits/word)

Step 2:
Form the product CX_i, $2b$ bits long.
Discard b higher-order bits of the product.
Set $X_{i+1} = b$ lower-order bits.

Step 3:
Form the pseudo-random number,

$$r_{i+1} = \frac{X_{i+1}}{2^b}$$

Note: division by 2^b is achieved by shifting the decimal point of X_{i+1} to the left by b positions.

Step 4:
  Set $i = i + 1$ and go on repeating Step 2 to Step 4.

```
FUNCTION  RANDM (IASEED)
IASEED   = IASEED * 630360016
RANDM    = IASEED
RANDM    = RANDM * 0.46566613 E-9
END
```

Figure 6.3   General format of computer program for random number generation.
Notes:
1. A word size of 31 bits assumed.
2. IASEED is a global integer variable.
3. Guard against overflow/underflow checks during integer multiplication in line 2 and ensure that a non-negative integer given by the 'b' lower-order bits are correctly stored in IASEED on the left.
4. Floating point operations in lines 3 and 4 produce random numbers in the range (0,1).
5. Check the features of the machine and the programming language before implementation.

Example

For simplicity, we set $C = 7$, $b = 4$ and $X_0 = 3$.

Iteration 1:
  $i \quad = 0$
  $X_0 \quad = 3 = 0011$ (binary)
  $CX_0 = 21 = 00010101$
  $X_1 \quad = 0101 = 5$
  $r_1 \quad = 5/16 = 0.3125$ (decimal)
  $\qquad\qquad = 0.0101$ (binary)

Iteration 2:
  $i \quad = 1$
  $CX_1 = 35 = 00100011$
  $X_2 \quad = 0011 = 3$
  $r_1 \quad = 3/16 = 0.1875$
  $\qquad\qquad = 0.0011$ (binary)

Iteration 3:
  etc.

6.6   Other pseudo-random number generators

In addition to the mixed and multiplicative linear congruential generators discussed earlier, several other generators have been developed with a view to increase the period and randomness of the numbers. *Additive generators* producing Fibonacci sequences, *quadratic congruential generators* (Knuth, 1969), and *composite generators* (Marsaglia, 1965; Westlake, 1967) are some examples. Marsaglia used two congruential generators where one generator shuffles the sequence produced by the other. A modification of this method which uses only one generator has been suggested by Bays and Durham (1976). These generators are comparatively more complex and the results are slightly better. However, the simplicity and ease of implementation make linear congruential generators more attractive for most practical applications.

6.7 Pseudo-random number generators for microcomputers

A variety of microcomputers are currently being used (Crookes and Valentine, 1982) for simulation work. Unlike mainframe computers, random number generators are not very often available as standard routines on micros, and users have to write their own routines. Even though the linear congruential generators are primarily designed for implementation on mainframe machines with long words, adaptations of multiplicative generators of the form

$$X_{n+1} = (5^{13}X_n) \bmod 2^{35}$$

have been successfully implemented on 8-bit and 16-bit microcomputers. The Pascal implementation on Apple 11 (Jennergren, 1983) produced uniformly distributed sequences of integers in the range 0 to 32,767 and statistical tests on these numbers were found to be satisfactory. It is very important to note that the *kn* bit numbers produced by simple *concatenation* of the output of *k* microprocessors with *n* bit long words, and using different congruential generators, are not *random*, and Mueller *et al.* (1977) recommend a *modified algorithm* to assure randomness and uniformity.

Several other papers (Francis, 1985; Gordon, 1985; Thesen, 1985) on the subject of generating random numbers on a variety of micros have recently appeared in the literature. The paper due to Modianos *et al.* (1984) is highly critical of some of the *vendor-supplied* generators on several popular microprocessors.

6.8 Testing of pseudo-random numbers

The output of pseudo-random number generators must be tested for uniformity and independence and several statistical tests are available (Knuth, 1969; Fishman, 1973; Fishman and More, 1982; IBM, 1969) for this. But none of these tests is powerful enough to guarantee perfect randomness; therefore each generator should be tested in the context of its intended use. Some of the *validation* and *verification* procedures discussed in Chapter 4 are useful here.

The congruential methods discussed in Sections 6.4 and 6.5 are deterministic processes and the sequence of numbers generated by these methods is completely determined by the starting value of the seed. Then, how do we justify the use of pseudo-random numbers as true random numbers in modelling, simulation, and other work? The true random numbers generated by a chance device are statistically independent (i.e. do not depend upon other numbers) and each number over the interval (0,1) is equally likely to occur. If the pseudo-random numbers generated by algebraic methods satisfy the same statistical tests usually applied to the true random numbers, then for all practical purposes we can treat the pseudo-random numbers as true random numbers (Knuth, 1969; Marsaglia and Maclaren, 1965). The statistical methods usually applied for testing the *randomness* of numbers are

Moments test
Frequency test
Serial test
Runs tests
Gap test
Kolmogorov–Smirnov Test
Other tests

6.8.1 Moments test

For random numbers r_i, $0 \leq r_i < 1$ the first (Figure 6.4), second, and third moments should be 1/2, 1/3, and 1/4 respectively. That is,

$$\frac{1}{n} \sum_{i=1}^{n} r_i = 1/2$$

$$\frac{1}{n} \sum_{i=1}^{n} r_i^2 = 1/3$$

$$\frac{1}{n} \sum_{i=1}^{n} r_i^3 = 1/4$$

where n is very large.

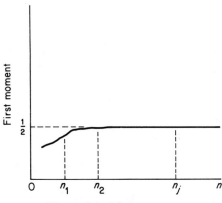

Figure 6.4 Moments test.

114

6.8.2 *Frequency test using chi-square method*

The frequency test is applied to check the uniformity of a set of random numbers. The discrepancy between the observed and theoretical frequencies is measured by means of a chi-square test, which is basically a test for goodness-of-fit between a sample and its theoretical probability distribution. Suppose $r_1, r_2, \ldots r_n$ to be a sequence of n pseudo-random numbers (sample) generated over the interval (0,1) and the unit interval is divided into subintervals (classes.). Let f_i ($i = 1, 2, \ldots s$) be the observed frequency of pseudo-random numbers in the ith interval. For a uniform distribution the theoretical expected frequency for any interval is n/s. Then, the number

$$\chi_1^2 \text{ (chi-square)} = \frac{s}{n} \sum_{i=1}^{s} \left(f_i - \frac{n}{s}\right)^2 = \frac{\sum (\text{actual-expected})^2}{\text{expected}} \qquad (6.3)$$

is known as chi-square statistic, and this gives a measure of the degree of fit between observed (actual) and expected (theoretical) frequencies. A small value for chi-square implies good fit between experiment and prediction. The squaring operating on the right-hand side of the equation (6.3) assures positivity of chi-square statistic. Since

$$\sum_{i=1}^{s} f_i = n,$$

there are only $(s - 1)$ independent frequencies or classes in the sample and the number $d = (s - 1)$ is known as the degrees of freedom. In general, $n \geqslant 100$ and $(n/s) \geqslant 5$. The theoretical value of χ^2 for a specified value of d and significance level α (Section 5.15) can be read directly from chi-square tables (Table 6.2). If $\chi_1^2 < \chi^2$, we accept the hypothesis that the set of numbers $r_1, r_2 \ldots r_n$ are uniformly distributed.

Example

The output of a random number generator was found to have the following distribution:

Digit	0	1	2	3	4	5	6	7	8	9
Observed frequency f_i	30	20	35	36	17	14	29	20	18	31

Here
$$n = \sum f_i = 250$$

$$s = 10; \frac{n}{s} = 25$$

$$\chi_1^2 = \frac{1}{25} \sum_{i=1}^{10} (f_i - 25)^2$$

$$= \frac{1}{25} [(30 - 25)^2 + (20 - 25)^2 + \ldots (31 - 25)^2]$$

$$= 23.29$$

Table 6.2 Chi-square table.

	p				
d	0.5%	1%	5%	97.5%	99.5%
1	7.8794	6.6349	3.8414	0.0982	0.0392
2	10.5966	9.2103	5.9914	0.05063	0.01002
3	12.8381	11.3449	7.8147	0.21579	0.07172
4	14.8602	13.2767	9.4877	0.48441	0.20699
5	16.7496	15.0863	11.0705	0.83121	0.41174
6	18.5476	16.8119	12.5916	1.23734	0.67572
7	20.2777	18.4753	14.0671	1.68987	0.98926
8	21.9550	20.0902	15.5073	2.17973	1.34441
9	23.5893	21.6660	16.9190	2.70039	1.73492
10	25.1882	23.2093	18.3070	3.24697	2.15585
11	26.7569	24.7250	19.6751	3.81575	2.60321
12	28.2995	26.2170	21.0261	4.40379	3.07382
13	29.8194	27.6883	22.3621	5.00874	3.56503
14	31.3193	29.1413	23.6848	5.62872	4.07468
15	32.8013	30.5779	24.9958	6.26214	4.60094

For 9 degrees of freedom and 5% significance level (i.e. $\alpha = 0.05$), we have, from chi-square table (Table 6.2), χ^2 16.919. Since $\chi_1^2 > \chi^2$, we conclude that the output of the one-digit random number generator is not unformly distributed.

6.8.3 *Serial test*

The serial test is applied to check the randomness or independence of successive pseudo-random numbers. This is an extension of the chi-square test to higher dimensions. The first member in the sequence is compared with the second, third, fourth, etc., and checked for frequency deviations from theoretical values. The experiment is repeated for all other numbers in the sequence and the hypothesis that the numbers are randomly distributed is tested by computing the chi-square statistic.

In its simplest form the serial test can be applied to pairs of consecutive numbers in the sequence or pairs of consecutive digits in the sequence. One can form n pairs of numbers of the form (r_1,r_2), (r_3,r_4), (r_5,r_6) . . . (r_{2n-1},r_{2n}) from a sequence of $2n$ numbers and the observed frequency of pairs is recorded. If the computer used is capable of generating d distinct numbers (e.g. a four-bit machine can generate 2^4 distinct numbrs), then d^2 distinct pairs of numbers are possible and the theoretical frequency of each pair is $1/d^2$ (n/d^2 for n pairs). As before, the chi-square statistic is computed and the sequence is tested for randomness at a specified significance level. The experiment is repeated on sets of 3, 4, . . . successive numbers.

116

6.8.4 Runs test

This is primarily oriented towards testing the independence of numbers. A sequence of identical results preceded and followed by non-identical results is called a *run*.

Example

+	+	−	−	−	+	−	+	+	+
H	H	T	T	T	H	T	H	H	H
0	0	1	1	1	0	1	0	0	0

Here we have two runs of length 1, one run of length 2, and two runs of length 3. 'zero' (+ or H) runs are called *runs up* and 'one' (− or T) runs are called *runs down*. Runs can be generated from a sequence of random numbers $r_1, r_2, \ldots r_n$ in many ways by forming a binary sequence (Knuth, 1969; Gorenstein, 1967).

Method 1

ith term in the sequence is 1 if $r_i \geqslant 0.5$
ith term in the sequence is 0 if $r_i < 0.5$

For n random numbers, the expected total number of runs is $(n + 1)/2$ and the expected number of runs of length K is

$$\frac{(n - K + 3)}{2^{K+1}}$$

Method 2

ith term in the sequence is 1 if $r_i \geqslant r_{i+1}$
ith term in the sequence is 0 if $r_1 < r_{i+1}$

For a truly random sequence, theoretical values for the expected number of runs are

Total number of runs $= \dfrac{(2n - 1)}{3}$

Runs of length $K < (n-1)$ $= \dfrac{2[(K^2+3K+1)n - (K^3+3K^2-K-4)]}{(K + 3)!}$

Runs of length $(n - 1)$ $= \dfrac{2}{n!}$

The number of occurrences of runs of different lengths in the sequence can be counted; the corresponding theoretical values are known and therefore the chi-square goodness-of-fit test can be easily applied. A very small number of runs in a sequence indicates non-randomness.

Example

Suppose we generated the following binary sequence by the Method 2 from a set of 20 numbers.

01111001010001010100

Then the chi-square statistic can be computed from the data given in Table 6.3.

Table 6.3   Data for runs test.

Runs	Theoretical	Observed
Total no. of runs	13	13
Runs of length 1	8.4	9
Runs of length 2	3.43	2
Runs of length 3	0.925	1
Runs of length 4	0.09	1

6.8.5   Gap test

Suppose we have a set of numbers $a, c_1, c_2, \ldots c_K, b$ in the interval (α, β) such that

1. $a,b \geq \alpha; a,b \leq \beta$
2. $c_i < \alpha$ or $c_i > \beta; \quad i = 1, 2, \ldots K$

then K is the length of the gap. The gap length is zero if there is no c_i between a and b.

For a random sequence the theoretical probability of getting a gap of length K is given by Knuth (1969):

$$p(K) = (\beta - \alpha)(1 - \beta + \alpha)^K$$

The actual number of gaps of lengths $0, 1, 2, \ldots$ is computed for the given sequence of numbers, and χ^2 goodness-of-fit test is applied as before.

Example

$$0 < \alpha < \beta < 1$$
$$\alpha = 0.5; \quad \beta = 0.77$$

For a sequence of $n = 12$ numbers

$$\underline{0.599} \quad 0.1085 \quad \underline{0.557} \quad 0.0926 \quad \underline{0.7626} \quad 0.0327 \quad 0.3528$$

$$0.9418 \quad 0.199 \quad 0.3395 \quad 0.155 \quad \underline{0.751}$$

we get

Length of gap	Theoretical probability $p(K)$	Theoretical frequency $p(K) \cdot (n)$	Observed frequency
1	0.197	2.364	2
6	0.1513	1.816	1

6.8.6 Kolmogorov–Smirnov test (KS test)

This is a general *goodness-of-fit* test using *cumulative* probability distribution (Knuth, 1969; Schmidt and Taylor, 1970) and is good for all sample sizes n, in contrast to the chi-square test which converges only when n is very large. The procedure is very similar to the chi-square test except that instead of the chi-square table we use the KS table to test the hypothesis at a given significance level α. The chi-square table entries are only approximations, whereas KS table entries are exact and valid for both small and large values of n. Unlike the chi-square test, the KS test requires no classes or groups of data and is used when the hypothesized distribution function $F(X)$ is continuous. However, to date, there is no conclusive evidence to show that the KS test is better than the chi-square test for testing sequence of random numbers.

For a sample of observations $X_1 \leqslant X_2 \leqslant X_3 \ldots \leqslant X_n$ we can define an empirical distribution function

$$F_n(X) = \frac{\text{number of } X_i \leqslant X}{n}$$

$$= \begin{cases} 0 & \text{for } X < X_1 \\ i/n & \text{for } X_i \leqslant X < X_{i+1} \\ 1 & \text{for } X \geqslant X_n \end{cases}$$

The KS statistic K_n gives a measure of the deviation of the empirical distribution function $F_n(X)$ from the hypothesized or fitted continuous theoretical distribution function $F(X)$, and is given by

$$K_n = \underset{X}{\text{Supremum}} \, [\,|F_n(X) - F(X)|\,]$$

The computational algorithm for the KS statistic is

(a) compute

$$K_n^+ = \max_{1 \le j \le n} [j/n) - F(X_j)]$$
$$K_n^- = \max_{1 \le j \le n} [F(X_j) - ((j-1)/n)]$$

(b) $K_n = \max[K_n^+, K_n^-]$

6.8.7 Other tests

Several other tests have been developed for checking the randomness of any given sequence of numbers.

(a) Poker test. The individual digits of the pseudo-random numbers are checked, taking five digits at a time corresponding to a poker hand. The probability of occurrence of each hand is theoretically and experimentally determined; then proceed as before.

(b) Maximum test. This is used to check abnormally high or low numbers in the sequence.

(c) Autocorrelation tests. Used to test the dependence of one number on another number in the sequence; also checks relationships among sets of random numbers.

6.9 Generation of random variates

If a *pseudo-random number Y* is used to generate another variable X, then X is called a *random variate* and the sequence X may be *uniformly* or *nonuniformly* distributed. The random variates from a given probability distribution representing the input to simulation models are generated in this way by using a set of uniformly distributed random numbers. In many simulation models, we use empirical data collected from the actual process being modelled as input either directly or after approximating it with a well-known distribution function. If at all possible it is preferable to fit a family of curves to data rather than using the empirical distribution directly.

The random variates may be generated in many ways. *Inverse, composition, rejection,* and *table look-up* (Mitchell and Stone, 1975; Walker, 1977) methods, as well as *algorithms* which use special properties (Schmeiser, 1980), have been developed. More recently, Hora (1983) has reported a *regression method* for estimating the inverse of a continuous cumulative probability function, and this is found to be useful for generating random variates from an arbitrary continuous distribution function. The most commonly used methods for the generation of random variates are (a) the inverse transformation method, and (b) the rejection method.

6.10 Inverse transformation method

We know that the cumulative distribution function $F(X)$ is defined (Section 5.8) over the interval $(0,1)$. If r is a sequence of uniformly distributed random numbers in the range $(0,1)$, then we can generate numbers X from the distribution $F(X)$ by setting $F(X) = r$, provided the inverse transformation $F^{-1}(r)$ exists. Unfortunately several distribution functions cannot be analytically inverted, and we may have to look for approximate numerical or empirical methods.

Example

$$f(X) = 4x^3 \text{ for } 0 < x \leqslant 1$$

$$= 0 \text{ elsewhere}$$

$$F(X) = \int_0^X 4x^3 \, dx = X^4$$

Setting $F(X) = r$, we get

$$X^4 = r$$

or

$$X_i = F^{-1}(r_i) = (r_i)^{1/4}; \quad 0 \leqslant r_i < 1$$

6.11 Rejection method

Suppose the probability density function $f(X)$ is completely enclosed in a rectangle with base (a,b) and height h (Figure 6.5), such that

$$a \leqslant X \leqslant b; \quad 0 \leqslant f(X) \leqslant h; \quad 0 \leqslant f(X)/h \leqslant 1$$

Then, for $0 \leqslant r \leqslant 1$,

$$p[r \leqslant f(X)/h] = f(X)/h$$

The rejection method of computing the random variates X_i can be summarized as follows.

1. Generate random numbers r_i and r_{i+1}
2. Compute $X_i = a + (b - a)r_i$
   $$Y_i = hr_{i+1}$$
3. If $Y_i > f(X_i)$, repeat from Step 1; otherwise output X_i.

The principle employed here is very simple, but the method, in general, is very inefficient (Tocher, 1963).

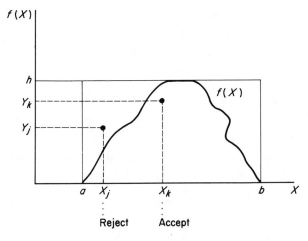

Figure 6.5   Random variates by rejection method.

6.12   Generation of continuous random variates

6.12.1   Uniform distribution

In the absence of additional information, we always assume that the given distribution is uniformly distributed. For uniform distribution, we have (Section 5.9):

$$f(X) = \begin{cases} 1/(b - a) & \text{for } a < X \leq b \\ 0 & \text{elsewhere} \end{cases}$$

Using the inverse transform method

$$F(X) = \frac{X - a}{b - a} = r; \quad 0 \leq r < 1$$

and

$$X = a + r(b - a)$$

For different values of $r = r_i$ we get random variates X_i over the interval (a,b).

If X_i are restricted to take only integer values, then we use

$$X_i = a + [r_i\{(b - a) + 1\}] = a + [\cdot] \tag{6.4}$$

where $[\cdot]$ is the largest integer value of $[r_i\{(b - a) + 1\}]$

Example

$$a = 1; \quad b = 5$$

Then

r_i	X_i
0	1
0.6	4
0.999	5

Some generators produce random numbers in the interval (0,999) and in this case equation (6.4) should be modified as follows:

$$X_i = a + [\{r_i/1000\}\{(b - a) + 1\}]$$

where $a \leqslant X_i \leqslant b$ and $0 \leqslant r_i < 1000$.

6.12.2 Exponential distribution

Exponential distributions are generally used to represent occurrences of events such as arrivals and departures of customers (supermarkets, banks, computer centres), failure of machines and components, births, deaths, accidents, etc. If the events are independent, and if the probability of occurrence of an event in a small interval of time is very small, then the time interval between occurrences of these events is *exponentially distributed* (Morse, 1958; Kleinrock, 1975) and this is known as a *Poisson process*. The probability density function is of the form (Figure 6.6):

$$f(X) = \begin{cases} \lambda e^{-\lambda X} & \text{for } \lambda > 0 \text{ and } X \geqslant 0 \\ 0 & \text{elsewhere} \end{cases}$$

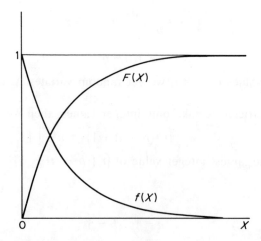

Figure 6.6 Exponential density and distribution functions.

$$F(X) = \int_0^X \lambda e^{-\lambda t}dt = 1 - e^{-\lambda X}$$

$$\text{mean} = E(X) = \frac{1}{\lambda}; \quad \text{variance} = \frac{1}{\lambda^2}$$

Using the inverse transformation technique,

$$r = 1 - e^{-\lambda X}; 0 \leqslant r < 1$$

$$X = -\frac{1}{\lambda} \log (1 - r)$$

$$= - (\text{mean}) \cdot \log (1 - r)$$

and this is shown in Figure 6.7 and Table 6.4. Notice that, if the random number r is uniformly distributed on (0,1), then so is (1 − r) and the sequence

$$X = -\frac{1}{\lambda} \log r$$

will have the same distribution. Thus the interevent time X for an exponential distribution can be computed from the mean of the distribution.

6.12.3 Normal distribution

One of the most important and commonly used distributions in modelling and simulation is the *normal distribution*, which is continuous and symmetric

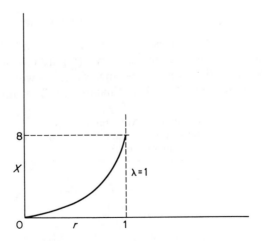

Figure 6.7 Exponential random variates.

Table 6.4 Table of r versus $-\log(1 - r)$.

r	$-\log(1 - r)$
0	0
0.1	0.104
0.2	0.222
0.4	0.509
0.6	0.915
0.8	1.6
0.95	2.99
0.98	3.9
0.995	5.3
0.999	7.0
0.9997	8.0

about the mean. The output data from many physical experiments are known to have normal distribution. It is defined by

$$f(X) = \frac{1}{\sigma(2\pi)^{\frac{1}{2}}} e^{-\frac{1}{2}(X-\mu)^2/\sigma^2} \tag{6.5}$$

mean $= \mu$; variance $= \sigma^2$ standard deviation $= \sigma$

$$e = 2.7183; \quad \pi = 3.1416$$

when $\dfrac{(x-\mu)}{\sigma} = Z$, equation (6.5) becomes

$$f(Z) = \frac{e^{-\frac{1}{2}Z^2}}{(2\pi)^{\frac{1}{2}}} \tag{6.6}$$

mean $= 0$; variance $=$ standard deviation $= 1$

The equation (6.6) is known as the standard form and Z is the standard unit. The total area bounded by the curve (Figure 6.8) and the Z axis is one. The area under the standard normal curve between the ordinates at $Z \pm K$ is shown in Table 6.5. The function $F(Z)$ is not invertible and

Table 6.5 Area under standard normal curve between ordinates at $Z = \pm K$.

K	Area
0	0
1	0.6826
2	0.9546
3	0.9974
3.87	1.0

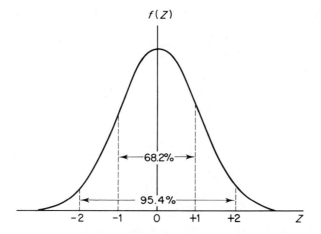

Figure 6.8 Standard normal distribution.

therefore X cannot be found analytically. However, several indirect methods have been developed (Bray and Marsaglia, 1964). The joint probability density function for two independent standard normal deviates X_1 and X_2 is

$$f(X_1, X_2) = \frac{1}{2\pi} e^{-\frac{1}{2}(X_1^2 + X_2^2)}$$

Substituting

$$X_1 = r \cos \theta \text{ and } X_2 = r \sin \theta,$$

Box and Muller (1958) derive the following algorithm:

(a) Generate uniformly distributed random variables r_i and r_{i+1} in the range (0,1)
(b) Compute

$$X_i = (-2 \log r_i)^{\frac{1}{2}} \cos 2\pi r_{i+1}$$
$$X_{i+1} = (-2 \log r_i)^{\frac{1}{2}} \sin 2\pi r_{i+1}$$

Then the variates X_i and X_{i+1} are normally distributed.

An approximate method for computing normally distributed random variates is summarized below:

1. Construct a table of Z versus $F(Z)$ by using Table 6.5.
2. For a given value of $r=F(Z)$, read out the value of Z from the table constructed in Step 1 (interpolation may be necessary).
3. Compute the random variate X from the relation $Z=(X-\mu)/\sigma$.

Another approximate method is due to Tocher (1963). He shows that,

$$f(X) = \frac{1}{(2\pi)^{\frac{1}{2}}} e^{-X^2/2}; \quad -\infty \leqslant X \leqslant \infty$$

$$e^{-X^2/2} \simeq \frac{2e^{-KX}}{(1+e^{-KX})^2} \quad \text{for } X > 0 \text{ and } K = \sqrt{8/\pi}$$

Then

$$F(X) = \frac{2}{1+e^{-KX}} - 1 = r; \quad 0 \leqslant r < 1$$

and

$$X_i = \frac{1}{K} \log\left(\frac{1+r_i}{1-r_i}\right)$$

The variables X_i together with a random sign give the desired normal variates.

6.12.4 Empirical distributions

Suppose the data for a simulation model have been obtained from experiments at a finite number of points and it is not possible to fit a well-known distribution to data. Then one could generate random variates from the distribution *empirically* by means of linear interpolation techniques. From Figure 6.9:

$$\tan \theta = S_i = \frac{X_{i+1} - X_i}{Y_{i+1} - Y_i}$$

Any point X_j between X_i and X_{i+1} is given by

$$X_j = X_i + [(Y_j - Y_i)S_i] \tag{6.7}$$

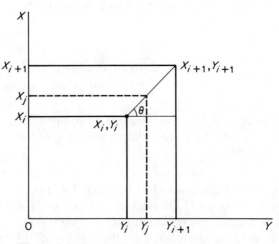

Figure 6.9 Interpolation between two points.

The random variates from the empirical distribution are generated as follows:

(a) Generate uniformly distributed random numbers r where $0 \leqslant r < 1$
(b) If $r_i = Y_i$, then output X_i
(c) If $r_i = Y_j$ such that $Y_i < r_i < Y_{i+1}$, then compute X_j from equation (6.7)

Example 1

X_i		0	2	5	4
$Y_i = F(X_i)$		0	0.3	0.5	1

Let $r = 0.4 = Y_j$

$$X_i = 2; \quad X_{i+1} = 5; \quad Y_i = 0.3; \quad Y_{i+1} = 0.5$$

Then, $F(2) < r < F(5)$

$$S_i = \frac{(5-2)}{(0.5-0.3)} = 15$$

Therefore $X_j = 2 + [(0.4 - 0.3)15] = 3.5$.

Example 2

The interarrival time distribution of 50 customers in a car park is shown in Table 6.6. Determine the interarrival time X_j (random variate) of a customer corresponding to the random number $r = 0.52$.

Table 6.6   Distribution of interarrival times.

Interarrival time X (minutes)	Number of arrivals	Relative frequency	Cumulative distribution $Y = F(X)$
0– 9	14	0.28	0.28
10–19	10	0.20	0.48
20–29	12	0.24	0.72
30–39	14	0.28	1.00
	50	1.00	

We have, $r = 0.52$.
Therefore $Y_i = 0.48; \quad Y_{i+1} = 0.72; \quad X_i = 20; \quad X_{i+1} = 30$.

$$S_i = \frac{(30-20)}{(0.72-0.48)} = \frac{10}{0.24}$$

$$X_j = 20 + [(0.52 - 0.48)(10/0.24)]$$
$$= 22 \text{ minutes (approx.)}$$

6.12.5 Other distributions

(a) Erlang distribution. Erlang distribution is generally used in queuing theory and inventory control problems. It is the sum of K exponential variables, each with an expected value of $1/K$. The probability density function is

$$f(X) = \lambda^K X^{K-1} \frac{e^{-\lambda X}}{(K-1)!}; \quad \lambda, X \geqslant 0 \text{ and } K = 1, 2, 3 \ldots$$
$$\text{mean} = K/\lambda; \quad \text{variance} = K/(\lambda^2).$$

When $K = 1$ we get the density function for the negative exponential distribution.

(b) Beta distribution. The probability density function is defined over the interval $(0,1)$; it is useful in fitting empirical distributions and widely used in project management applications.

(c) Gamma distributions. This is a very flexible and positively skewed distribution (Schriber and Tadikamalla, 1977) with many applications in engineering, maintenance scheduling, and reliability studies.

(d) Weibull distribution. Weibull distribution is a generalization of exponential distribution (Schriber and Tadikamalla, 1977) and it has applications in reliability studies, queuing theory and inventory control.

6.13 Generation of discrete random variates

6.13.1 Poisson distribution

The discrete probability distribution

$$p(X) = \frac{\lambda^X e^{-\lambda}}{X!}; \quad X = 0, 1, 2 \ldots$$

is known as Poisson distribution, where

$$\lambda = \text{constant}; \quad \text{mean} = \lambda; \quad \text{variance} = \lambda$$

Here the interevent times are exponentially distributed and the expected number of occurrences per unit time is λ. Variates from Poisson distribution can be generated as follows

(a) Generate random variates $X_1, X_2, \ldots X_{i+1}$ from the exponential distribution (Section 6.12.2) by using $X_i = (-1/\lambda) \log r_i$ such that

$$\sum_{i=1}^{x} X_i \leqslant 1 \leqslant \sum_{i=1}^{x+1} X_i$$

(b) Then x is the desired Poisson variate.

6.13.2 Binomial (Bernoulli) distribution

If p is the probability of success and $q = 1 - p$ is the probability of failure in an experiment, then the probability of X successes in n experiments is given by

$$p(X) = \binom{n}{X} p^X q^{n-X}; \quad X = 0, 1, 2, \ldots n$$

$$\text{mean} = np; \quad \text{variance} = npq$$

This is known as binomial distribution since for $X = 0, 1, \ldots n$, the value of $p(X)$ corresponds to the successive terms in the binomial expansion of $(q + p)^X$. The following steps generate the binomial variates with parameters p and n:

(a) Generate n uniformly distributed random numbers in the range $(0,1)$.
(b) Count the number N of uniform variates greater than p.
(c) Then the value of binomial variate is $(n - N)$.

Another approach is to use an integer version of the normal distribution as an approximation to the binomial distribution.

6.13.3 Empirical distributions

The random variables in this case take only discrete non-negative values. The cumulative distributive function is (Figure 6.10),

$$F(X) = p(X \leqslant x) = \sum_{j=0}^{x} p(j)$$

$$\text{where } p(j) = p(X=j); \quad j = 0, 1, 2, \ldots K$$

$$\sum_{j=0}^{k} p(j) = 1; \quad p(0) = 0$$

The random variates can be computed as follows:

(a) Generate uniformly distributed random numbers r $(0 \leqslant r < 1)$.
(b) Compute X_i such that

$$\sum_{j=0}^{X_i} p(j) \leqslant r < \sum_{j=0}^{X_{i+1}} p(j)$$

(c) Then X_i is the desired random variate.

Example

There are for pumps ($j = 1$ to 4) at a petrol station, and on an average $1/3$ of the customers used Pump 1, $1/6$ of them used Pump 2, another $1/3$ of

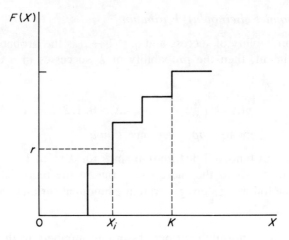

Figure 6.10 Discrete random variates.

them used Pump 3, and the remaining 1/6 of the customers used Pump 4. Outline a procedure for the selection of pumps by various customers.

From the definition of the problem we have

j	1	2	3	4
$p(j)$	1/3	1/6	1/3	1/6
$F(j)$	1/3	1/2	5/6	1

The following procedure accomplishes the random selection of pumps:

If:
$0 \leqslant r < 1/3$,   select Pump 1
$1/3 \leqslant r < 1/2$,   select Pump 2
$1/2 \leqslant r < 5/6$,   select Pump 3
$5/6 \leqslant r < 1$,   select Pump 4

Note that we have modified step c of the algorithm and used $(1 + X_i)$ instead of X_i since j cannot take the value of zero.

6.14 Summary

Random numbers are used for problem-solving in many areas of science, engineering, operations research, economics, and computer science. Random numbers can be generated in many ways—physical and algebraic methods. Algebraic methods (congruential methods) are currently popular because of their simplicity, computational speed, and reproducibility of the numbers generated. The computer-produced numbers cannot be truly random and are therefore known as pseudo-random numbers, which are satisfactory for most practical applications provided the constants in the algebraic formulae are selected according to certain rules. Random numbers have to satisfy a series of statistical tests for uniformity and randomness. Several methods for the generation (on mainframe and microcomputers) and testing of pseudo-random numbers, together with numerical examples, are presented.

Uniformly and nonuniformly distributed random variates are generated by means of uniformly distributed random numbers. In general, simulation models are stochastic in nature and random variates form the input to many simulation models. Two commonly used methods for generating random variates are the inverse transformation method and the rejection method. Algorithms for the generation of both discrete and continuous random variates from well-known probability distributions, as well as empirical distributions, are given. The operation of the algorithms is illustrated by means of several numerical examples.

6.15 Exercises

1. What is meant by pseudo-random numbers? What are the characteristics of a good random number generator? Explain various methods for the generation of pseudo-random numbers.
2. (a) Write a computer program in Fortran or Pascal to generate three-digit random numbers in the range 0 to 0.999 by (a) multiplicative generators and (b) mixed generators.
   (b) Show that the performance of the generators depends upon the selection of constants.
   (c) Select 100 numbers, divide the unit interval into 10 equal parts, and count the frequencies of numbers falling into each interval.
   (d) Apply the Frequency test and compare the output of the two generators.
   (e) Generate binary sequences from the random numbers and apply the Runs test.
3. Generate all numbers in one cycle using the following algorithm and test the numbers for uniformity and randomness:

$$X_{i+1} = (11 X_i) \bmod 16; \quad X_0 = 3$$

4. Generate a set of random numbers using the built-in function on your computing system. Apply various statistical tests and verify whether the generator is a good one.
5. Read 100 numbers in the range 0 to 1 from random number tables and then
   (a) Count the number of numbers falling into each of the ten intervals 0 to 0.1, 0.1 to 0.2, 0.2 to 0.3, etc.
   (b) Compute the theoretical frequency for each interval.

(c) Compute chi-square statistic.

(d) Test the sequence for uniformity at $\alpha = 0.05$.

6. Using the inverse transform technique, find the random variates for the triangular density function defined by

$$f(X) = \begin{cases} \dfrac{2(X-a)}{(b-a)(c-a)} & \text{for } a \leqslant X \leqslant c \\[2mm] \dfrac{2(b-X)}{(b-a)(b-c)} & \text{for } c < X \leqslant b \\[2mm] 0 & \text{elsewhere} \end{cases}$$

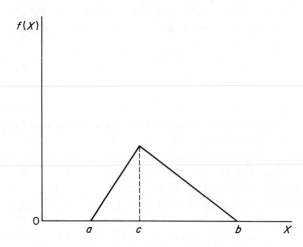

Figure 6.11   Triangular density function.

7. (a) Write a program in Fortran or Pascal to compute the value of π by the rejection method.

(b) Estimate the area under the curve $y = 0.7 \cos X$ for $0 \leqslant X \leqslant \pi$ by the rejection method.

8. Generate random numbers with the following probability density function by (i) the inverse transform and (ii) the rejection method.

(a) $f(X) = 2X^3 + 5$ for $1 < X < 10$ and zero elsewhere.

$f(X) = 10 - X$ for $3 \leqslant X\ 8$ and zero elsewhere.

9. (a) Generate 100 normally distributed random numbers with a mean of 8 and a standard deviation of 3.

(b) Plot the frequency distribution of the numbers.

(c) Compute the sample mean, variance, and standard deviation.

10. (a) If the arrival of jobs from remote terminals to a computing system is known to be random, show that the probability $p(K)$ of exactly

K arrivals occurring within an interval t is given by the Poisson distribution

$$p(K) = \frac{(t/\lambda)^K e^{-t/\lambda}}{K!}$$

where λ is the mean interarrival time.
(b) Compute $p(K)$ when

$$t = 10, \; \lambda = 3, \text{ and } K = 0, 1, \ldots 15$$

(c) Generate the arrival time of the first 20 jobs.
11. The processing time of jobs (in seconds) at the local computer centre is as shown below.

Processing time (seconds)	1	2	3	4	5	6	7
Number of jobs	153	220	145	250	300	270	195

Outline a random number generator which supplies the processing time of jobs to simulation model.

References

Bays, C., and Durham, S. D. (1976). "Improving a poor random number generator', *ACM Trans on Math. Soft*, **2**(1), 59–64.
Box, G. E. P. and Muller, M. E. (1958). 'A note on the generation of random normal deviates', *Ann. Math. Stat*, **29**(2), 610–611.
Bray, T. A., and Marsaglia, G. (1964). 'A convenient method for generating normal variables', *SIAM Rev*, **6**(3), 260–264.
Crookes, J. G., and Valentine, B. (1982). 'Simulation in microcomputers,, *J. Operational Res. Soc.*, **33**(9), 855–858.
Fishman, G. S. (1973). *Concepts and Methods in Discrete Event Digital Simulation*. Wiley-Interscience, New York.
Fishman, G. S., and More, L. R. (1982). 'A statistical evaluation of multiplicative congruential random number generators with modulus $2^{31} - 1$, *J. Am. Statist. Assoc.*, **77**(377), 129–136.
Francis, N. D. (1985). 'Generation of random numbers on micros—a simulation study', *Microprocessing and Microprogramming*, **15**(1), 17–19.
Gordon, T. J. (1985). 'Statistical simulation on the BBC microcomputer: significance tests of the pseudo-random number generator', *J. Appl. Statist.* **12**(2), 147–154.
Gorenstein, S. (1967). 'Testing a random number generator', *CACM*, **10**(2), 111–118.
Hora, S. C. (1983). 'Estimation of the inverse function for random variate generation', *CACM*; **26**(8), 590–594.
Hull, T. E., and Dobell, A. R. (1962). 'Random number generators', *SIAM Rev.*, **4**(3), 230–254.
Hutchinson, D. W. (1966). 'A new uniform pseudo random number generator', *CACM*, **9**(5), 432–433.

134

IBM (1969). *Random Number Generation and Testing*. IBM Publ. No. GC20–8011–0.
Jennergren, L. P. (1983). 'Another method for random number generation on microcomputers', *Simulation*, **41**(2), 79.
Kleijnen, J. P. C. (1986). 'Selecting random number seeds in practice', *Simulation*, **47**(1), 15–17.
Kleinrock, L. (1975). *Queuing Systems*, Vol.I: *Theory*. Wiley-Interscience, New York.
Knuth, D. E. (1969). *The Art of Computer Programming*, Vol. 2. A. Wesly, London.
Lehmer, D. H. (1951). 'Mathematical methods in large scale computing units', *Ann. Comp. Lab, Harvard Univ.*, **26**, 141–146.
Lewis, P. A., Goodman, A. S., and Miller, J. M. (1969). 'A pseudo–random number generator for IBM 360', *IBM SJ*, **8**(2), 136–146.
Marsaglia, G., and Maclaren, M. D. (1965). 'Uniform random number generators', *JACM*; **12**(1), 83–89.
Mitchell, R. L., and Stone, C. R. (1975). 'Table-look up methods for generating arbitrary random numbers', *IEEE Trans. on Comp.*, **C-26**, 10, 1006–1008.
Modianos, D. T., Scott, R. C., and Cornwell, L. W. (1984). 'Random number generation on microcomputers', *Interfaces*, **14**(4), 81–87.
Morse, P. M. (1958). *Queues, Inventories and Maintenance*. John Wiley, New York.
Mueller, R. A., George, D. D., and Johnson, G. R. (1977). 'A random number generator for microprocessor', *Simulation*, **28**(4), 123–127.
Naylor, T. H. (1971). *Computer Simulation Experiments with Models of Economic Systems*. John Wiley, New York.
Payne, W. H., Rabung, J. R., and Bogyo, T. P. (1969). 'Coding the Lehmer pseudorandom number generator', *CACM*, **12**(2), 85–86.
Rand Corporation (1955). *A Million Random Digits with 100,000 Normal Deviates*. Free Press, Glencoe, IL.
Schmeiser, B. (1980). 'Random variate generation: a survey'. In *Simulation with Discrete Models; a state of the art view* (eds T. I. Ören, C. M. Shub and P. F. Roth). IEEE Press, New York, pp. 79–104.
Schmidt, J. W., and Taylor, R. E. (1970). *Simulation and Analysis of Industrial Systems*. Richard D. Irwin, Homewood, Illinois.
Schriber, T. J., and Tadikamalla, P. R. (1977). 'Sampling from the Weibull and gamma distributions in GPSS', *Simuletter*, **9**(1), 39–45.
Thesen, A. (1985). 'An efficient generator of uniformly distributed random variates between zero and one', *Simulation*, **44**(1), 17–22.
Tocher, K. D. (1963). *The Art of Simulation*. English Universities Press, London.
Walker, A. J. (1977). 'An efficient method for generating discrete random variables with general distributions', *ACM Trans. Math. Soft*, **3**(3), 253–256.
Westlake, W. J. (1967). 'A uniform random number generator based on the combination of two congruential generators', *JACM*, **14**(2), 337–340.

7

Discrete System Simulation

7.1 Introduction

In the discrete approach to system simulation discussed in Chapter 1, state changes in the physical system are represented by a series of discrete changes or events at specific instants of time and such models are known as *discrete event models*. The *time* and *state* are the two important coordinates used in describing simulation models. Between *events*, the states of the *entities* remain constant. The change in state is brought about by events which form the driving force behind every discrete event simulation model. However, there exists considerable confusion in the literature on the definition of time and state relationships and in particular the terms 'event', 'activity', and 'process', which are fundamental to the development of simulation models.

7.2 Event, activity, and process

We will use the following definitions, due to Nance (1981)

Model: A model of a system consists of entities (objects) and their inter-relationships. Entities are described by attributes (e.g. customer in a shop model is an entity; the sex, age, priority, shopping time, queuing time, service time, and money spent are attributes).

Instant: A value of system time at which the value of at least one attribute of an entity can be altered.

Interval: Duration between two successive instants.

State: The state of an entity is the description of all attribute values of that entity at a specified instant.

Activity: The state of an entity over an interval. (An activity is bound by any two successive events which need not be related to the same entity.)

Object activity: The state of an entity (object) between two successive events which cause state changes for that entity (here, activity is bound by successive events related to the specified entity).

Actions: A set of operations that transform the state of an entity.

136

Event: A change in the state of an entity, occurring at an instant that initiates an activity (e.g. initiation or termination of service to a customer in a shop; arrival or departure of customers; creation or destruction of entities in a simulation model).

Process: A process is a succession of states of an entity over one or more contiguous intervals (or contiguous succession of one or more object activities.)

These concepts are illustrated in Figure 7.1.

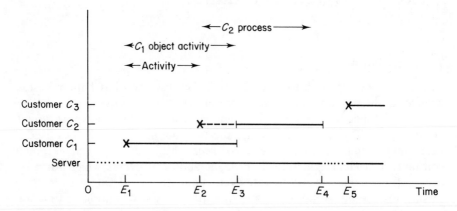

Figure 7.1 Event, activity, and process. (E = Event; X = customer arrival; . . . . , server idle; ---, customer in queue; ——, customer being served.)

7.3 Representation of time

The dynamic behaviour of the system is studied by tracing various system states as a function of time and then collecting and analysing the system statistics. The events that change the system state are generated at different points in time, and the passage of time is represented by an *internal clock* which is incremented and maintained by the simulation program (simulator).

The simulation time can be advanced in two ways. The first method is the *interval-oriented simulation* or the uniform time increment method (fixed time increment or synchronous method) where the clock is advanced from time t to $t + \Delta t$ where Δt is a uniform fixed time increment. The second method is the *event-oriented simulation* or the variable time increment method (next-event time increment or asynchronous method) where the clock is incremented from time t to the next event (most imminent event) time t', whatever may be the value of t'. The state changes are made at event time t, the next event time t', and this process is continuously repeated. Thus, only events are represented explicitly in a simulation model and the periods between events are treated as inactive or insignificant and therefore consume no time even though the interevent activities do consume time in the real world. The two approaches are shown in Figure 7.2

Obviously, method 1 detects the events that occur during the interval $(t, t+\Delta t)$ only at time $(t+\Delta t)$, thereby introducing errors in simulation. Another drawback of this method is that if the interval between two events is very large compared to Δt, then the simulator goes through several unproductive clock increments (during periods of inactivity) and the associated computing effort which will not bring about any change in system states. The activation time for each event is maintained in a list which is used for scheduling events, and thus the computer implementation of this method is comparatively less sophisticated. The second method involves sorting of event activation times and maintaining *current* and *future events* lists. In general, most of the discrete event simulation languages use variable time increments. The fixed time increment methods are suitable for the simulation of continuous systems and in particular systems with large numbers of state variables.

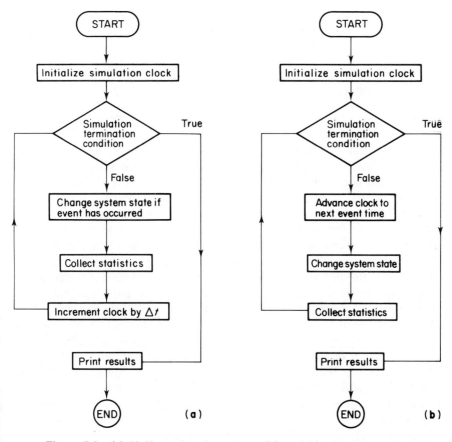

Figure 7.2 (a) Uniform time increment; (b) variable time increment.

7.4 Analysis of discrete systems—a simple example

A small post office (Figure 7.3) giving service to customers, one at a time, on a first-come–first-served basis (FIFO) was selected for this study. Customers arrive at random and wait in the queue whenever the postmaster (PM) is busy.

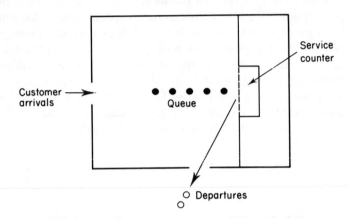

Figure 7.3   Post office system.

This is the classical single-server-single-queue system discussed in Section 5.17. The items of interest are the customer arrival rate, service rate, server (PM) utilization, average queue length, average number in the system, average waiting time, and the average time spent in the system. The state variables associated with this system are the time of arrival of each customer in the queue, the number of customers in the queue, and the state (idle or busy) of the server. Both the arrival and departure (on completion of service) of customers are events because they bring about changes in state variables. If the queue is empty on completion of serving a customer, the PM becomes idle; otherwise the next customer from the queue is selected for service.

Obviously, the PM works continuously as long as there are customers in the queue. The arrival, queuing, and service times of individual customers were observed for 2 hours and recorded as shown in Table 7.1. From this, a histogram (number of customers in queue or system versus time) of the type shown in Figure 7.4 was constructed. Table 7.2 was derived from this histogram, and it should be noted that the number of customers in the queue is always one less than the number in the system. We take the departure time T of the Nth customer ($N = 25$ here) as the period of study.

In order to gain confidence in simulation as a method of problem-solving, we will examine three possible approaches to the analysis of the post office system by using some or all of the observed data.

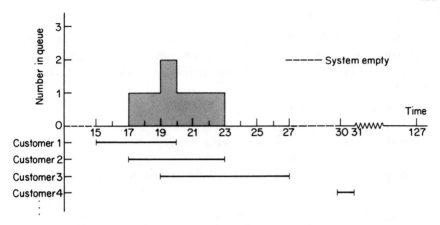

Figure 7.4 Observed number of customers in the queue.

Table 7.1 Observed data (time in minutes) for post office system.

Customer i	Arrival time	Inter-arrival time	Time service begins	Time service ends	Service time, S_i	Waiting time in queue, W_i	Time spent in system, $(W_i + S_i)$
1	15	15	15	20	5	0	5
2	17	2	20	23	3	3	6
3	19	2	23	27	4	4	8
4	30	11	30	31	1	0	1
.	.	.	.	.	.	.	.
.	.	.	.	.	.	.	.
.	.	.	.	.	.	.	.
25	120	3	122	127	5	2	7
					$\Sigma S_i =$ 71	$\Sigma W_i =$ 100	$\Sigma (W_i + S_i)$ = 171

Table 7.2 Observed cumulative times for customers in queue and in system.

i	No. of customers in queue, m_i	No. of customers in system, n_i	Cumulative time, t_i
1	0	0	56
2	0	1	21
3	1	2	15
4	2	3	20
5	3	4	15
			$\Sigma t_i = T = 127$

7.4.1 Approximate method

The data given in Tables 7.1 and 7.2 are based upon a small sample of observations, and therefore the overall system statistics computed from these data is only an approximation to the true performance measures. From Table 7.1 we have

Total number of arrivals $N = 25$
Arrival time of the last customer $T' = 120$.
Departure time of the last customer $T = 127$.

Average arrival rate $\lambda = \dfrac{N}{T'} = \dfrac{25}{120} = 0.208$ arrivals/minute.

Average interarrival time $\dfrac{1}{\lambda} = 4.8$ minutes.

Average service rate $\mu = \dfrac{N}{\Sigma S_i} = \dfrac{25}{71} = 0.352$ services/minute.

Average service time $= \dfrac{1}{\mu} = 2.84$ minutes/service.

Utilization of server $= \dfrac{\lambda}{\mu} = 0.59$.

Average waiting time in queue $W_q = \dfrac{\Sigma W_i}{N} = \dfrac{100}{25} = 4$ minutes/customer.

Average time spent in system $W = \dfrac{\Sigma(S_i + W_i)}{N} = \dfrac{171}{25} = 6.84$ minutes/customer.

Using Table 7.2, we compute

Average number of customers in queue $L_q = \dfrac{\Sigma(m_i\, t_i)}{T}$

$$= \frac{[(0) \cdot (56) + (0) \cdot (21) + \ldots + (3) \cdot (15)]}{127}$$

$$= \frac{100}{127} = 0.79$$

Average number of customer in system $L = \dfrac{\Sigma(n_i t_i)}{T}$

$$= \frac{[(0) \cdot (56) + (1) \cdot (21) + \ldots + (4) \cdot (15)]}{127}$$

$$= \frac{171}{127} = 1.35$$

If these performance measures are socially, economically, or otherwise unacceptable, then the post office system will have to be redesigned so as to achieve the desired results.

7.4.2 Theoretical method

Section 5.17 gave analytical formulae for computing statistics for single-queue–single-server systems. These formulae are based upon the assumptions: (a) unlimited queue length, (b) arrivals from an infinite source, (c) negative exponential interarrival and service time distributions, and (d) observations are made over a long period of time. Therefore the theoretical results of Section 5.17 are applicable to our post office system only if we can show that the interarrival and service time data given in Table 7.1 are negative exponentially distributed. This is done by constructing a table of observed and theoretical frequencies of interarrival and service time distributions and then performing the chi-square test discussed in Sections 5.15 and 6.8.2.

The cumulative distribution function $F(t)$ for the negative exponential distribution $f(t) = \lambda e^{-\lambda t}$ is given by (see Section 6.12.2):

$$F(t) = 1 - e^{-\lambda t}$$

λ (observed) $= 0.208$
Theoretical (expected) frequency in an interval $=$

$$\begin{pmatrix} \text{total no. of} \\ \text{occurrences} \end{pmatrix} \begin{pmatrix} \text{theoretical probability of} \\ \text{occurrence in that interval} \end{pmatrix}$$

Now, the theoretical frequency of interarrival times in a given interval can be computed as follows:

When:

$t = 0; F(t) = 0$

$t = 2; F(t) = 0.343$

interval $(0-2)$; theoretical frequency $= (25) \cdot (0.343) = 8.6$

interval $(2-4)$; theoretical frequency $= (25) \cdot (0.564 - 0.343) = 5.5$

$t = 4; F(t) = 0.564$

interval $(4-10)$; theoretical frequency $= (25) \cdot (0.875 - 0.564) = 7.8$

$t = 10; F(t) = 0.875$

interval $(10- \;)$; theoretical frequency $= (25) \cdot (1 - 0.875) = 3.1$

$t > 10; F(t) = 1.0$

Table 7.3 Chi-square test to compare theoretical negative exponential distribution and the observed interarrival time distribution.

Interarrival times	Observed frequency, o_i	Theoretical frequency, e_i	$\dfrac{(o_i - e_i)^2}{e_i}$
0–2	9	8.6	0.0186
2.01–4	5	5.5	0.04545
4.01–10	8	7.8	0.005128
Over 10.01	3	3.1	0.0032258
	25	25	0.0724038

$\chi_1^2 = 0.0724$ (observed)

$\chi_{0.95}^2$ (d.o.f. = 2) = 5.99 (critical)

Table 7.4 Chi-square test to compare theoretical negative exponential distribution and observed service time distribution.

Service time	Observed frequency, o_i	Theoretical frequency, e_i	$\dfrac{(o_i - e_i)^2}{e_i}$
0–2	12	13.07	0.08759
2.01–4	7	6.23	0.09516
4.01–10	5	4.95	0.0005
Over 10.01	1	0.75	0.0833
	25	25	0.2666

$\chi_1^2 = 0.2666$ (observed)

$\chi_{0.95}^2$ (d.o.f. = 2) = 5.99 (critical)

Similar computations are carried out on service time distributions with $\mu = 0.352$ and the results are recorded in Tables 7.3 and 7.4. The observed frequencies are divided into four categories and each closed interval consists of (in general, classes with expected frequencies smaller than five should not be used in chi-square test) at least five frequencies.

The negative exponential distribution is a one-parameter distribution (since mean = standard deviation) and we used two sample statistics, mean and sample size, in computing the expected class frequencies. The degrees of freedom (d.o.f.) are therefore $4 - 2 = 2$. From standard tables (Table 6.2), at 5% significance level and two degrees of freedom, the critical value of χ^2 is found to be 5.99. Since the observed values of chi-square (χ_1^2) in Tables 7.3 and 7.4 are both less than 5.99, we accept the hypothesis that the interarrival time and service time are negative exponentially distributed.

Therefore the theoretical values of system statistics (Section 5.17.2) are:

$$\lambda = 0.208; \quad \mu = 0.352; \quad \frac{\lambda}{\mu} = \rho = 0.59$$

$$W_q = \frac{\rho}{(1-\rho)\mu} = 4.08$$

$$W = \frac{1}{\mu - \lambda} = 6.94$$

$$L_q = \frac{\rho^2}{1-\rho} = 0.84$$

$$L = \frac{\rho}{1-\rho} = 1.43$$

Inadequate sample size and invalid assumptions are two major sources of errors. Considering the small size of the sample used, the degree of fit between the observed results (Section 7.4.1) and the theoretical results is reasonably good.

7.4.3 Simulation

The representation of arrivals of new entities into the modelled system, representation of what happens to these entities within the model, and mechanisms for the termination of simulation are the three essential components of a simulation model. A flowchart for the study of our post office system by simulation is shown in Figure 7.5 and the operations of the event routines R_1 and R_2 are summarized below.

Event routine R_1

(a) Compute the length of time and the number of customers in the system between events.
(b) Update clock to next arrival time.
(c) Record arrival time of this customer.
(d) If the system is empty, then:
 1. start service and record time service begins for this customer,
 2. generate service time from appropriate distribution and compute next discharge time.
(e) Increase number in system by one.

Event routine R_2

(a) Compute the length of time and the number of customers in the system between events.
(b) Update clock to next discharge time.
(c) Record time service ends for this customer.
(d) Increase number serviced by one.
(e) Decrease number in system by one.

144

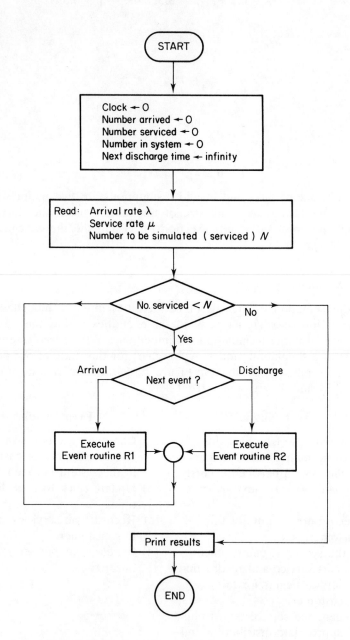

Figure 7.5 Flowchart for the simulation of post office system.

(f) Increase number arrived by one.

(f) If the system is not empty, then:
1. record time service begins for the next customer,
2. generate service time from appropriate distribution and compute next discharge time.

(g) Generate interarrival time from appropriate distribution and compute next arrival time.

(g) If the system is empty, then set next discharge time to infinity.

The occurrence of events in the system is simulated by generating the next event time which is expressed in terms of interarrival or service time distributions. Variable time increment method is used to update the clock as the simulation proceeds. Several conditions can be used to terminate the simulation. The clock time, total number of arrivals, total number of departures, or until everything in the model has come to rest are some of the possible choices. In Figure 7.5 the simulation is terminated when N customers have sucessfully completed service. Note that the number of arrivals may be greater than N when simulation is terminated. Events are scheduled dynamically (next event is scheduled only after the occurrence of the previous event) and there is no question of generating and storing of all possible events (e.g. arrivals) in advance.

A Pascal program (VAX–11/780) for simulating the post office system is shown in Figure 7.6 where $\lambda = 0.208$, $\mu = 0.352$, $N = 150$ and the interarrival time and service time are described by negative exponential distributions (see Section 7.5). A comparison of results obtained by the approximate method, theoretical method and simulation method is given in Table 7.5. As discussed in Chapter 4, verification and validation must always be part of all simulation modelling exercises.

7.5 Generation of the time and type of next event

A simulation program must provide efficient mechanisms for the generation of the time (e.g. service time) and the type (buying stamps, buying postal orders, etc.) of the next event. We will examine methods for generating the time and the type of the next event from four categories of distributions as a function of the input data and the output from the built-in random number generators.

7.5.1 Standard statistical event distributions

If the interarrival and service time (or other random variates) are known to have some standard statistical distributions (e.g. exponential, normal), then

```
PROGRAM POST_OFFICE(INPUT,OUTPUT);
   (* Simulation of.. M/M/1/infinity.. Postoffice system *)

CONST   INFINITY = 99999;

TYPE    RECTYPE = RECORD (* to store statistics about each customer *)
                  ARRIVALTIME,SERVICEBEGINS,SERVICEENDS :INTEGER;END;
        INDEX = 0..250; (* array index:no.of arrivals must be <250 *)
        SYS_STATS_ARRAY = ARRAY [INDEX] OF RECTYPE; (* customer statistics array *)
        TIME_LENGTH_ARRAY = ARRAY [INDEX] OF INTEGER; (* time length statistics array *)

VAR     LENGTH : TIME_LENGTH_ARRAY; (* Length(i)=length of time i customers in system *)
        INFO : SYS_STATS_ARRAY; (* to store customer information *)
        I, (* counter *)
        NUMBER_SERVICED,NUMBER_ARRIVED,NEXT_ARRIVAL_TIME,
        INTER_ARRIVAL_TIME,NEXT_DISCHARGE_TIME,SERVICE_TIME,
        NUMBER_IN_SYSTEM,CLOCK,N: INTEGER; (* N=no.of customers simulated *)
        SEED1,SEED2, (* for Random number generators *)
        LAMBDA,MU, (* arrival rate and service rate *)
        L, Lq,W,Wq,T,U : REAL ;     (* queue statistics *)

   PROCEDURE INTERVAL(VAR VALUE:INTEGER); (* inter arrival time generation *)
      VAR    RN : REAL;
      FUNCTION MTH$RANDOM(VAR I:REAL):REAL;EXTERN; (* external Fortran function *)
   BEGIN
    RN := MTH$RANDOM(SEED1);
    VALUE := TRUNC(-LN(RN)/LAMBDA+0.5);
   END; (* Interval *)

   PROCEDURE SERVICE(VAR VALUE:INTEGER); (* Service time generation *)
      VAR    RN : REAL;
      FUNCTION MTH$RANDOM(VAR I:REAL):REAL;EXTERN;
   BEGIN
    RN := MTH$RANDOM(SEED2);
    VALUE := TRUNC(-LN(RN)/MU+0.5);
   END; (*Service *)

BEGIN (*Mainline *)

  WRITELN(' enter arrival rate LAMBDA :  '); READLN(LAMBDA) ;
  WRITELN('enter service rate    MU :  '); READLN(MU) ;
  WRITELN('enter no. of customers simulated    N : '); READLN(N) ;

  SEED1 :=12457913 ;SEED2:=39315747 ;
  CLOCK:=0;
  NEXT_DISCHARGE_TIME:=INFINITY;
  INTERVAL(INTER_ARRIVAL_TIME);
  NEXT_ARRIVAL_TIME :=INTER_ARRIVAL_TIME ;
  NUMBER_SERVICED := 0;
  NUMBER_IN_SYSTEM := 0;
  NUMBER_ARRIVED := 0;

  WHILE (NUMBER_SERVICED < N) DO
   BEGIN
     (* simulation stops after servicing N customers;no.of arrivals may be > N *)
     IF (NEXT_ARRIVAL_TIME < NEXT_DISCHARGE_TIME)
        THEN BEGIN (* handle arrival *)
             LENGTH[NUMBER_IN_SYSTEM]:= LENGTH[NUMBER_IN_SYSTEM]+NEXT_ARRIVAL_TIME-CLOCK;
             CLOCK := NEXT_ARRIVAL_TIME;
             INFO[NUMBER_ARRIVED].ARRIVALTIME := NEXT_ARRIVAL_TIME; (* store statistics *)
             IF (NUMBER_IN_SYSTEM = 0)  (* post master idle;none in queue *)
                THEN BEGIN (* start service *)
                     INFO[NUMBER_ARRIVED].SERVICEBEGINS := NEXT_ARRIVAL_TIME;
                     SERVICE(SERVICE_TIME);
                     NEXT_DISCHARGE_TIME := SERVICE_TIME + CLOCK;
                     END;
             NUMBER_IN_SYSTEM := NUMBER_IN_SYSTEM + 1;
             NUMBER_ARRIVED := NUMBER_ARRIVED + 1;
             INTERVAL(INTER_ARRIVAL_TIME); (* get next arrival time *)
             NEXT_ARRIVAL_TIME :=INTER_ARRIVAL_TIME + CLOCK;
             END
```

Figure 7.6   Pascal program for simulating post office system.

```
      ELSE BEGIN (* handle discharge *)
            LENGTH[NUMBER_IN_SYSTEM]:=LENGTH[NUMBER_IN_SYSTEM]+NEXT_DISCHARGE_TIME-CLOCK;
            CLOCK := NEXT_DISCHARGE_TIME; (* increment Clock *)
            INFO[NUMBER_SERVICED].SERVICEENDS := NEXT_DISCHARGE_TIME;
            NUMBER_SERVICED := NUMBER_SERVICED + 1;
            NUMBER_IN_SYSTEM := NUMBER_IN_SYSTEM - 1;
            IF (NUMBER_IN_SYSTEM <> O)
                THEN BEGIN
                        INFO[NUMBER_SERVICED].SERVICEBEGINS := CLOCK;
                        SERVICE(SERVICE_TIME);
                        NEXT_DISCHARGE_TIME := SERVICE_TIME + CLOCK;
                        END
                ELSE NEXT_DISCHARGE_TIME := INFINITY;
            END;
  END;

WRITELN('LAMBDA =',LAMBDA:7:4,'    MU =',MU:7:4,'    N =',N:4);
  WRITELN('                            time      time                       time');
  WRITELN(' customer    arrival int-arriv  service  service    service  queuing      in');
  WRITELN('   no.        time     time     began    ended      time      time    system');

WITH INFO[O] DO
  BEGIN
    WRITE('   1',ARRIVALTIME,ARRIVALTIME,SERVICEBEGINS,SERVICEENDS);
    WRITELN(SERVICEENDS-SERVICEBEGINS,SERVICEBEGINS-ARRIVALTIME,SERVICEENDS-ARRIVALTIME);
    T :=  LENGTH[O];
    L := O;
    Lq := O;
    W := SERVICEENDS-ARRIVALTIME;
    Wq := SERVICEBEGINS-ARRIVALTIME;
    U := SERVICEENDS-SERVICEBEGINS;
  END;

FOR I := 1 TO (N-1) DO
  BEGIN
    WITH INFO[I] DO
      BEGIN
        WRITE(I+1:6,ARRIVALTIME,ARRIVALTIME-INFO[I-1].ARRIVALTIME,SERVICEBEGINS);
        WRITE(SERVICEENDS,SERVICEENDS-SERVICEBEGINS);
        WRITELN(SERVICEBEGINS-ARRIVALTIME,SERVICEENDS-ARRIVALTIME);
        L := L + I * LENGTH[I];
        U := U + SERVICEENDS-SERVICEBEGINS;
        W := W + SERVICEENDS-ARRIVALTIME;
        Wq := Wq + SERVICEBEGINS - ARRIVALTIME;
        Lq := Lq + (I-1)*LENGTH[I];
        T := T + LENGTH[I];
      END;
  END;

L := L/T; (* compute system statistics *)
Lq := Lq/T;
U := U/INFO[(N-1)].SERVICEENDS;
W := W/N;
Wq := Wq/N;

I := O;
WRITELN('number in system    time');
WHILE LENGTH[I] <> O DO
  BEGIN
    WRITELN(I,'    ',LENGTH[I]);
    I := I + 1;
  END;

WRITELN(' average number of customers  in the system  : ',L:10:8);
WRITELN(' average number of customers  in queue       : ',Lq:10:8);
WRITELN(' average time spent in the system            : ',W:10:8);
WRITELN(' average time spent in the queue             : ',Wq:10:8);
WRITELN(' utilisation of facility                     : ',U:10:8);

END. (* mainline *)
```

Figure 7.6 *con't*

LAMBDA = 0.2080   MU = 0.3520   N = 150

customer no.	arrival time	int-arriv time	time service began	time service ended	service time	queuing time	time in system
1	2	2	2	4	2	0	2
2	10	8	10	11	1	0	1
3	13	3	13	27	14	0	14
4	13	0	27	35	8	14	22
5	14	1	35	42	7	21	28
.	.	.	.	.	.	.	.
.	.	.	.	.	.	.	.
.	.	.	.	.	.	.	.
146	720	3	720	725	5	0	5
147	723	3	725	732	7	2	9
148	727	4	732	735	3	5	8
149	729	2	735	742	7	6	13
150	744	15	744	745	1	0	1

number in system	time
0	328
1	154
2	83
3	90
4	45
5	33
6	11
7	1

average number of customers in the system : 1.35302019
average number of customers in queue   : 0.79328859
average time spent in the system   : 6.71999979
average time spent in the queue   : 3.94000006
utilisation of facility   : 0.55973154

Figure 7.6 *con't*

Table 7.5 Comparison of results (post office) by different methods.

	Approximate method	Theoretical method	Simulation method
Average no. of customers in system, L	1.35	1.43	1.353
Average no. of customers in queue, L_q	0.79	0.84	0.793
Average time spent in system, W	6.84	6.94	6.72
Average time spent in queue, W_q	4.0	4.08	3.94
Utilization of postmaster ρ	0.59	0.59	0.56

we can use the appropriate analytical function to generate (Sections 6.12.1, 6.12.2, and 7.4.2) the next event time. For example, exponentially distributed interarrival times t with mean value λ can be generated from

$$t = (-1/\lambda) \log(r)$$

where r is uniformly distributed random numbers in the range (0,1).

7.5.2 Interpolated continuous event distributions

If it is not possible to fit a well-known distribution to observed data, then the continuous random variates representing interarrival times, service times, or other variables can be generated empirically from a finite number of data points by using interpolation techniques (Figure 7.7) as described in Section 6.12.4.

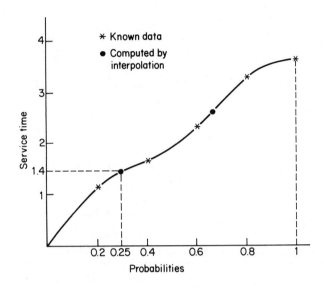

Figure 7.7   Interpolated continuous service time distribution function.

7.5.3 Discrete event distributions

If Y is continuous and X is discontinuous, then X values are defined only for a finite number of Y values. However, the simulation program must return X values for every Y value. If Y values are the uniformly distributed random numbers in the range $(0,1)$, then the method for the generation of X values from a discrete distribution is given in Section 6.13.3. In Figure 7.8 the symbols A, B, C, . . . may take either numerical (e.g. service time) or symbolic (type of business or transaction) values as illustrated in Table 7.6.

7.5.4 List-type event distributions

Here, both X and Y are discrete variables and their values are defined only at specified points as shown in Table 7.7. The simulation program is constrained to generate only the specified X values; the corresponding Y values are read from a table. For example, when $X = 2$ a value of -4 is always returned for Y.

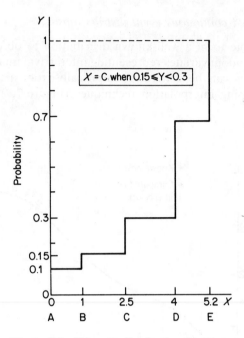

Figure 7.8   Discrete distribution function.

Table 7.6   Time or type of transaction.

Y probability	Symbol	X Service time (minutes)	Type of transaction
$0 \leq Y < 0.1$	A	Negligibly small	Buy stamps
$0.1 \leq Y < 0.15$	B	1	Buy postal orders
$0.15 \leq Y < 0.3$	C	2.5	Registered letters
$0.3 \leq Y < 0.7$	D	4	Pay bills
$0.7 \leq Y < 1$	E	5.2	Other

Table 7.7   List function.

X	1	2	6	9
Y	5	−4	2	3

7.6   Simulation strategies

We have already mentioned in Section 7.3 that the next event time increment method is generally used in most of the discrete event simulation languages, for advancing simulation time. In some simulation languages such as GPSS (see below) the advance of time is restricted to integer clock units and here care must be taken in choosing the simulation time units so as to avoid truncation errors. The scheduling of the next event and updating the system state by the next event time increment method can be implemented in several ways (Zeigler, 1976; Fishman, 1973). The major event sequencing approaches (Figures 7.1 and 7.9) are: (a) *event scheduling*, (b) *process interaction*, and (c) *activity scanning*.

The general structure of discrete event simulation systems is shown in Figue 7.10 and any of the three methods can be used for practical implementation. The event scheduling, activity scanning, or the activation of processes and the execution of appropriate program segements continue until no more state change can occur at the current clock time. Then, and only then, is the simulation time advanced. I will use the post office system as an example to illustrate these concepts further.

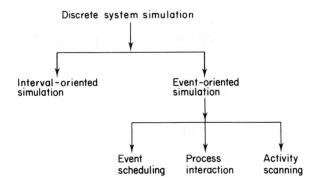

Figure 7.9   Simulation strategies.

7.6.1   *Event scheduling*

Figure 7.5 is an example of simulation by event scheduling (sometimes called event-oriented simulation). The time is advanced to the time of occurrence of the next event and simulation is accomplished by the execution of ordered (by time) event sequences. An ordered list of events 1, 2, . . . k and the time of their occurrences t_1, t_2, . . . t_k, are maintained (Wyman, 1975) and the appropriate event routine R_i (e.g. collect statistics, update system state, update event list) is executed at simulation time t_i where $t_i = \min (t_1, t_2, \ldots t_k)$. The event scheduling approach takes a global view of the entire system; a complete description of everything that happens in the model when an indvidual event occurs is given, and the events are scheduled explicitly by specifying their time of occurrence. The event scheduling approach is used in the design of the simulation languages GASP (Pritsker, 1975) and SIM-SCRIPT (Markowitz *et al.*, 1963).

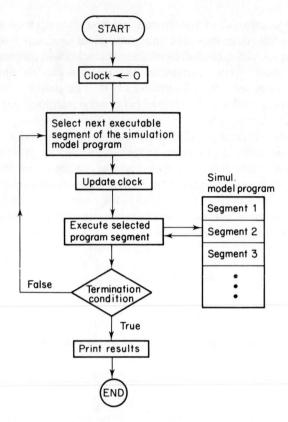

Figure 7.10   General structure of discrete event simulation system.

7.6.2   Process interaction

In Section 7.2 we defined activities and processes in terms of events and entities. For example, the process for customer 2 (Figure 7.1) begins with queuing activity followed by service activity. A *process* represents an entity and the sequences of actions it experiences during its life in the model. The behaviour of the system can be described by a set of processes (instances or copies of the same process plus other processes) which consist of a collection of mutually exclusive activities (Figure 7.1). Not more than one activity can be initiated at a particular point in time.

Processes may overlap (several customer processes competing for scarce system resources) and the interaction between processes is exploited here in describing the system being modelled. Thus the process interaction method is based upon the flow of entities (transactions or objects) through the model, in time, along operation paths created by interactive parallel processes. The emphasis is on scheduling of processes and the events are detected and handled implicitly. A list of processes, each ordered according to the time of occurrence of next event, is maintained and the collection of all event sequences together describes all events that occur in the system. Therefore the generation of the next event time and the scheduling of the next event can be achieved indirectly by activating the process (scheduling and executing the routines which describe the actions of the process) at the head of the list. Entities move through various blocks (processes) which operate on them and the current state of each entity including the conditions (e.g. server-free) under which it is admitted to the next block is maintained. Unlike the event scheduling method, a process (sequence of interrelated events ordered by time) can be interrupted and the process routines have multiple entry points, called *reactivation* points. The conflict between overlapping processes is resolved by using wait (wait in queue until selected) and delay (service time) procedures. Thus, unlike the event scheduling method, the time flow is explicitly included in the description of process routines.

Figure 7.11 shows the process interaction method of simulating the post office system of Section 7.4. Conceptually, modelling by the process inter-action method (Franta, 1977) is simpler, but it offers less programming control and flexibility compared to the event scheduling method. The pro-

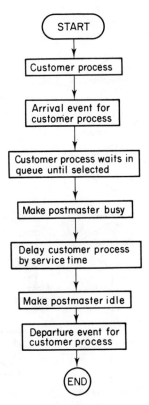

Figure 7.11   Simulation of post office by process interaction method.

gram structure is very similar to the model structure and the programming and debugging are generally easier. Two well-known simulation languages which follow this method are GPSS (Schriber, 1974) and SIMULA (Birtwistle *et al.*, 1973). SIMSCRIPT II.5 (Russell, 1983) offers a user the choice of either event scheduling or process interaction approach to modelling.

7.6.3 Activity scanning

Here, no event list is maintained and simulation progresses from event to event by scanning activities. In Section 7.2 an activity is defined as the state of an entity over an interval and an activity is bound by any two successive events. The change in system state is brought about by actions. Associated with each activity there is a condition which is set true or false depending upon the simulation time and the overall system state. For example, beginning of customer service operations (Figure 7.12) is a *condition* that can occur either at '*an arrival event if the server is idle and queue is empty*' or '*at a departure event if the queue is not empty*'. At every time step the status

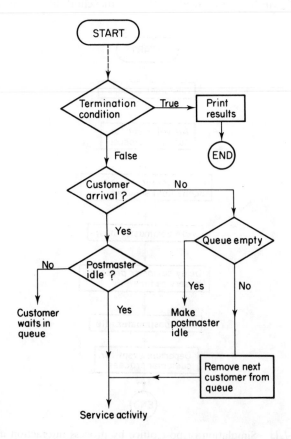

Figure 7.12   Activity scanning approach.

of all activities in the model is scanned (i.e. checking the state of each transaction or customer in the model) and those activities which satisfy the necessary boolean conditions are immediately scheduled and the appropriate action segments executed. Thus the events are scheduled implicitly.

The number of events in a model is a function of the number of activities. As the number of activities grows, the number of events grows, and therefore the activity scanning approach becomes more attractive than event scheduling, which requires the maintenance of an up-to-date future events list. The activity scanning method is used in the implementation of the languages AS (Parslow, 1967) and CSL (Buxton, 1966). However, most of the currently popular languages do not use this method for simulation modelling.

7.7 Computer languages for simulation

Simulation programs can be written in a variety of computer languages. Subsets of several programming languages are now available on micros which are becoming popular for small-scale simulation studies. The availability of inexpensive machines and user-friendly languages is bound to offer new opportunities for the application of simulation in several untried areas.

7.7.1 Characteristics of a good language

In addiion to the normal requirements of a good computer language, programming languages for simulation must also provide efficient mechanisms for:

1. describing the system being modelled;
2. advancing simulation time;
3. keeping track of events, activities, and process interactions;
4. creation and deletion of events and maintenance of associated data structures;
5. scanning operations and execution of appropriate program segments;
6. database management (for storing and retrieving data, results, and the model);
7. detection and correction of errors;
8. generation of stochastic variates from appropriate distributions;
9. interactive graphical simulation;
10. Collection, analysis, and presentation (flexible reports, colour graphics, animation) of results;
11. self-documentation (listing must be understood by analysts who are not programmers).

7.7.2 General-purpose versus simulation languages

Discrete event simulation programs can be written in a high-level general-purpose language or in a higher-level simulation language. Some of the widely used languages for simulation are shown in Table 7.8. A catalogue of micro, mini, and mainframe simulation software can be found in SCS (1985).

The translation of a model into a computer program is made simpler, cheaper, and faster by the use of special-purpose simulation languages, especially in view of the current trend in rising labour charges and falling computer prices. The simulation languages have eased the burden of programming simulation problems and popularized the practice of simulation. On the other hand, programming in general-purpose languages is comparatively more difficult and labour-intensive, but the resulting programs are more efficient in terms of speed of execution and flexibility in program control. Frequent use of a model for simulation may justify programming in a general-purpose language. Unlike simulation languages, the general-purpose languages do not have built-in routines for the generation of stochastic variates and the collection, analysis, and display of results.

Table 7.8   Computer languages for simulation.

General-purpose language	Simulation language	
Fortran	SIMSCRIPT (Fortran-based)	Event scheduling
PL/1	SIMSCRIPT II.5 (compiler)	
Pascal	GASP IV (Fortran-based)	
Basic		
Ada	GPSS V (interpreter)	Process interaction
	GPSS/H (compiler)	
	SIMSCRIPT II.5	
	SIMULA (Algol-based)	
	CSL	Activity scanning
	AS	

7.7.3 Comparison of major simulation languages

GPSS and SIMSCRIPT are probably the most widely used discrete event simulation languages and they are treated in more detail in Chapters 8 and 9. The Algol-based SIMULA is also gaining popularity. GASP IV (Pritsker, 1974) and SLAM II (Pritsker, 1984) can be used not only for discrete event simulation, but also for continuous and combined discrete–continuous simulations. SIMSCRIPT II.5 (Russell, 1983) ad SLAM can perform both event oriented and process-oriented simulations. GPSS/H (Henriksen, 1979) is a compiler- (not an interpreter- or pre-processor-based language) which is considered to be several times faster than GPSS V (Gordon, 1975).

Depending upon the design concepts, a particular simulation language is likely to be best for a specific type of application. For example, SIMULA, SIMSCRIPT and GASP are oriented towards general system simulation, whereas GPSS is biased towards queuing sytems. Programming experience in a general-purpose language need not necessarily be very helpful in understanding the logic of simulation languages such as GPSS. It is extremely difficult to compare various simulation languages. The language generality, programming power, ease of use, machine efficiency, and availability are some of the criteria generally used for comparing simulation languages. GPSS has good debugging facilities, inflexible I/O (input/output), poor execution efficiency, facilities for automatic generation of output statistics, and it is extremely easy to learn the language. SIMSCRIPT II.5 has extensive general-purpose programming capabilities, flexible I/O, high execution efficiency, excellent statistical data collection facilities, and probably it is the most machine-independent general-purpose simulation language. SIMULA is a complex language which is comparatively more difficult to learn; it has good debugging facilities, flexible I/O, high execution efficiency, and good statistical data collection facilities.

7.7.4   Selection of a simulation language

The selection of a simulation language (Fishman, 1978; Law and Kelton, 1982) depends upon several factors. The following points (together with the discussions in Sections 7.7.1 and 7.7.3) should serve as a guide in selecting a simulation language.

1. Nature of the problem under study.
2. The availability of the language.
3. Ease of installation and use.
4. Understanding of simulation concepts and ease of learning the language by the local staff.
5. Accuracy of simulation results.
6. Facilities for collection, analysis, and display of results.
7. Availability of user-friendly documentation.
8. Features that reduce cost of programming and simulation.
9. Cost-effective maintenance and enhancements facilities.

7.8   Summary

Time and state relationships form the core of discrete event simulation model representations. The fundamental concepts of event, activity, and process are introduced. Fixed-time increment and variable-time increment are the two methods used for advancing the simulation clock (time). In order to gain confidence in simulation, three possible approaches to the study of a simple post office system are presented in detail, and it is shown that the simulation results are comparable to the results obtained by approximate and theoretical methods. The time and type of the next event are two of the

158

parameters required by simulation programs. Methods for the generation of the time and type of the next event from four categories of event distributions are described. The scheduling of the next event by variable time increment method can be implemented 'in several ways. The principles behind the implementation of event scheduling, process interaction, and activity scanning methods are examined. Simulation programs are generally written either in a high-level general-purpose language or in a higher-level special-purpose simulation language. The characteristics of a good language for computer simulation, the strengths and weaknesses of some of the popular simulation languages, and the selection of a simulation language for local use are discussed. The development of simulation languages (for mainframe and microcomputers) has eased the burden of programming simulation problems and popularized the practice of simulation.

7.9 Exercises

1. Explain what is meant by:
   (a) event, activity, and process
   (b) uniform time incremnent method
   (c) variable time increment method
   (d) discrete event simulation strategies.
2. Draw flowcharts for the simulation of the following systems:
   (a) supermarket with five checkouts
   (b) self-service restaurant with a single cash register
   (c) bank with single queue and four tellers.
3. Write a Pascal or Fortran program to simulate the operation of a garage with two petrol pumps. Assume that the service times are uniformly distributed in the range 4 ± 1 minutes and the interarrival times are uniformly distributed in the range 6 ± 2 minutes.
4. The observed data on the use of programming languages at a computer centre were found to be as follows:

Number of jobs	Language used
99	Fortran
178	Pascal
40	GPSS
79	Other
396	

A program which simulates the operation of the computing system uses random numbers r ($0 \le r < 1$) to select the appropriate programming language for processing each job. What programming language will be used for processing the incoming job, if the random number generated by the simulation program was $r = 0.595$.

5. The service time of patients at a casualty department are shown below:

Service time (minutes)	Frequency
1 – 2	3
2.1 – 3	5
3.1 – 4	15
4.1 – 5	23
5.1 – 6	33
6.1 – 7	25
7.1 – 8	37
8.1 – 9	17
9.1 – 10	11
10.1 – 11	9
11.1 – 12	1

Graph the cumulative distribution (probability versus time) and read out the service time when the random number generated by the simulation program was 0.732. Compare the result with the service time obtained analytically by interpolation tecnhiques.

6. (a) What are the characteristics of a good language for computer simulation?

(b) Comment on the merits and demerits of the discrete event simulaton languages: SIMULA; SIMSCRIPT, and GPSS.

(c) How do you go about selecting a simulation language for an industrial client?

7. Discuss the important features of event scheduling, process interaction, and activity scanning methods for discrete event simulation.

References

Birtwistle, G. M., Dahl, O. J., Myhrhaug, B., and Nygaard, K. (1973). *SIMULA Begin*. Auerbach, Philadelphia, PA.

Buxton, J. N. (1966). 'Writing simulations in CSL', *Comp. J.*, **9**(2), 137–143.

Fishman, G. S. (1973). *Concepts and Methods in Discrete Event Digital Simulations*. John Wiley, New York.

Fishman, G. S. (1978). *Principles of Discrete Event Simulation*. John Wiley, New York.

Franta, W. R. (1977). *The Process View of Simulation*. North Holland, New York.

Gordon, G. (1975). *The Applications of GPSS V to Discrete System Simulation*. Prentice Hall, Englewood Cliffs, NJ.

Henriksen, J. O. (1979). *The GPSS/H User's Manual*. Wolverine Software Corp., Annandale, VA 22003.

Law, A. M., and Kelton, W. D. (1982). *Simulation Modelling and Analysis*. McGraw-Hill, New York.

Markowitz, H. M., Hausner, B., and Karr, H. W. (1963). *SIMSCRIPT, A Simulation Programming Language*. Prentice Hall, Englewood Cliffs, NJ.

Nance, R. E. (1981). 'The time and state relationships in simulation modelling', *CACM*, **24**(4), 173–179.

Parslow, R. D. (1967). 'AS: an Algol simulation language'. IFIP working conference on simulation languages. Oslo, Norway.

Pritsker, A. A. B. (1974). *The GASP IV Simulation Language*. John Wiley, New York.

Pritsker, A. A. B. (1975). GASP. In *Encyclopedia of Computer Science and Technology* (eds Belzer, J., Holzman, A. G., and Kent, A.). Dekker, New York.

Pritsker, A. A. B. (1984). *Introduction to Simulation and SLAM II*. John Wiley, New York.

Russell, E. C. (1983). *Building Simulation Models with SIMSCRIPT II.5*. CACI, Inc., Los Angeles, CA.

Schriber, T. (1974). *Simulation Using GPSS*. John Wiley, New York.

SCS (1985). 'Catalog of simulation software', *Simulation*, **45**(4), 196–209.

Wyman, F. P. (1975). 'Improved event scanning mechanisms for discrete event simulations', *CACM*, **18**(6), 350–353.

Zeigler, B. P. (1976). *Theory of Modelling and Simulation*. John Wiley, New York.

8

General-purpose Simulation System (GPSS)

8.1 Introduction

GPSS was originally developed by IBM (Gordon, 1962) and was intended for use by non-computer specialists. In 1967, GPSS/360 was introduced and the name was changed from 'General-purpose system simulator' to 'General-purpose simulation system'. GPSS-V, which is a super set of GPSS/360, contains several new features including free-form coding and interface to Fortran and PL/1. Identical results may be obtained when a GPSS/360— Version 2 simulation model is run under GPSS-V. A comparison of GPSS/360 is given in Appendix 7 of Gordon (1975).

The GPSS language (Gordon, 1981) is structured as a *block-oriented language* and the design was influenced by *block diagram* and *flowchart* concepts. Simulation is carried out by creating temporary entities called *transactions*; moving them through a network of blocks (GPSS statements or instructions) connected in the same order as a sequence of events, and finally destroying them and removing them from the system. The block diagram approach to simulation is less flexible and therefore unsuitable for certain types of applications. Several versions of GPSS are currently available on a variety of computers including microprocessors. Important features of GPSS (with emphasis on GPSS/360) will be discussed in this chapter and further details can be found in Schriber (1974) and Bobillier *et al.* (1976) and user's manuals prepared by software vendors and computer manufacturers.

8.2 Basic concepts and overview

GPSS uses the *process interaction* approach to the simulation of *discrete systems*. The model structure is defined by entities and the attributes of these entities at any given time describe the status of the system. Thus by measuring the numerical/logical values of the attributes one can evaluate the performance of the system being modelled. GPSS simulates the system by updating the *simulation clock* (absolute clock) to the time at which the next

161

most imminent event is to occur, and not by evaluating the model at each successive interval of time. GPSS maintains another clock time called *relative clock time* which can be externally addressed by the programmer.

There are *fourteen types of entities* (Figure 8.1) available in GPSS for model representation. The statements in a GPSS program are called blocks, and are basically subroutines or macro-instructions which perform a series of operations. GPSS block entities are used to define other entities and also to change their attributes. An entity referenced in a block operation is identified either by a number or a symbolic name. The *permanent entities* of the system (e.g. PM—postmaster in a post office) which remain throughout the simulation are represented by GPSS equipment entities (facilities, storages, logic switches, etc.) and these are created implicitly when first referenced in the program. The *temporary entities* (e.g. representation of customers in a post office) called *transactions* are created in GENERATE blocks during the execution phase of a GPSS program; they move through various blocks and are finally destroyed and removed from the system on entry to a TERMINATE block. Unlike other GPSS blocks, GENERATE block cannot be entered from other blocks and TERMINATE block has no exit. GPSS has facilities for entry and collection of data using SAVEVALUE and FUNCTION. Expressions involving system attributes can be evaluated using VARIABLE statement. Each system activity is represented by a group of interconnected blocks, and groups of blocks are connected together to achieve the desired sequence of execution of system activities.

The simulation process is initiated by creating transactions which may be assigned various levels of priorities, and the flow of transactions through the network of blocks is controlled by the operations and the interconnections of the blocks used. The blocks are activated by the entering transactions and simulation is accomplished by the movement of transactions through specified blocks which execute the actions associated with each block. The movement of transactions from block to block alters the system state and the change in state represents an *event*. The status of the model is altered by events by changing the attributes of the entities and GPSS keep a record of the times at which these events are due to occur on ordered lists called chains. The *current events chain* and *future events chain* are the two lists automatically defined and maintained by GPSS. The current events list (chain) contains all events that can take place at the present simulation clock time if conditions are favourable, and the future events chain holds events that can take place only at future points in time.

All times in the model must be specified as *integers* and fractional time units are not allowed. This means that the smallest time interval encountered in the model must be used as the unit of time, and obviously this interval may have to be estimated. Proper scaling of time variable is essential in order to ensure accuracy of results consistent with the speed of simulation.

At any point in time a transaction may be in *active state* (managed by control program), *suspended state* (waiting on current events or future events chain

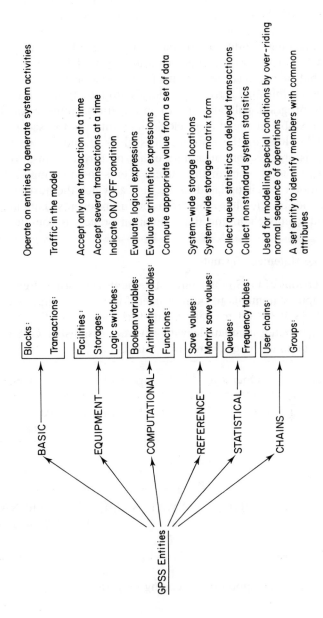

Figure 8.1 GPSS entities for model representation.

until certain conditions are met), *passive state* (waiting on user chain and can be activated only by another transaction under program control), or *terminated state* (removed from the system). The flow of transactions through certain types of blocks takes place instantaneously, while some other types of blocks may delay the transactions for a specified period of time or until the blocking conditions in the next logical blocks are removed. An ADVANCE block always assigns a positive time delay to each transaction entering that block. The movement of a transaction may alter the status of the model and this may activate previously stopped transactions. In general, the GPSS program will attempt to move transactions through as many blocks as possible at the current clock time until the transaction reaches an ADVANCE block or the transaction is blocked and unable to move any further. This process continues until either no further transaction can move into the next logical block or the current events chain is empty. At this point the simulation clock is updated to the time at which the next most imminent event is to occur; eligible events from the future events chain are merged to the current events chain and the simulation process is continued.

8.3 Source statement format

In some versions of GPSS the source statements are format-free, while others demand input statements to be in a fixed format. For improved readability we use GPSS/360 fixed format in our discussions, and this has the added advantage of being compatible with several versions of GPSS. The input statements defining blocks consist of four fields:

Label	Operator	Operands	Comments
(Col. 2 to 6)	(Col. 8 to 18)	(Col. 19 onwards)	(At least one space after operands)

Example

TICKT	TRANSFER	0.25, NAME1, NAME2	75% go to NAME1 and 25% to NAME2
(label)	(operator)	(operands)	(comments)

The following rules apply to the coding of various fields:

Label:
optional; usually consists of symbolic names, 3 to 5 characters long; first three characters must be alphabetic; coded in columns 2 to 6 and must begin in column 2. Care must be taken in the use of numbers as labels

as they may be in conflict with numbers automatically assigned by the program.

Operator:

coded in columns 8 through 18; must begin in column 8. Control codes associated with some types of blocks are coded in the operator field after a blank space.

Operands:

operands (A, B, C . . .) begin in column 19 and individual operands is separated by a comma with no embedded blanks. The absence of operands is indicated by successive commas if they are accompanied by one or more operands.

Comments:

the characters following the first blank in the operands field will be treated as comments. Columns 72 to 80 are unused. The entire statement is treated as a comment if an asterisk (*) appears in column 1.

A sample of GPSS blocks and frequently used operands are shown in Figure 8.2.

8.4 A Simple GPSS simulation program—example 1

Microprocessors arrive at the test station of a manufacturing plant every 6 ± 2 minutes and the testing time per micro was found to be 5 ± 3 minutes. The service is on a first-come–first-served basis, and the units are placed in a queue whenever the test facility is busy. Assuming that the interarrival times and service times are uniformly distributed, simulate the processing of 1000 micros at the test station.

GPSS block diagram (see IBM manual for other block symbols) for the simulation of the microprocessor test station is shown in Figure 8.3. The corresponding GPSS source program listing appears in Figure 8.4, where the comment on each statement describes the function of the block. It is difficult to remember all the GPSS block symbols and many users may find it completely unnecessary to draw a GPSS block diagram and may prefer to write the GPSS program directly from the description of the problem.

The first and last two statements in Figure 8.4 are control statements which are necessary for the execution of GPSS programs. If SIMULATE statement is absent, the GPSS program will be compiled but not executed. The START statement specifies that the simulation is to continue until 1000 micros have been tested. The END statement signals the end of the GPSS program.

The GENERATE block creates the transactions (micros) or traffic in the model and the interarrival times are uniformly distributed in the range 4 to 8 minutes. The transactions wait in queue 1 defined by QUEUE block until the test station is free. A transaction gets control of the test facility on entry to the SEIZE block and then moves into the DEPART block when one

Block name	Operands					Function of block
	A	B	C	D	E	etc.
GENERATE	mean	modifier		count	priority	Creates new transactions or traffic in the system
TERMINATE	units					Destroys transaction
SEIZE	facility no.					Engages facility if it is idle
RELEASE	facility no.					Remove transactions from facility
QUEUE	queue no.	units				Gathers statistics on delayed transactions
DEPART	queue no.	units				Reduces queue contents
ADVANCE	mean	spread				Delays transactions
ASSIGN	parameter no.	integer				Assigns numerical values to transaction parameter
TEST	argument 1	argument 2	next block			Tests arguments and control flow of transaction
TRANSFER	selection rule	next block A	next block B			Divert transactions to other blocks
TABULATE	table no.	units				Tabulates frequency distribution of an argument
SAVEVALUE	savevalue no.	attribute				Stores attributes in global storage locations

Figure 8.2 A sample of GPSS blocks and frequently used operands.

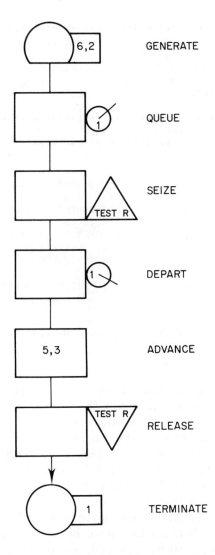

GENERATE

QUEUE

SEIZE

DEPART

ADVANCE

RELEASE

TERMINATE

Figure 8.3   GPSS block diagram for example 1.

transaction is removed from the top of queue 1. The queue statistics are automatically collected by the GPSS system. The transaction then moves into the ADVANCE block where it is delayed by 2 to 8 minutes (5 ± 3) representing the processing time in the test facility. On completion of testing a micro, the transaction moves out of the ADVANCE block and enters the RELEASE block, where it gives up the test station which is now made available to the next transaction waiting in the QUEUE block. The next block is the TERMINATE block where the transactions are destroyed and removed from the simulation model. Whenever a transaction enters the

168

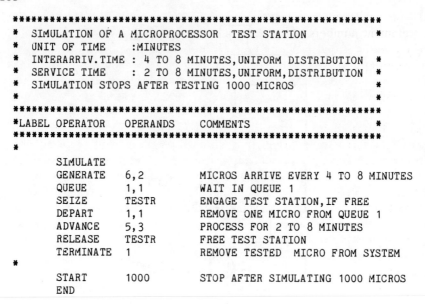

```
***************************************************************
*   SIMULATION OF A MICROPROCESSOR  TEST STATION              *
*   UNIT OF TIME    :MINUTES                                  *
*   INTERARRIV.TIME : 4 TO 8 MINUTES,UNIFORM DISTRIBUTION     *
*   SERVICE TIME    : 2 TO 8 MINUTES,UNIFORM,DISTRIBUTION     *
*   SIMULATION STOPS AFTER TESTING 1000 MICROS                *
*                                                             *
***************************************************************
*LABEL OPERATOR   OPERANDS    COMMENTS                        *
***************************************************************
*
         SIMULATE
         GENERATE   6,2        MICROS ARRIVE EVERY 4 TO 8 MINUTES
         QUEUE      1,1        WAIT IN QUEUE 1
         SEIZE      TESTR      ENGAGE TEST STATION,IF FREE
         DEPART     1,1        REMOVE ONE MICRO FROM QUEUE 1
         ADVANCE    5,3        PROCESS FOR 2 TO 8 MINUTES
         RELEASE    TESTR      FREE TEST STATION
         TERMINATE  1          REMOVE TESTED  MICRO FROM SYSTEM
*
         START      1000       STOP AFTER SIMULATING 1000 MICROS
         END
```

Figure 8.4   GPSS source program listing for example 1.

TERMINATE block, the value of the first operand (operand A) of the START statement is decremented by the value of the first operand of the TERMINATE block and the simulation stops when the value of the operand A of the START statement becomes zero.

Normally transactions move sequentially and pass through as many blocks as possible instantaneously until they are delayed or denied entry to a block. For example, if the test facility in Figure 8.4 is free at the time of the creation of a transaction, then that transaction will move through GENERATE, QUEUE, SEIZE, DEPART blocks in zero time and straight away enter the ADVANCE block, where of course it will be delayed for the specified period of time. Several blocks such as QUEUE and DEPART, GENERATE and TERMINATE, SEIZE and RELEASE, appear as pairs in GPSS programs. The pairing of blocks allows activities to take place between the initiation and termination of the same phase.

8.4.1   GPSS output

The GPSS program goes through two stages—the assembly phase and the execution phase. The listing of the source program, cross-reference list, and the assembled program listing are the output from the assembly stage. The source statements are numbered sequentially on the left-hand side and the control statements are excluded from the sequential numbering on the right-hand side (Figure 8.5a). The cross reference list gives the symbolic names and their equivalent numerical values used by the assembler together with the statement numbers where the symbolic names are used. The assembled program is the actual program used for the execution phase.

The output of a successful GPSS execution phase is shown in Figure 8.5b. GPSS automatically collects items of interest such as 'average queue length', 'average waiting time', 'utilization of facilities', 'average time per transaction', etc. The model was run for 5945 simulated time units (minutes, here) as indicated by both relative and absolute clocks. The number of transactions successfully passed through each block, as well as the number of transactions currently present in each block at the termination of simulations are shown in the output. 1003 transactions were created by the GENERATE block, 1000 of them went through the TERMINATE block, and 2 of the transactions are still waiting in the QUEUE block. The utilization of the test station (i.e. fraction of time the facility was in use) was 0.8257 and the average testing time per micro was 4.91 minutes.

The maximum number of micros waiting in the queue at any time during the simulation was 3, and on an average there were 0.28 micros in the queue. A total of 1002 micros entered the queue; of these 512 did not wait at all and on an average each micro waited in the queue for 1.68 minutes (3.44 minutes if only nonzero waiting times are included in the statistics). For a full description of GPSS output statistics, the reader is referred to GPSS manual (IBM, 1975).

8.4.2 Possible errors

Like any other language, GPSS gives both assembly and execution errors. The current number of entities remaining in individual blocks gives an indication of the bottlenecks in the system, and this is useful in checking logical errors in the program during the initial simulation runs. The omission of one of the pairs of a block is a common source of error. Obviously a transaction cannot be terminated unless it was created earlier; a transaction cannot depart a queue unless it was entered, and a facility cannot be released unless it was seized. Similarly, the queue will be flooded with transactions if there is no DEPART block in the program and eventually simulation will be terminated either because of too many transactions in the system or time limit exceeded. In a GPSS program, if a GENERATE block is used without at least one TERMINATE block with nonzero value for operand A, the simulation will go on until the task time limit is exceeded, since the operand A of the START statement will never be decremented.

8.4.3 Effects of deleting selected blocks from GPSS program

The omission or incorrect sequencing of blocks in a GPSS program may result in the simulation of entirely different systems. The following two cases illustrate the effect of deleting certain blocks from our GPSS program (Figure 8.4) for Example 1.

170

```
      **********************************************
      *  SIMULATION OF A MICROPROCESSOR TEST STATION    *
      *  UNIT OF TIME    :MINUTES                        *
      *  INTERARRIV.TIME : 4 TO 8 MINUTES,UNIFORM DISTRIBUTION  *
      *  SERVICE TIME    : 2 TO 8 MINUTES,UNIFORM,DISTRIBUTION  *
      *  SIMULATION STOPS AFTER TESTING 1000 MICROS      *
      *                                                  *
      **********************************************
      *LABEL OPERATOR   OPERANDS   COMMENTS              *
      **********************************************
      *
```

GPSS Assembly
```
 1
 2
 3
 4
 5
 6
 7
 8
 9
10
11
12              SIMULATE
13              GENERATE   6,2       MICROS ARRIVE EVERY 4 TO 8 MINUTES
14              QUEUE      1,1       WAIT IN QUEUE 1
15              SEIZE      TESTR     ENGAGE TEST STATION,IF FREE
16              DEPART     1,1       REMOVE ONE MICRO FROM QUEUE 1
17              ADVANCE    5,3       PROCESS FOR 2 TO 8 MINUTES
18              RELEASE    TESTR     FREE TEST STATION
19              TERMINATE  1         REMOVE TESTED MICRO FROM SYSTEM
20          *
21              START      1000      STOP AFTER SIMULATING 1000 MICROS
22              END
```

GPSS Assembly

```
SYMBOL NAME    VALUE   CROSS REFERENCE

    TESTR        1      15      18

NO ERRORS DETECTED
```

Figure 8.5(a) Output from GPSS assembly phase.

CLOCK TIME   5945   5945

BLOCK COUNTS

BLOCK CURRENT	TOTAL	BLOCK CURRENT	TOTAL	BLOCK CURRENT	TOTAL	BLOCK CURRENT	TOTAL
1 1	1003	2 2	1002	3 0	1000	4 0	1000
5 0	1000	6 0	1000	7 0	1000		

QUEUE	MAXIMUM CONTENTS	AVERAGE CONTENTS	TOTAL ENTRIES	ZERO ENTRIES	PERCENT ZEROS	AVERAGE TIME/TRANS	$AVERAGE TIME/TRANS	TABLE NUMBER	CURRENT CONTENTS
1	3	0.28	1002	512	51.098	1.68	3.44	0	2

FACILITY	AVERAGE UTILIZATION	NUMBER ENTRIES	AVERAGE TIME/TRANS	SEIZING TRANS. NO.	PREEMPTING TRANS. NO.
TESTR	0.8257	1000	4.91	0	0

Figure 8.5(b) Output from GPSS execution phase.

Case 1

On deleting the QUEUE and DEPART blocks, we get (comments are excluded for clarity):

```
SIMULATE
GENERATE    6,2
SEIZE       TESTR
ADVANCE     5,3
RELEASE     TESTR
TERMINATE   1
START       1000
END
```

Whatever may be the values of operand A and operand B, the GENERATE block creates a new transaction only when the previously created transaction succeeds in entering the next sequential block. Since the revised model has no queuing facility, the GENERATE block will create and hold at most only one new micro (transaction) whenever the test facility (SEIZE block) is busy. In other words, the revised model simulates a directly coupled system where the output of subsystem 1 (production line) is directly coupled to the input of subsystem 2 (test station) and subsystem 1 automatically switches itself off whenever subsystem 2 fails to accept the output of subsystem 1.

Case 2

We will now delete SEIZE and RELEASE blocks from the GPSS program obtained in case 1 and we have

```
SIMULATE
GENERATE    6,2
ADVANCE     5,3
TERMINATE   1
START       1000
END
```

The ADVANCE block never denies entry to a transaction and therefore the micros created in the GENERATE block will move straight into the ADVANCE block where they are delayed by a positive period of time representing the processing time at the test station. Here, in effect, we are simulating a system where there are an infinite number of test stations and the testing of each micro is initiated as soon as it is created; therefore the question of queuing does not arise.

8.5 Parameters and Savevalues

The parameters are attributes of transactions, and associated with each transaction there are several parameters which can be used for recording data and later on referenced as standard numerical attribute or SNA (see Section 8.6). For example, integer-coded information about a student's sex, nationality, courses chosen, etc., can be stored in transaction parameters. The number of each type of parameters (halfword, fullword, byte size, and floating point in GPSS-V) required is specified in the F through I fields on the GENERATE block. Up to 100 parameters are allowed in GPSS/360 and up to 255 parameters of each type allowed in GPSS-V. The default is 12 halfword parameters.

GENERATE   6,1,,,,8,F

will generate transactions every 6 ± 1 minutes and 8 fullword parameters will be assigned to each transaction. In GPSS-V the above will be written as

GENERATE   6,1,,,,8PF

The parameter values are initially set to zero, but can be modified by means of ASSIGN statement (see also Section 8.13).

ASSIGN   2,FN1

will assign the value of FN1 (function 1) to parameter 2 of the entering transaction. Note that the use of

ASSIGN   P2,FN1

is illegal. The values of several operands can be defined in terms of parameters j which are referenced as $*j$, Pj or $P*j$ as explained in Section 8.8 (indirect addressing).

DEPART *3

will remove one transaction from the top of queue K where K is the current value of parameter 3 of the entering transaction.

The savevalues are system-wide storage locations where data can be stored for later use by the simulation program. The contents of savevalue locations are modified when a transaction enters SAVEVALUE or MSAVEVALUE block. The general format of savevalue is

SAVEVALUE   A,B,C

where

A: name or number of the savevalue location;
B: the value to be stored, added, or subtracted from savevalue location;

C: optional field which defines the type of savevalue referenced (fullword, halfword, byte, floating point—default is fullword)

and *Xj* is the SNA associated with the savevalue.

Example

SAVEVALUE   5,25

The number 25 is stored in the fullword savevalue location 5

SAVEVALUE   5-,25,H

will subtract 25 from halfword savevalue location 5 (GPSS-V uses XH instead of H)

SAVEVALUE   P2,S1

will store the current contents of storage 1 in fullword savevalue location whose number is the value of parameter 2 of the entering transaction. The use of MSAVEVALUE is similar to that of SAVEVALUE except that it modifies the elements of matrix savevalue locations. The INITIAL statement can be used to initializse savevalue locations before a simulation run.

8.6   Standard Numerical Attributes (SNA)

The entities have attributes, and some of these attributes are automatically recorded and updated by the simulator while others can be modified by the user. Attribute values such as block counts and average queue contents are automatically collected and printed at the end of simulation. The priority and parameter values can be changed by the user under program control. The attributes of several entities can be monitored during a simulation run and based upon the values of these attributes the course of simulation can be controlled. An attribute is called a standard numerical attribute, or SNA for short.

The SNAs associated with some of the most frequently used entities are given in Figure 8.6, where j in SNAj stands for the number or name of the SNA. The SNAs are denoted by one or two letters followed by a number or symbolic name. The SNA for priority (PR) is an exception. The symbolic names must be separated by $ sign. For example, FN1 represents function 1 while FN$BETA represents the function named BETA. Most of the SNAs take positive or negative integer values, but some of them are restricted to 0 or 1. The status of a facility is indicated by 0 or 1 and the contents of a queue can take any non-negative integer. Nj and Wj are two of the SNAs exclusively associated with blocks. C1 and RNj (plus AC1 and TG1 in

GPSS notation	Standard numerical attribute
BVj	Value of boolean variable j (O or 1)
Fj	Status of facility j (O or 1)
FNj	Value of function j (integer part only)
M1	Transit time of transaction
Pj	Parameter j of transaction
PR	Priority of transaction (O to 127)
Qj	Length of queue j
Rj	Remaining free space in storage j
Sj	Contents of storage j
Vj	Value of variable j (integer or floating point)
Xj	Value of fullword Savevalue location j
Nj	Total no. of transactions that have entered block j
Wj	Number of transactions currently in block j
C1	Relative clock time
RNj	The output of random no. generator j (usually 1 to 999; O to 1 when used in a function)

Figure 8.6   Frequently used standard numerical attributes (SNA).

(GPSSV) are general in nature, and therefore said to belong to the system as a whole.

The SNAs can be used as arguments in GPSS statements. For example,

QUEUE   P1

will make a transaction to wait in the queue whose number is given by the value of parameter 1 of the entering transaction.

DEPART   2,Q2

will empty queue 2.

8.7   Tabulated output

Statistical attributes of permanent entities are automatically collected and printed by the system. GPSS automatically produce block counts and facility, storage, and queue statistics. In addition there are blocks such as MARK and TABULATE that are designed to collect a variety of other statistics which can be presented in tabulated form under program control. The TABULATE block produces a table of values (distributions), the contents and format of which is defined in a TABLE statement.

TABLE   A,B,C,D

where A: SNA to be tabulated
      B: upper limit of lowest frequency interval
      C: interval width
      D: no. of intervals

For example,

          TABULATE   LABL
LABL   TABLE   P1,2,5,20

will tabulate the values of P1 in table LABL showing the distribution of P1 (values of parameter 1) in frequency intervals 0–2, 3–7, 8–12, . . . up to 20 intervals. The TABULATE block causes printing of several other statistics, including number of entries, mean, and standard deviation. The MARK, TABULATE, and TABLE statements can be used to produce (see Section 8.13) the distribution of the time required for a transaction to pass between two points in the GPSS program. Such information is vital for monitoring the progress of entities in the simulation model.

8.8   Indirect addressing

In GPSS it is possible to specify the number of SNA by another SNA, and this method of using SNAs is referred to as indirect addressing. The SNA can be used as block operands directly or by referring to SNAs whose index number is stored in a transaction parameter. The *indirect addressing* of SNAs is conveyed to GPSS by means of an asterisk (*). The parameter j of a transaction can be referenced in three ways:

*j or PJ   (value of parameter j)
P*j   (value of parameter whose number is the current value of
               parameter j)

If P5 = 8 and P8 = 1, then P*5 = 1 and therefore, the statements

QUEUE   P*5

and

QUEUE   1

would produce the same result. GPSS allow only one level of indirect addressing to define attributes of entities. This means that indirect addressing of attributes can be achieved only through the medium of transaction parameters. For example, to find the contents of a storage whose number is the contents of savevalue location 6, we have to store the value of X6 (savevalue 6) in a parameter (say P4) by means of ASSIGN statement and then we can access the content of the storage by referring to S*4 in the program. In other words, the use of SP4, SX6, and S*X6 are all illegal in GPSS. However, SNA*SNAj form of indirect addressing of attributes is allowed.

8.9 Random numbers, Variables, and Functions

8.9.1 Random number generators in GPSS

In simulation, we know that uniformly distributed random numbers are essential for the generation of events from various distributions. GPSS generates random numbers whenever required using the multiplicative congruence method, and they are not stored as SNA. GPSS has eight built-in independent generators which produce uniformly distributed random numbers in the range 0 through 999 (0 through 0.999999 when used with FUNCTION block) and referenced in the program by RN1,RN2, . . . RN8. The generator RN1 is used to generate random numbers for internal use (e.g. in TRANSFER, GENERATE, and ADVANCE blocks) and therefore it is desirable to use only RN2 to RN8 in user programs so as to avoid correlation and related errors. The results obtained from simulation experiments using the same sequence of random numbers as well as different sequences of random numbers may be required (see Chapter 10) for statistical analysis of simulation output. The sequence of random numbers can be altered by changing the initial seed using RMULT statement.

    RMULT   ,,,2153,,101

will set the initial seed of random number generator RN4 to 2153, RN6 to 101, and all others to their default value of 37. An analysis of GPSS produced random numbers is given in Reitman (1971).

8.9.2 Arithmetic, floating point, and boolean variables

The variable statement defines an expression consisting of constants and SNAs and the value of the variable is evaluated by simulation program when referenced during the simulation process. The general form of arithmetic and floating point variables is as follows:

    label   VARIABLE   arithmetic expression
    label   FVARIABLE   arithmetic expression

where $+$, $-$, $*$, $/$, and @(modulo division) are used in forming the expression on the right-hand side. The intermediate result obtained by evaluating the expression in VARIABLE statement is truncated to an integer after the evaluation of each operator in the expression. The intermediate computations in FVARIABLE statement are carried out in floating point arithmetic and only the final results are truncated to an integer.

Examples

2   VARIABLE   S2+Q2

will compute the value of V2 (variable 2) as the sum of the contents of storage 2 and the contents of queue 2.

LABL   VARIABLE   P8+X6*5
       ADVANCE   V$LABL

will result in delaying transactions entering ADVANCE block by the value of (parameter 8 + 5 times the value of savevalue 6).

8   VARIABLE   (10/6+3)*5

will give V8 = 20 and

8   FVARIABLE   (10/6+3)*5

will set V8 = 23.

The boolean variables are used to perform logical computations in boolean algebra and the individual elements involved in the computations will have a value of 0 or 1. The boolean variable statement has the form

label   BVARIABLE   logical expression.

The operators in the logical expression can be conditional operators ('E', 'L', 'G', 'NE', 'LE', 'GE'), boolean operators ($*$,$+$) and logical operators such as SEj (storage j empty) and FUj (facility j in use).

Example

1   BVARIABLE   Q3'L'8

will set boolean variable 1 (BV1) to 1 if the contents of queue 3 (Q3) is less than 8; otherwise BV1 = 0.

8.9.3 Discrete, Continuous, and List functions

As discussed in Chapter 7, functions are required to generate events from various probability distributions. Functions are evaluated when they are referenced in the GPSS program. Functions define the relationship between two variables x_i, y_i which may be positive or negative and the value of the variables need not be integers. Seven types of functions are available in GPSS, but only the three most frequently used functions are discussed here. The value of the function is truncated to an integer after computations except when it is used as a function modifier in ASSIGN, ADVANCE, and GENERATE blocks or when used as a floating point value. A FUNCTION statement followed by one or more function follower statements is required to define a function. The function follower statements contain the values of x_i, y_i beginning in column 1 and the x_i values must be given in ascending order. If RNj is used as an argument, then the x_i values must be in the range 0 to 1. The general format of a FUNCTION statement is

```
label   FUNCTION   A,B
x₁,y₁/x₂,y₂/ . . . /xₙ,yₙ
```

$x_1,y_1/x_2,y_2/ \ldots /x_n,y_n$

where A: the argument
      B: type of function and number of data points in the function (C: continuous with linear interpolation, D: discrete, L: list, E: discrete attribute mode, M: list attribute mode, S: entity mode)

Example

```
1   FUNCTION   RN3,C5
0,0/.1,5/.3,8/.7,12/1,10
```

is an example of a continuous function (FN1) defined by five data points and the output of random number generator 3 (RN3) is used as the argument.

```
2   FUNCTION   P1,D4
5,1/10,7/15,5/25,2
```

defines a discrete function consisting of four data points and the value of parameter 1 (P1) is used as the argument.
   A list function defined by six data points has the form

```
TCKT   FUNCTION        V5,L6
1,5/2,7/3,12/4,10/5,15/6,11
5         VARIABLE        RN4@6+1
```

Here we have used the value of variable 5 as the function argument and the value of V5 is in the range 1 to 6. When the value of V5=5, the function returns the value of 15.

180

8.10 GPSS example 2

Passengers arrive at the immigration control section of an airport every
7 seconds and join one of the two queues—queue 1 for aliens and queue 2
for local citizens. Sixty per cent of the arrivals were found to be local citizens
and they have priority over aliens for service. The immigration control desk
is manned by a single officer who takes 3 minutes to process local passports
and 7 ± 3 minutes (uniformly distributed) to process alien passports. Simulate
the operation of the immigration control section until 1000 passengers have
gone through the system, with a view to studying the queues of the passengers
and the utilization of the immigration officer.

I will develop three different GPSS program to solve the above problem
and in each case I present the output from the GPSS assembly stage together
with a portion of the statistical output. In section 8.10.1, I show a simple
GPSS program; in section 8.10.2, the use of VARIABLE, ASSIGN, PRI-
ORITY, and standard numerical attributes are illustrated. The use of FUNC-
TION is shown in section 8.10.3. The three GPSS programs (jobs) were run
as a single task. This is achieved by separating the first two programs by
JOB statements (no END statement) and only the last (third) program is
terminated by the END statement as shown below.

```
┌─────────────────┐
│    Program 1    │
└─────────────────┘
        JOB
┌─────────────────┐
│    Program 2    │
└─────────────────┘
        JOB
┌─────────────────┐
│    Program 3    │
└─────────────────┘
        END
```

8.10.1 A simple GPSS program for example 2

A simple GPSS program and a portion of the output are given in Figure 8.7a.
The local passengers are given higher priority over aliens by sending them
through a PRIORITY block (see Section 8.13). Queue 1 and queue 2 statistics, as well as the utilization of the immigration officer, are printed out.

8.10.2 Another GPSS program for example 2

The GPSS program shown in Figure 8.7b illustrates the use of modulo
division in computing the value of V1; the ASSIGN statement assigns a
specified value (field B) to a parameter (field A) and the last seven state-

GPSS Assembly

```
 1  ***************************************************************
 2  * SIMULATION OF IMMIGRATION CONTROL AT AIRPORT - ONE OFFICER  *
 3  * PASSENGERS ARRIVE EVERY 7 MINUTES                           *
 4  * 40% PASSENGERS ARE ALIENS--LOWER PRIORITY FOR SERVICE       *
 5  * OFFICER NEEDS 4 TO 10 MINUTES FOR ALIENS AND 3 MINUTES FOR LOCALS *
 6  * SERVICE TIMES ARE UNIFORMLY DISTRIBUTED                     *
 7  * STOP AFTER SIMULATING 1000 PASSENGERS                       *
 8  ***************************************************************
 9  *LABEL OPERATOR  OPERANDS      COMMENTS
10  ***************************************************************
11        SIMULATE
12        GENERATE    7             PASSENGERS ARRIVE EVERY 7 MINUTES
13        TRANSFER    .600,,LOCAL   40% ALIENS ARE SEPARATED
14        QUEUE       1             ALIENS STAND IN QUEUE 1
15        SEIZE       OFFCR         ENGAGE IMMIGRATION OFFICER IF FREE
16        DEPART      1             REMOVE ONE ALIEN PASSENGER FROM QUEUE 1
17        ADVANCE     7,3           IMIGRATION OFFICER TAKES 4 TO 10 MINUTES
18        RELEASE     OFFCR         MAKE IMMIGRATION OFFICER FREE
19        TERMINATE   1             REMOVE 1 ALIEN PASSENGER FROM SYSTEM
20  LOCAL PRIORITY    1             GIVE PRIORITY 1 TO LOCAL PASSENGER
21        QUEUE       2             LOCAL PASSENGER STAND IN QUEUE 2
22        SEIZE       OFFCR         ENGAGE IMMIGRATION OFFICER, IF FREE
23        DEPART      2             REMOVE ONE LOCAL PASSENGER FROM QUEUE 2
24        ADVANCE     3             IMMIGRATION OFFICER TAKES 3 MINUTES
25        RELEASE     OFFCR         MAKE IMMIGRATION OFFICER FREE
26        TERMINATE   1             REMOVE 1 LOCAL PASSENGER FROM SYSTEM
27        START       1000          STOP AFTER SIMULATING 1000 PASSENGERS
```

QUEUE	MAXIMUM CONTENTS	AVERAGE CONTENTS	TOTAL ENTRIES	ZERO ENTRIES	PERCENT ZEROS	AVERAGE TIME/TRANS	$AVERAGE TIME/TRANS	TABLE NUMBER	CURRENT CONTENTS
1	2	0.03	393	311	79.135	0.52	2.48	0	0
2	1	0.04	607	483	79.572	0.43	2.11	0	0

FACILITY	AVERAGE UTILIZATION	NUMBER ENTRIES	AVERAGE TIME/TRANS	SEIZING TRANS. NO.	PREEMPTING TRANS. NO.
OFFCR	0.6492	1000	4.55	0	0

Figure 8.7(a) Simple GPSS program for example 2.

GPSS ASSEMBLY

```
 1
 2            JOB
 3            ****************************************************************
 4          * BEGINNING OF SECOND JOB                                       *
 5          * ANOTHER GPSS PROG.TO SIMULATE IMMIGR.CONTROL PROBLEM OF FIGURE 8.7a *
 6            ****************************************************************
 7   1        VARIABLE   4+RN3%7              GENERATES INTEGER IN THE RANGE 4 TO 10
 8            GENERATE   7                    PASSENGERS ARRIVE EVERY 7 MINUTES
 9            TRANSFER   .600,,LOCAL          40% ALIENS ARE SEPARATED
10            ASSIGN     1,V1                 ASSIGN VALUE OF V1 TO PARAMETER P1
11            ASSIGN     2,1                  ASSIGN  1  TO PARAMETER P2
12            TRANSFER   ,LINK                GO TO LINK
13    LOCAL   ASSIGN     1,3                  ASSIGNS 3 TO PARAMETER 1
14            ASSIGN     2,2                  ASSIGNS 2 TO PARAMETER 2
15            PRIORITY   1                    GIVE PRIORITY 1 TO LOCAL PASSENGER
16    ******** P2=1 FOR ALIENS AND P2=2 FOR LOCAL PASSENGERS  ***************
17    LINK    QUEUE      P2                   PASSENGERS STAND IN QUEUE P2
18            SEIZE      OFFCR                ENGAGE OFFICER IF FREE
19            DEPART     P2                   REMOVE ONE PASSENGER FROM QUEUE P2
20    ***** P1=3 FOR LOCALS AND 4 TO 10 MINUTES FOR ALIEN PASSENGERS ********
21            ADVANCE    P1                   IMMIGRATION OFFICER TAKES P1 MINUTES
22            RELEASE    OFFCR                MAKE IMMIGRATION OFFICER FREE
23            TERMINATE  1                    REMOVE ONE PASSENGER FROM SYSTEM
24            START      1000                 STOP AFTER SIMULATING 1000 PASSENGERS
```

QUEUE	MAXIMUM CONTENTS	AVERAGE CONTENTS	TOTAL ENTRIES	ZERO ENTRIES	PERCENT ZEROS	AVERAGE TIME/TRANS	$AVERAGE TIME/TRANS	TABLE NUMBER	CURRENT CONTENTS
1	1	0.02	383	312	81.462	0.40	2.15	0	0
2	1	0.04	617	493	79.903	0.46	2.31	0	0

FACILITY	AVERAGE UTILIZATION	NUMBER ENTRIES	AVERAGE TIME/TRANS	SEIZING TRANS. NO.	PREEMPTING TRANS. NO.
OFFCR	0.6468	1000	4.53	0	0

Figure 8.7(b) GPSS program 2 for example 2.

ments of the program are shared by both local and alien passengers and the program has become shorter. The output statistics is more or less the same as that of Figure 8.7a.

8.10.3 Third GPSS program for example 2

The GPSS program of Figure 8.7c is shorter than those in Figures 8.7a and 8.7b, and most of the GPSS statements are common to both local and alien passengers. This is achieved by clever usage of standard numerical attributes FN1, PR, and V1. The function FN1 takes a value of 2 in 60% of cases and 1 in 40% of cases, and these values are assigned as priorities of transactions when they are created in the GENERATE block. The three different GPSS programs discussed in Section 8.10 are designed to solve the same problem; however, they handle transactions differently and therefore, as expected, the output statistics from the three programs vary slightly.

8.11 Generation and Termination of transaction (temporary entities)

The GPSS transactions are the temporary entities and they simulate the traffic in the system. Transactions are created by GENERATE blocks and destroyed by TERMINATE blocks. GPSS programs must contain at least one GENERATE block. The GENERATE block has the form

GENERATE   A,B,C,D,E,F,G

where the operands are defined as follows:
A: mean inter-generation time;
B: spread ($\leq$ mean) or function modifier;
C: the time at which the generation process begins;
D: maximum number of transactions to be created (default is infinity);
E: priority of transaction (default is zero; highest priority is 127);
F: number of parameters associated with each transaction;
G: parameter type (H for halfword and F for fullword).

The F to I operands in GPSS-V define fullword, halfword, byte, and floating point type of parameters and symbols used for coding are slightly different.

Example

GENERATE   12,3,10,,,15,F

will keep on generating transactions with priority zero at intervals of 9 to 15 time units (uniformly distributed); starting at GPSS clock time 10 and 15 fullword parameters will be allocated to each transaction.

GENERATE   10,FN1

GPSS Assembly

```
 1
 2                JOB
 3     **********************************************************
 4     * BEGINNING OF THIRD JOB                                 *
 5     * ANOTHER GPSS PROG.TO SIMULATE IMMIGR.CONTROL PROBLEM OF FIGURE 8.7a *
 6     **********************************************************
 7          SIMULATE
 8     ********** FN1=2 IN 60% CASES AND FN1=1 IN 40% CASES **********
 9  1       FUNCTION  RN2,D2        DISCRETE FUNCTION
10  .6,2/1,1
11     ***** V1=4 TO 10 WHEN PR=1 AND V1=3 WHEN PR=2 **********
12  1       VARIABLE  ((4+RN3%7)*(2-PR))+(3*(PR-1))
13          GENERATE  7,,,FN1       ARRIVALS EVERY 7 MINUTES WITH PRIORITY FN1
            ******QUEUE 1 FOR ALIENS AND QUEUE 2 FOR LOCALS **********
14          QUEUE     PR            PASSENGERS STAND IN QUEUE PR=FN1
15          SEIZE     OFFCR         ENGAGE OFFICER, IF FREE
16          DEPART    PR            REMOVE ONE PASSENGER FROM QUEUE PR
17          ADVANCE   V1            IMMIGRATION OFFICER TAKES V1 MINUTES
18          RELEASE   OFFCR         MAKE IMMIGRATION OFFICER FREE
19          TERMINATE 1             REMOVE ONE PASSENGER FROM SYSTEM
20          START     1000
21          END
```

QUEUE	MAXIMUM CONTENTS	AVERAGE CONTENTS	TOTAL ENTRIES	ZERO ENTRIES	PERCENT ZEROS	AVERAGE TIME/TRANS	$AVERAGE TIME/TRANS	TABLE NUMBER	CURRENT CONTENTS
1	1	0.03	405	311	76.790	0.53	2.27	0	10
2	1	0.04	595	460	77.311	0.53	2.32	0	0

FACILITY	AVERAGE UTILIZATION	NUMBER ENTRIES	AVERAGE TIME/TRANS	SEIZING TRANS. NO.	PREEMPTING TRANS. NO.
OFFCR	0.6659	1000	4.66	0	0

Figure 8.7(c) GPSS program 3 for example 2.

will keep on generating transactions with priority zero, beginning at time zero; the inter-generation time is ten times the value of FN1 and 12 halfword parameters will be automatically allocated to each transaction.

The TERMINATE block has the following format

TERMINATE   A

where A is the termination count decrement (default is zero) and the termination count is specified on the START statement as described earlier.

Example

TERMINATE

or

TERMINATE   0

will remove the entering transaction from the system, but the START counter is not decremented and therefore the simulation will go on until the program time limit is exceeded.

TERMINATE   P5

will decrement the START counter by the value of the parameter 5 of the entering transaction which of course is destroyed.

8.12   Operations on permanent entities

The permanent entities include facilities, storages, queues, logic switches, chains, and groups. The chains and groups are generally required for modelling complex systems and they are not discussed here.

8.12.1   Facilities

This entity can be engaged only by one transaction at a time and is ideal for simulating single server in a queuing model. SEIZE–RELEASE and PREEMPT–RETURN are the blocks (GPSS–V has FAVAIL and FUNAVAIL) associated with facilities. A facility can only be released by the same transaction that seized it.

Example

```
SEIZE       MACHN
ADVANCE     5,2
RELEASE     MACHN
```

In its simplest form, the PREEMPT block interrupts the seizing transaction, if any, and takes control of the facility. On entering a RETURN block, the control of the facility is returned to the original seizing transaction and the suspended service is allowed to continue.

Example

```
PREEMPT    PHONE
RETURN     PHONE
```

8.12.2 Storages

A storage can be engaged by several transactions (e.g. telephone exchange, warehouse) at the same time. A facility is basically a storage with a capacity of one unit. ENTER and LEAVE are the two blocks (GPSS-V has SAVAIL and SUNAVAIL) associated with storages and they have the form

```
ENTER      A,B
LEAVE      A,B
```

where A: storage name or number,
     B: number of units to be added or removed from the storage (default is one).

Example

```
ENTER      LANE,100
ADVANCE    5,1
LEAVE      LANE,50
```

Here, 100 units are added to the storage named LANE by the entering transaction and after 5 ± 1 units of time 50 units are removed from the storage. The storage capacity is defined by the statement

```
label  STORAGE  A
```

where
     label: storage name or number,
         A: capacity of storage.

8.12.3 Queues

The operation of the queue entity is very similar to that of storage entity. The QUEUE and DEPART blocks are associated with queues, and the entering transactions modify the status of the queue.

Example

```
QUEUE      1,1
SEIZE      PHONE
DEPART     1,1
```

and

```
QUEUE  1
SEIZE  PHONE
DEPART 1
```

will have the same effect.

8.12.4 Logic switches

The LOGIC block can be used to set, reset, or invert the specified logic switch and the status of the switches can be tested by means of GATE blocks. The entering transaction will leave the switch undisturbed if it is already in the desired state. The general format of this block is

```
LOGIC  X  A
```

where A: logic switch name or number,
     X: S   set the logic switch,
         R   reset the logic switch,
         I   invert the logic switch.

Example

```
LOGIC  R  RED
```

will reset the logic switch named RED.

8.13 Manipulation of entity attributes

It was mentioned in Section 8.6 that the user has access to certain entity attributes which can be collected as data or can be used to control the course of simulation. The use of savevalues and logic switches has been discussed in Sections 8.5 and 8.12 respectively. I will now examine the use of MARK, PRIORITY, and ASSIGN blocks to modify the attributes of transactions.

Associated with every transaction there are words for recording transaction attributes. Some of these are called parameters. A word called 'mark time word' is used to record the current clock time at which a transaction entered the MARK block. Initially the mark time word is set to the creation time of the transaction and the *mark time* can be accessed by means of the standard numerical attribute M1.

Example

MARK

will replace the '*mark time*' of the transaction by the current clock time C1 (relative clock)

MARK 2

will store the current clock time in parameter P2 of the entering transaction without disturbing the contents of the '*mark time word*'. The MARK and TABULATE blocks together with the standard numerical attributes M1 or MPj are used (see Section 8.7) to tabulate the original '*mark time*' or the intermediate transit times of transactions.

The priority of transactions set (default is zero) at the time of creation can be modified by the PRIORITY block. The simplest form of PRIORITY block is

PRIORITY A

where A is the new priority (0 to 127; 0 is lowest priority) assigned to the entering transaction.

We can change the value of transaction parameters by means of ASSIGN block which has the following form

ASSIGN A,B,C,D

where A: parameter number;
       B: the value used to modify the parameter specified by A (stored, added, or subtracted);
       C: function modifier (optional); if present, values of B and C operands are multiplied and the truncated integer is used to modify A;
       D: specify different parameter types in GPSS-V.

Example

ASSIGN 5,Q6

will store the current value of queue 6 in parameter 5 of the transaction.

ASSIGN 5-,Q6

will subtract the value of queue 6 from parameter 5 of the transaction.

189

ASSIGN   3,P2,5

will store the product of P2 and FN5 (truncated to integer) in parameter 3.

8.14   Mechanism for transaction flow control

Normally GPSS transactions move sequentially from one block to another. The nonsequential execution of GPSS program statements can be achieved in several ways by branching randomly, logically, arithmetically, or unconditionally. I will discuss TRANSFER, GATE, and TEST blocks which are frequently used for transaction flow control. Branching on condition using PREEMPT has already been discussed in Section 8.12.

8.14.1   The TRANSFER block

The general format of TRANSFER block is as follows

TRANSFER   A,B,C,D

where   A: Selection mode (only four of the nine modes are discussed here).
(1) If absent, the transaction is unconditionally sent to the block specified by operand B.
(2) Three digit fraction f; the transaction makes a random choice between blocks specified by operands B and C with probability $(1 - f)$ and f respectively.
(3) BOTH: The transaction will attempt to move to the block specified by the operand B and if entry is denied then it will try to move to the block specified by operand C. If entry is refused by both the blocks, then the transaction waits at TRANSFER block and the process is repeated in that order until it succeeds in selecting one of the paths.
(4) SIM: The transaction is sent to the block specified by operand B if the delay indicator is zero; otherwise it is sent to the block specified by operand C. (The delay indicator of a transaction is initially zero and it is set to 1 whenever the transaction is refused entry to a block.)
B: The address of a block where the transaction can be sent depending upon the selection mode A.
C: The address of a block where the transaction can be sent depending on the selection mode A.
D: Used with selection mode A = ALL (not discussed here).

Examples

TRANSFER   0.25,CLAS1,CLAS2

Seventy-five per cent of the transactions, selected at random, are sent to location CLAS1, and 25% to location CLAS2. If operand field B is left blank, the program will assume that the next sequential block is intended.

TRANSFER ,CLAS3

All transactions are sent to location called CLAS3.

8.14.2 The GATE block

The GATE block allows the user to test the status of logic switches, facilities, and storages. The general format of GATE block is

GATE X A,B

where A: permanent entity name or number,
      B: alternate route for transaction, if condition indicated by X is not satisfied (optional),
      X: mnemonics associated with facilities, storages, and logical operators. For example, the mnemonics associated with facilities are:
         U: facility in use,
         NU: facility not in use,
         I: facility pre-empted,
         NI: facility not pre-empted.

Example

GATE U PHON,LOST

The entering transaction will be sent to location LOST if the facility PHON is not in use; otherwise sent to the next sequential block.

GATE U PHON

The transaction is allowed to enter the GATE block only if the facility PHON is in use.

```
AGAIN   GATE NU      PHON1
        GATE NU      PHON2
        TRANSFER     SIM,,AGAIN
        SEIZE        PHON1
        SEIZE        PHON2
```

The entering transaction will be able to seize PHON1 and PHON2 only if both PHON1 and PHON2 are free simultaneously; otherwise the TRANS-

FER block keeps on sending the transaction back to the GATE block in location AGAIN until the SIM delay indicator is zero.

8.14.3   The TEST block

The operation of TEST block is similar to that of GATE block. The TEST block tests the relationship between SNAs of entities, whereas the GATE block tests the status of an entity. The TEST block has the form

TEST X   A,B,C

where A,B: the SNAs to be compared using the logical operator X,

C: if present, indicates alternative exit route,

X: E   (equal)
NE   (not equal)
L   (less than)
LE   (less than or equal)
G   (greater than)
GE   (greater than or equal)

Example

TEST E   P1,P2

The transaction enters the TEST block only if P1=P2; otherwise waits in the previous block.

TEST GE   Q1,FN2,LABL

The transaction enters the TEST block and it is immediately sent to the next sequential block if Q1 ≥ FN2; otherwise sent to the block at location LABL.

8.15   Mechanisms for delaying transactions

The flow of transactions through GPSS model can be delayed for a specified period of time called *action time* by means of ADVANCE block. The action time need not be a constant and the transaction remains in the ADVANCE block for the period of action time before attempting to move to the next block. The ADVANCE block never refuses entry and several transactions can coexist in the ADVANCE block.

ADVANCE   A,B

where A: mean time,
       B: spread or function modifier.

Example

   ADVANCE 10,2

The entering transaction will be delayed by 10 ± 2 units of time, uniformly distributed between 8 and 12. The delays caused by model interaction cannot be predicted in advance. As explained in earlier sections, GATE, TEST, SEIZE, PREEMPT, and TRANSFER blocks test for arithmetic or logical conditions and may force the transactions to wait for an unspecified period of time.

8.16 Simulation control statements

SIMULATE, START, END, CLEAR, and RESET are the most important subset of control statements in GPSS. The presence of SIMULATE requests a simulation run after assembly. In GPSS–V the length of the simulation run can be specified on the SIMULATE card. The END statement signals the end of the GPSS program input which may contain several jobs separated by JOB statements.

The condition for the termination of simulation and the type of printed output required are specified on the START statement, which has the form

   START A,B,C,D

where A: run termination counter which is decremented when transaction
          enters the TERMINATE block with nonzero operand A; simul-
          ation stops when the value of the counter is less than or equal
          to zero;
       B: if NP, no statistics are printed at the end of a simulation run,
       C: interval count for intermediate printout of results,
       D: if 1, the status of current events chain, future events chain, etc.,
          are included in the standard output.

Example

   TERMINATE
   START 100

will cause simulation to continue for ever unless stopped by other means.

   TERMINATE   2
   START   1000,,100

whenever a transaction is terminated, the termination counter (operand A) of the START block is decremented by 2. Intermediate results are printed on termination of 50, 100, 150, 200, . . . 500 transactions.

The RESET statement wipes out all statistics and resets the relative clock (C1) to zero. The model itself (transactions, savevalues, logic switches, etc.) is left undisturbed. Selected entities such as storages, facilities, tables, and user chains are not affected by RESET, provided they are specified in the operand fields

RESET   S1,F2,Q5

will reset all statistics except those associated with storage 1, facility 2, and queue 5.

The CLEAR statement reinitialises the model by (a) erasing all statistics including contents of SAVEVALUES, (b) removing all transactions from the model, (c) resetting logical switches, and (d) resetting both relative and absolute clocks to zero. It does not reset the random number generators and the user has the choice of specifying those savevalues which should not be reset to zero.

Example

CLEAR   X5,X10–X15

will not reset the contents of savevalues X5 and X10 through X15. The RESET AND CLEAR blocks are useful in conducting simulation experiments.

8.17   GPSS example 3 and example 4

Here I show the use of several GPSS blocks which are useful in simulating complex systems. Example 4 is a modified version of example 3 by adding more details into the model.

8.17.1   Example 3—Use of STORAGE, GATE, and SAVEVALUE

A travel agency has three telephone lines. On an average, 100 travel enquires (incoming calls) arrive at the central switchboard every hour; connected calls last 0.031 hours and calls are lost whenever all the three lines are busy. Both the arrival and service times were found to be exponentially distributed. Simulate the processing of 1000 travel enquiries and determine the number of calls lost and the utilization of the phone system during that period.

The GPSS simulation program and output appear in Figure 8.8, where the exponential distribution is characterized by a continuous function consisting of 24 points. In order to improve the accuracy of simulation, we have selected

GPSS Assembly

```
      ***********************************************************
      *                                                         *
      *  SIMULATION OF A TRAVEL AGENCY WITH 3 TELEPHONE LINES   *
      *  UNIT OF TIME : 1/1000 HOUR                             *
      *  INTERARRIVAL TIME OF CALLS : 10 TIME UNITS,EXPON.DISTRI *
      *  SERVICE TIME OF CALLS      : 31 TIME UNITS;EXPON.DISTRI *
      *  STOP SIMULATION AFTER PROCESSING 1000 TRAVEL QUERIES   *
      *                                                         *
      ***********************************************************
     *LABEL OPERATOR  OPERANDS        COMMENTS

 1         STORAGE    3               3 PHONE LINES AVAILABLE
     EXPON FUNCTION   RN3,C24         EXPONENTIAL DISTRIBUTION
     .000,.000/.100,.104/.200,.222/.300,.355/.400,.509/.500,.690/
     .600,.915/.700,1.20/.750,1.38/.800,1.60/.840,1.83/.880,2.12/
     .900,2.30/.920,2.52/.940,2.81/.950,2.99/.960,3.20/.970,3.50/
     .980,3.90/.990,4.60/.995,5.30/.998,6.20/.999,7.00/.9997,8.0
           SIMULATE
           GENERATE   10,FN$EXPON     100 CALLS ARRIVE EVERY HOUR
           GATE SNF   1,LOST          TEST FOR A FREE LINE
           ENTER      1,1             CONNECT THE CALL
           ADVANCE    31,FN$EXPON     TALK FOR 31 UNITS OF TIME,EXP.DISTRIBUTED
           LEAVE      1,1             DISCONNECT CALL AND SET LINE FREE
           TERMINATE  1               REMOVE COMPLETED CALL FROM SYSTEM
           SAVEVALUE  1+,1            RECORD LOST CALL IN SAVEVALUE 1
     LOST  TERMINATE  1               REMOVE LOST CALL FROM SYSTEM
           START      1000            STOP AFTER SIMULATING 1000 TRAVEL QUERIES
           END
```

STORAGE	CAPACITY	AVERAGE CONTENTS	AVERAGE UTILIZATION	TOTAL ENTRIES	AVERAGE TIME/TRANS	CURRENT CONTENTS	MAXIMUM CONTENTS
1	3	1.94	0.6459	645	29.05	1	3

NON-ZERO FULLWORD SAVEVALUES

SAVEX	CONTENTS	SAVEX	CONTENTS	SAVEX	CONTENTS	SAVEX	CONTENTS	SAVEX	CONTENTS	SAVEX	CONTENTS
1	356										

Figure 8.8   GPSS program for example 3.

1/1000 of an hour as the basic time unit. The three telephone lines are represented by a storage with capacity 3 and the number of lost calls are recorded in savevalue 1. The GPSS output shows that, on an average, the telephone lines were busy 64.59% of the time and 356 calls were lost during the simulation period, which was found to be 9670 (not shown) time units.

8.17.2   Example 4—Use of TEST, RESET, and CLEAR

We modify example 3 by adding the following outgoing calls into the model and the purpose of simulation is to determine the number of lost calls as well as the number of outgoing calls.

If a line is free, the first outgoing call is made after 0.6 hours of operation. The next outside call is attempted 1 hour after the completion of the previous one. If a line is not free while attempting to make an outside call, keep on trying at intervals of 0.2 hours until a line is free. Assume that each outside call lasts for 0.125 hours and the dialled telephone is always free.

The modified GPSS program is shown in Figure 8.9 and the output immediately after the first RESET is shown in Figure 8.10. The GEN-ERATE block on line 34 generates only one transaction which simulates the attempt to make an outside call. This transaction is never terminated and loops around a small segment of the GPSS programme. Such a transaction is called *cyclic transaction*. The RESET statement eliminates all system statistics after a small warming-up period (10% of calls—to eliminate initial bias) and the values of savevalues are set to zero by the INITIAL statement. Figure 8.10 shows both relative (time after last RESET; 9573) and absolute clock (10,551) times; on an average telephone lines were busy 67.46% of the time; 363 calls were lost and 8 outside calls were successfully completed during the simulation of 1000 calls. The frequency distribution of the transit times of incoming calls is shown in Table 1 of the output, which also displays the mean and standard deviation. For a detailed explanation of GPSS output, the reader should consult the GPSS manual.

After CLEAR and RESET, the GPSS output was found to be

Relative clock: 9748
Absolute clock: 10,514
Average utilisation of phones: 69.13%
Number of lost calls: 428
Number of outside calls: 8

The simulation was repeated with 5 and 7 telephone lines and the following results were obtained:

Number of phone lines	3	5	7
Average utilisation of phones	0.6746	0.5672	0.4282
Number of calls lost	363	140	34
Number of outside calls made	8	8	8

GPSS Assembly

```
      *********************************************************
   1  * SIMULATION OF A TRAVEL AGENCY WITH 3 TELEPHONE LINES *
   2  * UNIT OF TIME : 1/1000 HOUR                            *
   3  * INCOMING CALLS                                        *
   4  *     INTER.ARR.TIME OF CALLS:  10 TIME UNITS,EXP.DISTR *
   5  *     SERVICE TIME OF CALLS  :  31 TIME UNITS,EXP.DISTR *
   6  * OUTGOING CALLS                                        *
   7  *     FIRST ATTEMPT AFTER .6 HOUR                       *
   8  *     KEEP ON TRYING EVERY  .2 HOUR,UNTIL LINE FREE     *
   9  *     INTER.ARR.TIME OF CALLS : 1 HOUR                  *
  10  *     SERVICE TIME OF CALLS  : .125 HOUR                *
  11  * STOP SIMULATION AFTER PROCESSING 1000 INCOMING CALLS  *
  12  *********************************************************
  13
  16  1   STORAGE   3         3 PHONE LINES AVAILABLE
  17  1   TABLE     M1,10,15,90   DEFINES FORMAT & CONTENT OF TABLE
  18  EXPON  FUNCTION  RN3,C24   EXPONENTIAL DISTRIBUTION
  19  .000,.000/.100,.104/.200,.222/.300,.355/.400,.509/.500,.690/
  20  .600,.915/.700,1.20/.750,1.38/.800,1.60/.840,1.83/.880,2.12/
  21  .900,2.30/.920,2.52/.940,2.81/.950,2.99/.960,3.20/.970,3.50/
  22  .980,3.90/.990,4.60/.995,5.30/.998,6.20/.999,7.00/.9997,8.0
  23      SIMULATE
  24      GENERATE  10,FN$EXPON  100 CALLS ARRIVE EVERY HOUR
1 25  GATE SNF   1,LOST        TRY FOR A FREE LINE
2 26  ENTER      1,1           CONNECT INCOMING CALL
3 27. ADVANCE    31,FN$EXPON   TALK FOR 31 TIME UNITS,EXPO.DISTR
4
```

```
28   5   LEAVE      1,1          DISCONNECT CALL AND SET LINE FREE
29   6   TABULATE   1            TABULATE TRANSIT TIMES IN TABLE 1
30   7   TERMINATE  1            REMOVE COMPLETED CALL FROM SYSTEM
31   8   LOST SAVEVALUE 1+,1     RECORD LOST CALL IN SAVEVALUE 1
32   9   TERMINATE  1            REMOVE LOST CALL FROM SYSTEM
34   10  GENERATE   600,,,1      FIRST ATTEMPT FOR AN OUTSIDE CALL
35   11  TRY  TEST L S1,3,WAIT   TEST FOR A FREE LINE
36   12  ENTER      1,1          CONNECT OUTGOING CALL
37   13  ADVANCE    125          TALK FOR 125 TIME UNITS
38   14  LEAVE      1,1          DISCONNECT CALL AND SET LINE FREE
39   15  SAVEVALUE  2+,1         RECORD OUTSIDE CALLS IN SAVEVALUE 2
40   16  ADVANCE    1000         TRY NEXT OUTSIDE CALL AFTER 1 HR.
41   17  TRANSFER   ,TRY         GO TO TRY
42   18  WAIT ADVANCE 200        WAIT .2 HR;THEN TRY OUTSIDE CALL AGAIN
43   19  TRANSFER   ,TRY         GO TO TRY
44       START      100          STOP AFTER SIMULATING 100 INCOMING CALLS
45  *****RESET SYSTEM STATISTICS AFTER 10% WARMING UP PERIOD *************
46       RESET                   RESET SAVEVALUES TO ZERO
47       INITIAL    X1-X2,0
48       START      1000         STOP AFTER SIMULATING 1000 INCOMING CALLS
49  *****USE CLEAR TO RE-INITIALISE SIMUL.MODEL WITH NEW RAND.NUMBERS **
50       CLEAR
51       START      100
52       RESET
53       START      1000
54       END
```

Figure 8.9 GPSS (assembly) program for example 4.

CLOCK TIME   9573   10551

BLOCK COUNTS

BLOCK	CURRENT	TOTAL	BLOCK	CURRENT	TOTAL	BLOCK	CURRENT	TOTAL	BLOCK	CURRENT	TOTAL
1	1	1003	2	0	1003	3	0	640	4	8	640
5	0	637	6	0	637	7	0	637	8	0	363
9	0	363	10	0	637	11	0	9	12	0	8
13	0	8	14	0	8	15	0	8	16	1	8
17	0	8	18	0	8	19	0	1			

STORAGE	CAPACITY	AVERAGE CONTENTS	AVERAGE UTILIZATION	TOTAL ENTRIES	AVERAGE TIME/TRANS	CURRENT CONTENTS	MAXIMUM CONTENTS
1	3	2.02	0.6746	648	29.90	3	3

TABLE 1

ENTRIES IN TABLE	MEAN ARGUMENT	STANDARD DEVIATION	SUM OF ARGUMENTS
637	28.653	29.332	18252.000

UPPER LIMIT	OBSERVED FREQUENCY	PER CENT OF TOTAL	CUMULATIVE PERCENTAGE	CUMULATIVE REMAINDER	MULTIPLE OF MEAN	NON-WEIGHTED DEVIATION FROM MEAN
10	215	33.75	33.8	66.2	0.349	-0.636
25	155	24.33	58.1	41.9	0.873	-0.125
40	112	17.58	75.7	24.3	1.396	0.387
55	58	9.11	84.8	15.2	1.920	0.898
70	38	5.97	90.7	9.3	2.443	1.410
85	28	4.40	95.1	4.9	2.967	1.921
100	7	1.10	96.2	3.8	3.490	2.432
115	10	1.57	97.8	2.2	4.014	2.944
130	11	1.73	99.5	0.5	4.537	3.455
145	1	0.16	99.7	0.3	5.061	3.967
160	1	0.16	99.8	0.2	5.584	4.478
175	0	0.00	99.8	0.2	6.108	4.989
190	0	0.00	99.8	0.2	6.631	5.501
205	0	0.00	99.8	0.2	7.155	6.012
220	0	0.00	99.8	0.2	7.678	6.524
235	0	0.00	99.8	0.2	8.202	7.035
250	1	0.16	100.0	0.0	8.725	7.546

REMAINING FREQUENCIES ARE ALL ZERO

NON-ZERO FULLWORD SAVEVALUES

SAVEX	CONTENTS	SAVEX	CONTENTS	SAVEX	CONTENTS	SAVEX	CONTENTS	SAVEX	CONTENTS
1	363	2	8						

Figure 8.10   GPSS output for example 4.

8.18 GPSS on microprocessors

GPSS/PC, a microprocessor-based GPSS, is currently available on any personal computer compatible with IBM PC or XT (Minuteman) using PC-DOS or MS-DOS operating system with at least 256K bytes of memory and one double-sided, double-density diskette.

Over 90% of GPSS blocks and several other features not available in GPSS–V are included (Cox and Cox, 1985; Karian, 1985) in GPSS/PC. Up to full memory usage there is no limit on the number of parameters, random number generators, entities, clock values, parameter values, and precision of statistical computations. The vendors claim that any number of full-period 32-bit random number generators may be used and the seeds can be set by the user. There are facilities to construct probability distributions without using GPSS functions. The simulation control commands, such as STOP, STEP, and CONTINUE, allow full interactive control of a running simulation. Mid-simulation modifications to values, entities, and block structures are permissible and there is a dynamic plot facility to observe values during a simulation run.

Barta (1985) has recently reported the use of a new version of GPSS/H for animated simulation graphics.

8.19 Summary

GPSS is powerful, and is one of the most widely used discrete system simulation languages currently implemented on several mainframes and microprocessors. The design of GPSS was influenced by block diagram and flowchart concepts. The language is less flexible than SIMSCRIPT and is particularly suitable for simulating queuing type problems. Important features of the language are presented and several examples, together with GPSS programs, are given to illustrate the use of GPSS in modelling and simulation. GPSS uses integer time units and therefore the selection of appropriate time scaling factors is important to ensure accuracy of simulations. GPSS is very easy to learn, and programs can be developed directly from the statement of the problem.

We have discussed only a subset of the GPSS language and its applications in systems simulation. After reading this chapter, the user should be in a position to attempt the modelling and simulation of complex systems. Advanced features of the language, and a detailed description of the output statistics, can be found in GPSS manuals. Several versions of GPSS are available on a variety of machines.

8.20 Exercises

1. (a) Write the function and function follower statements in GPSS for a distribution where the probability that y is 3, 1, 4, and 6 is 3/10, 4/10, 1/10, and 2/10 respectively.

(b) Using the list function in GPSS write the necessary statements to select one of the following numbers at random

$$5, 3, 0, -3, 21, -1, 2$$

(c) Write a continuous function and function follower statements in GPSS to represent the following data:

x	y
0	0
0.1	3
0.3	5
0.5	2
0.8	6
1.0	8

2. Read the GPSS manual and find out how the GPSS scan algorithm works. How is the GPSS clock updated to the next future event time? What are the functions of scan status indicators and status change flag?

3. Examine in detail how random numbers are generated in GPSS. How good are these numbers compared to other random number generator outputs you have come across? Generate 10,000 random numbers and test them for independence and uniformity as discussed in Chapter 6.

4. The manager of a savings bank wants to find the optimum stock of cash to hold on a daily basis. Carrying too much cash is unproductive, and moreover it poses a security risk. By carrying too little cash he runs the risk of not being able to give his customers the service they expect, and the consequent risk of losing business. Customers may deposit or withdraw cash and large transactions are dealt with separately by special arrangements. The following data are available:

probability of deposit: p
probability of withdrawl: $(1-p)$
opening stock of cash: $\$C$

The cumulative distribution of 10,000 withdrawals/deposits is shown below:

Less than than $	5	20	60	100	200	400	600	800	1000
No. of deposits	500	3000	6500	8000	9500	9750	9960	9975	9999
No. of withdrawals	150	300	1750	4500	7000	9500	9800	9970	9999

Simulate the daily closing stock, minimum stock, and maximum stock for different values of C and p, starting with $C=\$7500$ and $p=55\%$. What should be the ideal opening stock for smooth operation of the bank. Note that negative stock implies shortage of cash.

5. Jobs are submitted from terminals at the rate of one every 150 to 164 seconds for processing on the local computer. The types of jobs and their characteristics are as follows:

Jobs		Processing priority	Run time per job (minutes)
Type	Probability		
Pascal	0.5	1	3
Fortran	0.2	2	4
Others	0.3	3	2

Write a GPSS program to simulate the operation of the computer centre for 24 hours and output the following:
(a) utilization of the computer,
(b) average turnaround time for each type of job,
(c) number of each type of job processed.
Comment on the usefulness of these and other related simulation results in improving the efficiency of the computer centre.

6. Four identical processing machines in a food processing plant are arranged around a turntable (Figure 8.11) which carries the packets of food, and the processing is done on the first available machine. The processing time on each machine was found to be between 25 and 35 seconds, uniformly distributed. Processed food is not returned to the turntable, which is fed via a conveyor belt at the rate of one packet every 40 seconds. The turntable has a maximum capacity for 15 items and additional items are automatically rejected whenever the turntable is full. The rejected items are not recycled. It takes 20 seconds for a packet of food placed on the turntable to reach the first machine and 30 seconds are required for an item to move between any two adjacent machines.

Simulate the operation of the processing plant for a period of 8 hours; count the number of items rejected; examine the utilization of machines and suggest possible methods for improving the efficiency of the plant.

7. At the university computer centre, jobs arrive every 5 ± 1 minutes, and they are processed on a first-in–first-out basis. The distribution of processing time is as follows:

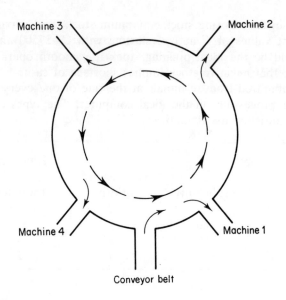

Figure 8.11 Arrangement of machines around turntable.

Probability	Processing time (minutes)
0.4	1
0.3	2
0.2	5
0.1	10

The computer breaks down, on an average, every 38 ± 5 hours and the expected repair times are shown below. Interrupted jobs, if any, are restarted from the point of interruption.

Time of day	Repair time (hours)
7 a.m.–7 p.m.	5 ± 2
7 p.m.–7 a.m.	14 ± 3

Starting at 7 a.m. on a given day, simulate the computing system for a period of 7 days. Comment on the usefulness of this sort of simulation study in the managerial decision-making process.

8. A manufacturing process consists of two stages: production and packaging of items. All items are produced on machine A which operates continuously and packaged on either machine B or machine C as shown in Figure 8.12. The output of machine A is always fed into hopper A if it is not full; fed into hopper B only if it is not full and hopper A is full, and fed into a bin with infinite capacity only if both the hoppers are full. Hopper A has a maximum capacity of 30 items and hopper B has a maximum capacity of 20 items. The processing time of items on machine A depends upon various characteristics of the items, and is shown in the following table:

Processing time (minutes) on machine A	Probability
4	0.29
6	0.21
7	0.13
9	0.2
11	0.17

The items in hopper A are packaged on machine B, items in hopper B are packaged on machine C, and the items collected in the bin are

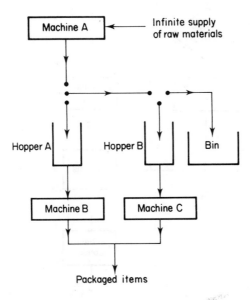

Figure 8.12 Production and packaging at a plant.

packaged by an external contractor. The packaging times were found to be 5 ± 1 minutes on machine B and 6 ± 1 minutes on machine C, uniformly distributed.

Starting from a completely idle state, simulate the operation of the manufacturing system for a period of 7200 minutes and estimate (a)

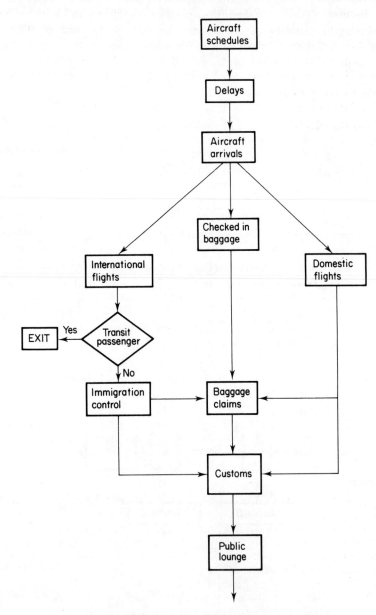

Figure 8.13 Passenger flow through arrivals terminal.

utilization of machine B and machine C, (b) the number of items packaged by the external contractor.

9. Two cities are connected by a canal, a section of which is narrow and cannot be used for sailings in both directions at the same time. At present the sailings in the two directions are interleaved one for one, while there are ships waiting. It has been suggested that the total number of sailings through the narrow part of the canal can be increased by batching the sailings in each direction since the second and subsequent sailings may be overlapped.

Examine the usefulness of this suggestion by simulating the traffic through the narrow part of the canal system. You may assume realistic data to illustrate various points.

10. The flow of passengers through the arrivals terminal of an airport is shown in Figure 8.13.

   (a) Collect the necessary data from the local airport authority and then write a GPSS program to simulate the operation of the arrivals terminal for a 24-hour period. Identify bottlenecks in the system and suggest possible solutions to improve the overall efficiency and smooth flow of passengers.

   (b) Redesign the queuing area at the immigration control point so that there will always be sufficient queuing space which is set at 3 ft per person (maximum expected queue length multiplied by 3 will give the required linear queuing space). Assume that

   no. of immigration control points = 21,
   average processing time per passenger = 3 minutes,
   passenger arrival rate into immigration = 10 per minute,
   no. of passengers in international flights = 400,
   interarrival time of international flights:

10 a.m.	to	4 p.m.:	60 ± 10	minutes
4 p.m.	to	6 p.m.:	25 ± 5	minutes
6 p.m.	to	10 a.m.:	50 ± 8	minutes

   and the queue length at each control point is roughly the same.

References

Barta, T. A. (1985). 'Animated simulation graphics with GPSS', in SCS *Conference on Modelling and Simulation on Microcomputers* (ed. R. G. Lavery), pp. 51–54.

Bobillier, P. A., Kahan, B. C., and Probst, A. R. (1976). *Simulation with GPSS and GPSS V*, Prentice Hall, Englewood Cliffs, NJ.

Cox, S. and Cox, A. J. (1985). 'GPSS/PC(tm): a user oriented simulation system', In *Modelling and Simulation on Microcomputers*, (pp. 48–50. SCS Conference, San Diego, CA.

Gordon, G. (1962). 'A general purpose system simulator', *IBM Syst. J*, **1**(1).

Gordon, G. (1975). *The Application of GPSS V to Discrete System Simulation*. Prentice Hall, Englewood Cliffs, NJ.

Gordon, G. (1981). 'The development of the GPSS'. In *History of Programming Languages* (ed. R. Wexelblat). Academic Press. London, pp. 403–407.

IBM (1975). *General Purpose Simulation System/360: GPSS and GPSS V User's Manual.* IBM Corp., White Plains, N.Y.

Karian, Z. A. (1985). 'GPSS for microcomputers: a software review of GPSS/PC', *Am. J. Math. Manag. Sci.,* **5**, 93–101.

Minuteman (1985). *GPSS/PC*, Minuteman Software, PO Box 171, Stow, MA 01775–0171.

Reitman, J. (1971). *Computer Simulation Application: discrete-event simulation for the synthesis and analysis of complex systems.* John Wiley, New York.

Schriber, T. J. (1974). *Simulation using GPSS.* John Wiley, New York.

9

SIMSCRIPT

9.1 Introduction

SIMSCRIPT was originally developed by RAND Corporation in the early 1960s and since then several versions of SIMSCRIPT have been developed for both mainframe and personal computers. The latest and the most comprehensive version is SIMSCRIPT II.5 (Kiviat *et al.*, 1983). The language is divided into *five levels*: the first three levels provide general-purpose programming capability; the fourth level contains powerful list processing facilities for entity manipulations, and the fifth level is oriented towards discrete system simulation. The free-form syntax and self-documenting English-like program statements are attractive features of the language. SIMSCRIPT has been implemented on several machines including IBM, CDC, DEC, Honeywell, UNIVAC, PRIME, NCR, and IBM mainframes and IBM PC compatible personal computers.

Important features of SIMSCRIPT II.5 language and its use for discrete-event simulation are described here. Further details can be found in Kiviat *et al.*, (1983); and Russell, (1983). We use the terms SIMSCRIPT II.5 and SIMSCRIPT synonymously.

The *process concept* plays the central role in defining a model in the SIMSCRIPT language. A process represents an object and the sequences of actions it experiences during its life in a simulation. There may be many instances of a process type, and many different process types representing different objects. A process object (e.g. a customer in a post office) enters the simulation model at the time of its creation and becomes active either immediately or at a specified activation time. The process routine contains the description of object activities.

Resource is used to model *passive objects* (e.g. postmaster in a post office) which are required by the process objects. A simulation may contain many different resources. Multiple units of a resource can be added to the model in two ways. Add more identical units of the resource serving processes from a single queue or add more separate units of the resource, each serving processes waiting in separate queues. The process object waits in a queue whenever the resource is not available on request, and the first process

207

ct waiting in the queue is reactivated as soon as the resource becomes
available. The *activation* or *reactivation* of a process constitutes an *event* and
thus the events are basically instantaneous processes. The ordered lists of
entities, processes, or resources are called *sets* in SIMSCRIPT. Processes
have evolved from events and therefore the descriptions of events and
processes in SIMSCRIPT are very similar.

A timing routine is at the heart of every discrete-event simulation package.
The processes (events) are ordered by *time* and *priority* on a *pending list*
(event list) which drives the simulation model. On completion of executing
the process routines (event routines) for all processes scheduled for a given
time period, the simulation clock is advanced to the process with earliest
activation (reactivation) time on the pending list. This process continues
until either the pending list becomes empty or an abnormal condition occurs.
Simulation can also be stopped at a predetermined time.

A SIMSCRIPT II.5 program consists of three segments, as shown in
Figure 9.1. Each segment begins with a keyword and ends with an END
statement.

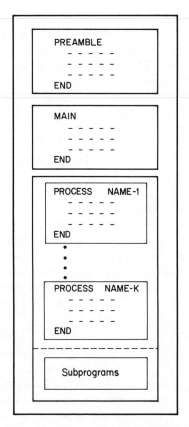

Figure 9.1   Program structure in SIMSCRIPT.

PREAMBLE:
The static description of all model components such as processes, resources, entities, events, and sets are given here. All global variables and the statistics to be collected are defined in this section.

MAIN:
The execution of the SIMSCRIPT program begins with the first statement in this section. The resources are created and initialized here before they are used by the processes. The control is passed to the timing routine by executing the START SIMULATION statement and the simulation begins by scheduling the first event. The statements following the START SIMULATION (e.g. statements for outputs, new simulation run, etc.) if any, are executed only at the end of the simulation run.

PROCESS routines:
Each process defined in the PREAMBLE is further described in this section. The process routines (event routines) give a complete logical description of the process, including the values of local variables, reactivation time, reactivation point, and the amount of resources the process currently holds, and describe the action to be taken when events occur.

Each simulation program in SIMSCRIPT must contain only one PREAMBLE, one MAIN, and one or more process routines. In addition, a SIMSCRIPT programme may have one or more subprograms which serve the same purpose as subroutines in Fortran.

A sample of SIMSCRIPT declarations, executable statements, I/O statements, and entity, array management, and process interaction statements are shown in Table 9.1.

9.2 A simple SIMSCRIPT simulation program: example 1

Let us consider the same problem of simulating a telephone system of the travel agency, discussed in Section 8.17.1. The GPSS program was given in Figure 8.8 and the corresponding SIMSCRIPT program appears in Figure 9.2a. The first thing to notice is that the SIMSCRIPT program is considerably longer than its GPSS counterpart.

Figures 9.2b to 9.2d show the compiler listing of SIMSCRIPT program including line numbers and cross-reference for each section of the program. Note that the line numbers are not included in the source program but are added by the SIMSCRIPT compiler for identification purposes. The printouts are reasonably self-explanatory; however, the reader should refer to the SIMSCRIPT manual for further explanation of some of the symbols used.

The global variables are declared in the PREMABLE. Unlike GPSS, the simulation statistics are not automatically collected by SIMSCRIPT. The percentage utilization of the phone system is collected by means of the ACCUMULATE statement in the program. The two process routines in the model, GENERATOR and INCOMING.CALL are also declared in the

210

Table 9.1 Some declarations and statements in SIMSCRIPT.

Declaration/ statement	Function	Remarks
PROCESS . . .	Marks the beginning of process entity declarations	Preamble declaration
TEMPORARY ENTITIES	Marks the beginning of resource entity declarations	Preamble declaration
EVERY . . .	Entity–attribute–set structure declarations	Preamble declaration
DEFINE . . .	Defines properties of variables, routines, sets, etc	Preamble/Routine declarations
MAIN	Marks the beginning of main segment in a program	Main declaration
PROCESS . . .	Process routine heading	Routine declaration
LET . . .	Assignment statement	Executable statement
FOR . . .	Used for constructing program loops	Executable statement
START SIMULATION	Passes control to the timing mechanism	Executable statement
READ . . .	Read data	I/O statement
PRINT . . .	Print output with titles	I/O statement
CREATE . . .	Create temporary entity	Entity management
FILE . . .	Insert temporary entity into a set	Entity management
RELINQIUISH . . .	Make resource available for reallocation	Process interactions
WORK . . .	Delay process execution	Process interactions
SCHEDULE	Create a new process	Process Interactions

PREAMBLE. Unless declared otherwise, all variables are treated as REAL in SIMSCRIPT.

The program execution begins in the MAIN segment. The value of NO.OF.CALLS (variable representing total number of calls to be simulated) will be used to control the length of the simulation and the time units need not be integers. The SCHEDULE statement activates the process GENERATOR and the exact time of activation is generated from an exponential distribution using the built-in random number generator No. 4 of the SIMSCRIPT system. The START SIMULATION statement passes control to the built-in timing routine. The PRINT statement prints various outputs with titles in a specified order. The combination of asterisks and period define the format for outputting numerical values of variables.

The GENERATOR and INCOMING.CALL are the two processes in the program. Calls generated by the process GENERATOR are serviced by the process INCOMING.CALL. The GENERATOR keeps on activating the process INCOMING.CALL and the interval between activations is expo-

```
''*******************************************************************
''*   SIMULATION OF A TRAVEL AGENCY WITH 3 TELEPHONE LINES      *
''*  See Section 8.17.1 and Figure 8.8 for Problem Description *
''*******************************************************************
PREAMBLE
  PROCESSES INCLUDE GENERATOR AND INCOMING.CALL
  DEFINE LOST.CALLS,BUSY.LINES,NO.OF.LINES,ARRIVAL.RATE,
         AND NO.OF.CALLS AS INTEGER VARIABLES
  DEFINE SERVICE.TIME AS REAL VARIABLE
  ACCUMULATE UTILISATION AS AVERAGE OF BUSY.LINES
END
MAIN
  PRINT 2 LINES THUS
  PLEASE ENTER RUN PARAMETERS(Incoming Calls):
  NUMBER OF CALLS,NUMBER OF LINES,ARRIVAL RATE,SERVICE TIME
  READ NO.OF.CALLS,NO.OF.LINES,ARRIVAL.RATE,SERVICE.TIME
  SCHEDULE A GENERATOR IN EXPONENTIAL.F (1/ARRIVAL.RATE,4) HOURS
  START SIMULATION
  PRINT 4 LINES WITH NO.OF.LINES,ARRIVAL.RATE,SERVICE.TIME,NO.OF.CALLS,
         LOST.CALLS,(LOST.CALLS/NO.OF.CALLS)*100.0
         AND (UTILISATION/NO.OF.LINES) * 100.0 THUS
    NO.OF LINES        = ****
    MEAN ARRIVAL RATE  = *** CALLS/HR. ;  MEAN SERVICE TIME = **.*** HRS.
    NO.OF CALLS        = ****            ;  LOST CALLS        = ***
    PERCENTAGE LOSS    = ***.***  ; UTILISATION OF LINES    = **.*** %
END
PROCESS GENERATOR
  DEFINE COUNT  AS AN INTEGER VARIABLE
  FOR COUNT = 1 TO NO.OF.CALLS
  DO
    SCHEDULE AN INCOMING.CALL NOW
    WAIT EXPONENTIAL.F(1/ARRIVAL.RATE,4) HOURS
  LOOP
END
PROCESS INCOMING.CALL
  IF BUSY.LINES LT NO.OF.LINES
      ADD 1 TO BUSY.LINES
      WORK EXPONENTIAL.F(SERVICE.TIME,4) HOURS
      SUBTRACT 1 FROM BUSY.LINES
  ELSE
      ADD 1 TO LOST.CALLS
  ALWAYS
END
```

Figure 9.2(a)   SIMSCRIPT source listing for example 1.

nentially distributed. The activation of INCOMING.CALL comes to an end after NO.OF.CALLS activations and the simulation stops as soon as INCOMING.CALL completes the processing of all the calls generated. The WAIT or WORK statements have the effect of delaying processes by a specified period of time. COUNT is defined as a local variable and it has no meaning outside the GENERATOR routine. The DO and LOOP statements achieve repetitive execution of a program segment. The ALWAYS statement is used to end an 'IF' group of statements. The model has no queuing facility and calls are lost whenever all the lines are busy.

In order to make the intent of the program clearer, SIMSCRIPT allows optional choices for keywords such as A, AN, THE, or THIS.

212

```
1  '********************************************
2  '**  SIMULATION OF A TRAVEL AGENCY WITH 3 TELEPHONE LINES  *
3  '**  See Section 8.17.1 and Figure 8.8 for Problem Description  *
4  '********************************************
5  PREAMBLE
6  PROCESSES INCLUDE GENERATOR AND INCOMING.CALL
7  DEFINE LOST.CALLS,BUSY.LINES,NO.OF.LINES,ARRIVAL.RATE,
8          AND NO.OF.CALLS AS INTEGER VARIABLES
9  DEFINE SERVICE.TIME AS REAL VARIABLE
10 ACCUMULATE UTILISATION AS AVERAGE OF BUSY.LINES
11 END
```

C R O S S - R E F E R E N C E

NAME	TYPE		MODE	LINE NUMBERS OF REFERENCES
ARRIVAL.RATE	GLOBAL VARIABLE	ASG 1	INTEGER	7
BUSY.LINES	GLOBAL VARIABLE	ASG 7	INTEGER	7 10
GENERATOR	PROCESS NOTICE	ASG 16		6
INCOMING.CALL	PROCESS NOTICE	ASG 5		6
LOST.CALLS	GLOBAL VARIABLE	ASG 3	INTEGER	7
NO.OF.CALLS	GLOBAL VARIABLE	ASG 2	INTEGER	8
NO.OF.LINES	GLOBAL VARIABLE	ASG 19	INTEGER	7
SERVICE.TIME	GLOBAL VARIABLE	ASG 14	DOUBLE	9
UTILISATION	ROUTINE		DOUBLE	10

Figure 9.2(b) Compiler listing of PREAMBLE for example 1.

```
12  MAIN
13     PRINT 2 LINES THUS
PLEASE ENTER RUN PARAMETERS(Incoming Calls):
NUMBER OF CALLS,NUMBER OF LINES,ARRIVAL RATE,SERVICE TIME
16     READ NO.OF.CALLS,NO.OF.LINES,ARRIVAL.RATE,SERVICE.TIME
17     SCHEDULE A GENERATOR IN EXPONENTIAL.F (1/ARRIVAL.RATE,4) HOURS
18     START SIMULATION
19     PRINT 4 LINES WITH NO.OF.LINES,ARRIVAL.RATE,SERVICE.TIME,NO.OF.CALLS,
20        LOST.CALLS,(LOST.CALLS/NO.OF.CALLS)*100.0
21        AND (UTILISATION/NO.OF.LINES) * 100.0 THUS
NO.OF LINES       = ****
MEAN ARRIVAL RATE = *** CALLS/HR. ;   MEAN SERVICE TIME = **.*** HRS.
NO.OF CALLS       = ***        ;   LOST CALLS        = ***
PERCENTAGE LOSS   = **.***  ; UTILISATION OF LINES = **.*** %
26  END
```

C R O S S - R E F E R E N C E

NAME	TYPE			MODE	LINE NUMBERS OF REFERENCES
ARRIVAL.RATE	GLOBAL VARIABLE	ASG	1	INTEGER	16 17 19
EVENTS.V	PERMANENT ATTRIBUTE	SYS	11	INTEGER	12*
EXPONENTIAL.F	ROUTINE			DOUBLE	17
F.EV.S	PERMANENT ATTRIBUTE	SYS	13 (1-D)	INTEGER	12*
GENERATOR	PROCESS NOTICE				17
L.EV.S	+ GLOBAL VARIABLE	ASG	16	INTEGER	17*
	PERMANENT ATTRIBUTE	SYS	14 (1-D)	INTEGER	12*
LOST.CALLS	GLOBAL VARIABLE	ASG	3	INTEGER	19*
NO.OF.CALLS	GLOBAL VARIABLE	ASG	2	INTEGER	16 19*
NO.OF.LINES	GLOBAL VARIABLE	ASG	19	INTEGER	16 19*
SERVICE.TIME	GLOBAL VARIABLE	ASG	14	DOUBLE	16 19
UTILISATION	ROUTINE			DOUBLE	19

Figure 9.2(c) Compiler listing of MAIN routine for example 1.

```
27  PROCESS GENERATOR
28      DEFINE COUNT AS AN INTEGER VARIABLE
29      FOR COUNT = 1 TO NO.OF.CALLS
30      DO
31          SCHEDULE AN INCOMING.CALL NOW
32          WAIT EXPONENTIAL.F(1/ARRIVAL.RATE,4) HOURS
33      LOOP
34  END
```

C R O S S - R E F E R E N C E

NAME	TYPE			MODE	LINE NUMBERS OF REFERENCES
ARRIVAL.RATE	GLOBAL VARIABLE	ASG	1	INTEGER	32
COUNT	RECURSIVE VARIABLE	WORD	1	INTEGER	28 29*
EXPONENTIAL.F	ROUTINE			DOUBLE	32
GENERATOR	PROCESS NOTICE				34
	+ GLOBAL VARIABLE	ASG	16	INTEGER	27*
INCOMING.CALL	PROCESS NOTICE				31
	+ GLOBAL VARIABLE	ASG	5	INTEGER	31*
NO.OF.CALLS	GLOBAL VARIABLE	ASG	2	INTEGER	29
PROCESS.V	PERMANENT ATTRIBUTE	SYS	47	INTEGER	34*

```
35  PROCESS INCOMING.CALL
36      IF BUSY.LINES LT NO.OF.LINES
37          ADD 1 TO BUSY.LINES
38          WORK EXPONENTIAL.F(SERVICE.TIME,4) HOURS
39          SUBTRACT 1 FROM BUSY.LINES
40      ELSE
41          ADD 1 TO LOST.CALLS
42      ALWAYS
43  END
```

C R O S S - R E F E R E N C E

NAME	TYPE			MODE	LINE NUMBERS OF REFERENCES
BUSY.LINES	GLOBAL VARIABLE	ASG	7	INTEGER	36 37* 39*
EXPONENTIAL.F	ROUTINE			DOUBLE	38
INCOMING.CALL	PROCESS NOTICE				35
	+ GLOBAL VARIABLE	ASG	5	INTEGER	35*
LOST.CALLS	GLOBAL VARIABLE	ASG	3	INTEGER	41*
NO.OF.LINES	GLOBAL VARIABLE	ASG	19	INTEGER	36
PROCESS.V	PERMANENT ATTRIBUTE	SYS	47	INTEGER	43*
SERVICE.TIME	GLOBAL VARIABLE	ASG	14	DOUBLE	38

Figure 9.2(d) Compiler listing of PROCESS routines for example 1.

```
NO.OF LINES       =    3
MEAN ARRIVAL RATE = 100 CALLS/HR. ;  MEAN SERVICE TIME =   .031 HRS.
NO.OF CALLS       = 1000          ;  LOST CALLS        = 347
PERCENTAGE LOSS   = 34.700 ; UTILISATION OF LINES      = 66.276 %
```

Figure 9.2(e) SIMSCRIPT program output for example 1.

The SIMSCRIPT program output shown in Figure 9.2e is not identical to the output shown in Figure 8.8. Minor variations of this type are to be expected, especially because of the differences in the method and the seeds used in the generation of random numbers. The differences in the data structures and the order of computations are other contributing factors. The printed output includes the values of input parameters, the number of lost calls, percentage loss, and the utilization of the telephone system.

9.3 Source format

SIMSCRIPT is a *free-form*, *English-like* language, and every statement begins with a keyword. Keywords are *not reserved* words; variable names may be of any length; the period at the end of a variable is ignored; there are any number of lines per statement or statements per line, and there is no statement continuation mark or delimiter.

9.4 Variable and constants

All SIMSCRIPT system defined variables end with a period followed by a letter.

Example

TIME.V (current simulation time—variable)
EXP.C   (2.7182818284590452—constant)
ABS.F   (absolute value of expression—function)
SNAP.R (user-supplied routine called by SIMSCRIPT when an execution error occurs—routine)

User-defined variables consist of any combination of letters, digits, and periods which is not a number. The mode of variables may be defined as INTEGER, REAL, or ALPHA in the PREAMBLE. The default option is REAL.

The integer and real constants have the usual meanings; scientific constants cannot be used in the program, but may be included in the data. A string of non-numeric characters enclosed between quotation marks constitutes an ALPHA mode constant. The statements

DEFINE MACHINE AS AN INTEGER VARIABLE
DEFINE BUSY TO MEAN 1

define MACHINE as an integer variable and assigns the value '1' to the identifier BUSY.

The global variables are defined in the preamble. These variables are initialized to zero at the start of simulation and can be used anywhere in the program. The local variables are defined in a routine (MAIN, PROCESS, EVENT, or FUNCTION) or subroutine, and these (except process delays and 'saved' variables) are initialized to zero each time the routine is entered.

9.5 Simulation Clock

The current simulated time is represented by the system variable TIME.V and this is used in process scheduling or within a process. The default unit of time is days, but automatic conversion between minutes, hours, and days in provided by the system. New time units can be obtained by redefining the basic time unit in a DEFINE statement in the Preamble.

Examples

(a)
```
ACTIVATE  A customer NOW
ACTIVATE  A customer AT TIME.V + 100
WAIT    xx  DAYS
WORK    xx  DAYS
```

(b) The following statement in the preamble defines a new time unit.

```
DEFINE identifier TO MEAN [expression] UNITS
```

where

> expression: consists of either an * or / followed by
>   a constant (optional).
> identifier: time unit.

```
DEFINE YEARS TO MEAN *1000 UNITS
DEFINE MICROSECOND TO MEAN UNITS
```

9.6 Expressions

There are several operations involving expressions in SIMSCRIPT.

```
LET variable = expression
ADD expression TO variable
SUBTRACT expression FROM variable
```

Examples

    LET Y = A+B*SQRT(B**2+C)
    ADD TIME.V+25.0 TO EXIT.TIME
    SUBTRACT LOST+SALES FROM CURRENT.STOCK

9.7 IF, GO TO, and LOOP Statements

Several conditional operators (=, <, <=, set is EMPTY, entity IS IN set,
etc.) which describe the branching conditions are available for use with the
IF statement.

Examples

(a) The ALWAYS statement is used when no action needs to be taken
    when the condition is false.

    IF   X < Z
                LET A = A + 1
    ALWAYS

(b)
    IF   X < Z
                LET A = A + 1
    ELSE
                LET A = A − 2
    ALWAYS

The GO TO statement has the form

    GO TO label

where the statement 'label' is enclosed within single quotes.

Example

    GO TO TESTR
    − − − − −
    − − − − −
    − − − − −
    'TESTR' WORK 0.3 HOURS

The repetitive execution of a program segment in SIMSCRIPT is achived
through the LOOP statement which is of the form

218

```
FOR              specification
    DO
                 (loop body)
    LOOP
```

Where the specification (numeric, set or entity types) identifies a variable
whose value is altered during each iteration. The DO and LOOP statements
may be omitted if the loop body contains only one statement to be iterated.

Example

(a) For I = 1 to 20

```
    DO
                CREATE A CALL
                LET CALL.TIME = 5.0
                IF NO.OF.LINES < MAX.NUMBER
                   NO.OF.LINES = NO.OF.LINES + 1
                   STATUS = BUSY
                ALWAYS
    LOOP
```

(b) FOR EACH JOB IN THE JOB.QUEUE
```
    DO
                LET DELAY = DELAY + 1
                LET STATUS = 3
    LOOP
```

(c) X = 5.0
```
    FOR J = 1 TO 500
    LET X = J*X
```

9.8 Random distribution functions

There are several built-in random distribution functions in SIMCRIPT. In
addition, SIMSCRIPT supports user-defined distributions.

9.8.1 Built-in distributions

There are *ten* random number generators (generating uniformly distributed
random numbers in the range 0 to 1) numbered from 1 to 10 in SIMSCRIPT.
Some of the most frequently used built-in functions, including distribution
functions, are shown in Table 9.2. The general format and examples of some
of these functions are given below

(a) EXPONENTIAL.F (mean, generator no.)

Will generate *exponentially distributed* random numbers with given *mean* using the specified random number generator (integer in the range 1 to 10).

WORK EXPONENTIAL.F (1/SERVICE.RATE,2) MINUTES

(b) RANDOM.F (generator no.)

Will generate *uniform pseudo-random numbers* in the range 0 to 1 using the specified generator

LET SERVICE.TIME = 3*RANDOM.F(4)+10

(c) UNIFORM.F (lower limit, upper limit, generator no.)

Will generate *uniform random numbers* in the given range using the specified generator
SCHEDULE A CALL IN UNIFORM.F
(MIN.ARRIVAL,MAX.ARRIVAL,6)SECONDS

9.8.2 User-defined distributions

These are defined by THE SYSTEM HAS statement in the preamble. The discrete and continuous distributions are identified by the words STEP and LINEAR, respectively. Random STEP variable may be real or integer while LINEAR variables must be real. The mode of the distribution function is specified in a DEFINE statement

Table 9.2   Some of the built-in functions in SIMSCRIPT.

Function	Description
ABS.F	Returns absolute value of the expression
COS.F	Returns cosine of a real expression given in radians
LENGTH.F	Returns the length of a text variable in characters
DATE.F	Used for converting a calendar date to cumulative simulation time
BETA.F	Returns a random sample from a beta distribution
BINOMIAL.F	Returns a random sample from a binomial distribution
POISSON.F	Returns a random sample from a Poisson distribution
RANDI.F	Returns a random integer value, uniformly distributed between the specified range of values

Example

PREAMBLE
THE SYSTEM HAS A SERVICE.TIME RANDOM STEP VARIABLE
DEFINE SERVICE.TIME AS AN INTEGER VARIABLE

The data for a user-defined distribution function are supplied by the READ statement and the end of data is marked by an asterisk. The data are organized as an ordered (X,Y) pair where X is the cumulative probability and Y is the corresponding value from the distribution.

Example

READ SERVICE.TIME
0.1 2 0.4 3 0.6 4 0.75 8 1.0 10*

will assign the values 2, 3, 4, 8 and 10 to SERVICE.TIME with probabilities 10%, 30%, 20%, 15% and 25%, respectively.

9.9 SIMSCRIPT example 2

Example 2 is an extended version of example 1 discussed in Section 9.2. The description of the problem is given in Section 8.17.2 and the GPSS and SIMSCRIPT program appear in Figures 8.9 and 9.3a, respectively. The variable COUNT is defined as a global variable in Figure 9.3a and is used in the GENERATOR and OUTGOING.CALL routines to control the length of simulation. The SIMSCRIPT program output shown in Figure 9.3b is very similar to the GPSS results shown in Figure 8.10.

9.10 Creation and Termination of temporary entities

In simulation, the traffic in the system under study is simulated by entities that enter and leave the model at different points in time. Such entities are called 'temporary entities' because of the temporary nature of their existence in the model. The customers in a post office can be regarded as temporary entities, whereas the postmaster who remains in the model throughout the period of simulation is an example of a 'permanent entity'. The entities and their attributes are defined in the preamble as follows:

TEMPORARY ENTITIES
EVERY entity name HAS A attributes

Example

TEMPORARY ENTITIES
EVERY CAR HAS A MAKE, MODEL, PRICE AND REG. NUMBER

```
 1  ''************************************************************
 2  ''*  SIMULATION OF A TRAVEL AGENCY WITH 3 TELEPHONE LINES   *
 3  ''*  See Section 8.17.2 and Figure 8.9 for Problem Description *
 4  ''************************************************************
 5  PREAMBLE
 6    PROCESSES INCLUDE GENERATOR,INCOMING.CALL AND OUTGOING.CALL
 7    DEFINE COUNT,LOST.CALLS,BUSY.LINES,NO.OF.LINES,ARRIVAL.RATE,
 8           OUTSIDE.CALLS AND NO.OF.CALLS AS INTEGER VARIABLES
 9    DEFINE SERVICE.TIME AS REAL VARIABLE
10    ACCUMULATE UTILISATION AS AVERAGE OF BUSY.LINES
11  END
12  MAIN
13    PRINT 2 LINES THUS
PLEASE ENTER RUN PARAMETERS(Incoming Calls):
NUMBER OF CALLS,NUMBER OF LINES,ARRIVAL RATE,SERVICE TIME
16  READ NO.OF.CALLS,NO.OF.LINES,ARRIVAL.RATE,SERVICE.TIME
17  ACTIVATE A GENERATOR IN EXPONENTIAL.F (1/ARRIVAL.RATE,4) HOURS
18  SCHEDULE AN OUTGOING.CALL IN 0.6 HOURS
19  START SIMULATION
20  PRINT 4 LINES WITH NO.OF.LINES,OUTSIDE.CALLS,ARRIVAL.RATE,SERVICE.TIME,
21        NO.OF.CALLS,LOST.CALLS,(LOST.CALLS/NO.OF.CALLS)*100.0
22        AND (UTILISATION/NO.OF.LINES) * 100.0 THUS
NO.OF LINES      = **              ; NO.OF OUTSIDE CALLS = ***
MEAN ARRIVAL RATE = *** CALLS/HR. ;  MEAN SERVICE TIME  = ***.*** HRS.
NO.OF CALLS      = ****            ;  LOST CALLS         = ***
PERCENTAGE LOSS  = ****.**  ; UTILISATION OF LINES       = ***.*** %
27  END
28  PROCESS GENERATOR
29    FOR COUNT = 1 TO NO.OF.CALLS
30    DO
31      SCHEDULE AN INCOMING.CALL NOW
32      WAIT EXPONENTIAL.F(1/ARRIVAL.RATE,4) HOURS
33    LOOP
34  END
35  PROCESS INCOMING.CALL
36    IF BUSY.LINES LT NO.OF.LINES
37        ADD 1 TO BUSY.LINES
38        WORK EXPONENTIAL.F(SERVICE.TIME,4) HOURS
39        SUBTRACT 1 FROM BUSY.LINES
40    ELSE
41        ADD 1 TO LOST.CALLS
42    ALWAYS
43  END
44  PROCESS OUTGOING.CALL
45    IF COUNT <= NO.OF.CALLS
46    UNTIL BUSY.LINES LT NO.OF.LINES
47    DO
48      WAIT 0.2 HOURS
49    LOOP
50      ADD 1 TO BUSY.LINES
51      LET OUTSIDE.CALLS=OUTSIDE.CALLS+1
52      WAIT 0.125 HOURS
53      SUBTRACT 1 FROM BUSY.LINES
54      SCHEDULE AN OUTGOING.CALL IN 1 HOUR
55    ALWAYS
56  END
```

Figure 9.3(a)   SIMSCRIPT program for example 2.

222

```
NO.OF LINES        = 3          ; NO.OF OUTSIDE CALLS =   8
MEAN ARRIVAL RATE = 100 CALLS/HR. ; MEAN SERVICE TIME   =    .031 HRS.
NO.OF CALLS        = 1000       ; LOST CALLS          = 370
PERCENTAGE LOSS    =   37.      ; UTILISATION OF LINES = 68.184 %
```

Figure 9.3(**b**) SIMSCRIPT program output for example 2.

Whenever needed, the CREATE statement is used to create a temporary entity in a process routine and is removed from the model by means of DESTROY statement. The attributes of temporary entities may be referenced directly just like a subscripted variable.

Examples

(a) LET MODEL(CAR) = 1986
   LET PRICE(CAR) = PRICE(CAR)–1000
(b) CREATE A entity
   CREATE A CALL
(c) DESTROY THE entity
   DESTROY THE CALL

9.11   Creation of permanent entities

Permanent entities are those which remain in the model throughout the simulation and they are defined in the PREAMBLE as follows:

PERMANENT ENTITIES
EVERY POSTMASTER HAS A STATE AND OWNS A QUEUE

Permanent entities are never destroyed and they are created by CREATE EVERY statement which has the following form

CREATE EVERY entity (integer)

where

entity: name of permanent entity
integer: number of permanent enti-
           ties to be created

Example

CREATE EVERY LINE(3)

will create three LINE permanent entities. A variable number of LINE permanent entities can be created by the following statements.

READ N.LINE
CREATE EVERY LINE

Where 'N.entity' is a system variable which contains the number of entities. The attributes of permanent entities can be referenced as in the case of temporary entities.

In Section 9.4 we gave examples for system-defined variables. The SIMSCRIPT language system automatically defines several variables, constants, and attributes associated with entities. The following attributes generated by a SIMSCRIPT system in conjunction with user-defined entities are very useful in simulation modelling.

U.resource: number of units of resource currently available,
N.Q.resource: number of requests for the resource currently waiting,
N.X.resource: number of requests for the resource currently being satisfied.

9.12   The concept of Sets

A set is an ordered collection of entities with some logical relationships. Set owners may be the system, temporary entities, or permanent entities while the set membership is generally confined to temporary entities. A temporary entity may belong to several different sets, but only to one set of a given type. A set may be empty or may contain one or more members. For example, a queue of customers waiting for service in a post office can be modelled as a set. A set has only one owner and the ownership/membership is defined in the preamble. If there exists only one set of a particular type in the model, then that set is always owned by the system. The system-owned sets are defined by:

THE SYSTEM OWNS list of sets
THE SYSTEM OWNS A JOB.QUEUE

When multiple copies of a set exist, then the EVERY statement together with the phrases

MAY BELONG TO list of sets
OWN list of sets

are used to define set membership or ownership

Example

EVERY JOB HAS A DELAY AND EXECUTION.TIME
   AND MAY BELONG TO A JOB.QUEUE
EVERY MACHINE OWNS A JOB.QUEUE

All sets are initially empty. A set may be ordered in several ways (LIFO, FIFO, etc.). The default option is FIFO and may be changed by the programmer using a DEFINE statement

DEFINE JOB.QUEUE AS A LIFO SET

The FILE and REMOVE statements are used to insert and remove temporary entities from the set

Examples

(a) FILE THE JOB IN THE JOB.QUEUE
FILE THE JOB FIRST IN THE JOB.QUEUE
FILE THE JOB2 BEFORE JOB1 IN JOB.QUEUE

(b) REMOVE LAST JOB FROM JOB.QUEUE

9.13   READ, LIST, and PRINT statements

The READ statement has the form

READ list of identifiers

where the identifiers are variables or attributes.

READ NO.OF.LINES, MAX.NO.OF.CUSTOMERS

The LIST statement is useful in printing variable names together with their values

LIST list of identifiers
LIST BUSY.LINES, OUTSIDE.CALLS

will print each of the variable names and their numerical values underneath them.

The PRINT statement appears in the MAIN segment and is generally used for printing output with titles.

PRINT integer LINES WITH list of expressions THUS format of output lines
where

integer:	number of lines to be printed,
list of expressions:	list of variables or expressions to be printed,
format of output lines:	'integer' lines containing text and numeric output formats.

Note that there must be a one-to-one correspondence between expressions in the list and numeric output formats which consist of a series of asterisks indicating digits and a period indicating the decimal point in the appropriate position. Blank lines can be introduced by SKIP n LINES.

Example

PRINT 1 LINE WITH OUTGOING.CALLS THUS
NO OF OUTGOING CALLS = ****

Assuming that the variable OUTGOING.CALLS = 235, the above statements will produce the following output:

NO OF OUTGOING CALLS = 235

9.14 Collection of statistics

Unlike GPSS, the statistical quantities are *not automatically collected* and printed in SIMSCRIPT. The user must explicitly define (need not compute) the statistical quantities in the PREAMBLE and the results are printed as part of the user-generated output. The TALLY statement collects statistics on *time-independent* (sample-based; e.g. mean waiting time) variables while ACCUMULATE is usually used to gather *time-dependent* (value of variable change with respect to time; e.g. average queue length) variable statistics. TALLY is ideal for collecting statistics on global variables which do not depend on time. The following statistical quantities are collected by TALLY and ACCUMULATE statements.

NUMBER
SUM
MEAN
SUM.OF.SQUARES
MEAN.SQUARE
VARIANCE
STD.DEV
MAXIMUM
MINIMUM

Example

(a) TALLY AVERAGE.WAIT.TIME AS THE MEAN OF
WAIT.TIMES

Will assign the mean of WAIT.TIMES to the variable AVERAGE.WAIT.TIME which is printed as usual using the PRINT command

(b) ACCUMULATE AVERAGE.Q.LENGTH AS THE MEAN OF
N.JOB.QUEUE

Will compute the mean number of elements of the set JOB.QUEUE.
Note that N.set gives the number of entities in the set.

9.15 Simscript example 3

Example 3 is the same as the microprocessor test facility discussed in
Section 8.4. The GPSS program was given in Figure 8.4 and the corresponding SIMSCRIPT program is shown in Figure 9.4a. TEST.STATION
is defined as a RESOURCE in the preamble and the required units of the
resource is created in the MAIN routine. Items are queued whenever no
resource is available for service, on request. The system generated attributes
N.X.TEST.STATION and N.Q.TEST.STATION are used to gather time-
dependent statistics. The collection of time-independent variable statistics
using TALLY is also illustrated. The system-defined variable TIME.V is
explicitly included in the computation of the average waiting time. The
SIMSCRIPT program output is shown in Figure 9.4b, which is comparable
with the GPSS output given in Figure 8.5b.

9.16 SIMSCRIPT on microprocessors

PC-SIMSCRIPT II.5 is now available (CACI) for the IBM PC-XT and AT
with a minimum of 520K bytes of random access memory and the numeric
processor. All language features of SIMSCRIPT II.5 that are widely used
on mainframes are fully supported in PC-SIMSCRIPT II.5 and it is possible
to transfer programs between the PC and mainframes. PC-SIMSCRIPT II.5
provides automatic program overlays and thus problems of all sizes can be
simulated at the expense of extra computing time.

   In addition, the new programming environment, called SIMLAB, simplifies the development, verification, modification, and enhancement of
simulation models on personal computers. Some of these interactive features
of SIMLAB cannot be found on larger computing systems. With SIMLAB,
several tasks can be done concurrently—one can modify a routine while
another one is compiling. Windows allow the observtion of different tasks
simultaneously. A debugging window is automatically opened whenever an
execution error occurs, and with the help of the error descriptions provided
by the system the user can correct and resume the execution of the program.

   SimAnimation provides graphic facilities to enhance PC-SIMSCRIPT simulation models. SimAnimation has several graphics drawing aids and the user can
generate graphic output by including a few statements in the program.
Animated graphics representation of simulations provide deeper insight into
the behaviour of dynamic systems. With SimAnimation one can create and
display animations of simulated system in colour graphics. For example, the
arrival and departure of trucks, the loading and unloading of cargo, the

```
1    ''****************************************************************
2    ''*         SIMULATION OF A MICROPROCESSOR TEST STATION         *
3    ''*    See Section 8.4 and Figure 8.4 for Problem Description   *
4    ''****************************************************************

5    PREAMBLE
6     PROCESSES INCLUDE GENERATOR AND MICROPROCESSOR
7     DEFINE NO.OF.TEST.STATIONS AS INTEGER VARIABLE
8     DEFINE WAITING.TIME AS A  REAL VARIABLE
9     RESOURCES INCLUDE TEST.STATION
10    ACCUMULATE UTILISATION AS THE MEAN OF N.X.TEST.STATION
11    ACCUMULATE AVERAGE.Q.LENGTH AS THE MEAN OF N.Q.TEST.STATION
12    ACCUMULATE MAX.Q.LENGTH AS THE MAXIMUM OF N.Q.TEST.STATION
13    TALLY MEAN.WAITING.TIME AS THE MEAN OF WAITING.TIME
14   END

15   MAIN
16    PRINT 1 LINE THUS
PLEASE ENTER NO.OF.TEST.STATIONS:
18    READ NO.OF.TEST.STATIONS
19    CREATE EVERY TEST.STATION(1)
20    LET U.TEST.STATION(1) =NO.OF.TEST.STATIONS
21    SCHEDULE A GENERATOR IN UNIFORM.F (4.0,8.0,4) MINUTES
22    START SIMULATION
23    PRINT 5 LINES WITH NO.OF.TEST.STATIONS,AVERAGE.Q.LENGTH(1),
24         MAX.Q.LENGTH(1),MEAN.WAITING.TIME,
25         AND (UTILISATION(1)/NO.OF.TEST.STATIONS)*100 THUS
SIMULATION OF A  MICRO TEST SYSTEM WITH   ***   TEST STATIONS
AVERAGE MICROPROCESSOR QUEUE LENGTH     = ***.***
MAXIMUM MICROPROCESSOR QUEUE LENGTH     = ***
AVERAGE WAITING TIME IN QUEUE           = ***.**** MINUTES
AVERAGE UTILISATION OF TEST STATIONS    = ***.** % OF TIME
31   END

32   PROCESS GENERATOR
33    FOR J=1 TO 1000
34    DO
35       SCHEDULE A MICROPROCESSOR NOW
36       WAIT UNIFORM.F (4.0,8.0,4) MINUTES
37    LOOP
38   END

39   PROCESS MICROPROCESSOR
40    DEFINE ARRIVAL.TIME AS REAL VARIABLE
41    LET ARRIVAL.TIME = TIME.V
42    REQUEST 1 TEST.STATION(1)
43    LET WAITING.TIME = (TIME.V - ARRIVAL.TIME) * HOURS.V * MINUTES.V
44    WORK UNIFORM.F(2.0,8.0,8) MINUTES
45    RELINQUISH 1 TEST.STATION(1)
46   END
```

Figure 9.4(a)   SIMSCRIPT program for example 3.

stock situation in a warehouse, the status of workers, etc. can be seen alive on the graphics screen.

9.17 Summary

SIMSCRIPT II.5 is a powerful, general-purpose, English-like, free-form language, particularly suitable for discrete system simulation. Important

```
SIMULATION OF A MICRO TEST SYSTEM WITH      1  TEST STATIONS
AVERAGE MICROPROCESSOR QUEUE LENGTH      =    .245
MAXIMUM MICROPROCESSOR QUEUE LENGTH      =   3
AVERAGE WAITING TIME IN QUEUE            =   1.4586 MINUTES
AVERAGE UTILISATION OF TEST STATIONS     =  85.20 % OF TIME
```

Figure 9.4(**b**)   SIMSCRIPT program output for example 3.

features of the language are discussed and several examples are given to illustrate modelling and simulation in SIMSCRIPT which has been implemented on several types of machines. Compared to GPSS it is more difficult to learn, and programs tend to be larger in size. However, the language is highly flexible and the simulation of complex problems can be attempted with comparative ease. The collection of statistics is not automatic but likely to be more accurate than GPSS. The system-generated variables, names, and attributes of entities are useful in simulation programming. The time units need not be integers and there are several built-in functions in SIMSCRIPT.

Full version of SIMSCRIPT II.5 is now available for IBM-PC compatible systems. The interactive computer graphics and animation capabilities supported by the PC-SIMSCRIPT system have enhanced the power and appeal for simulation.

9.18   Exercises

1. Customers arrive at a supermarket every 3 ± 1 minutes. Each customer spends, on an average, 3 minutes per item for shopping and the number of items bought by customers was found to be exponentially distributed with a mean of 15 items per customer. There are seven regular checkouts, two express checkouts (for those with not more than 8 items) and another checkout reserved for handicapped customers. On an average, 2% of the customers were found to be handicapped. Excluding the queuing time, customers spend 10 second per item at the regular checkout, 8 seconds per item at the express checkout, and a total of 5 minutes at the checkout for handicapped people. Simulate, in SIMSCRIPT, the operation of the supermarket for a period of 8 hours. Experiment with the model by changing the values of various parameters. What will be your recommendations to improve the overall efficiency of the supermarket?

2. Four line printers are servicing a large batch computing system where, on an average, 20.3 jobs per hour need to be printed and each line printer is capable of printing only 5.9 jobs per hour. The interarrival time of jobs and the service time of printers are exponentially distributed. Simulate the system and determine the ideal number of printers required to offer a reasonably good service. What will be the effect of replacing one of the printers with a faster one capable of outputting 7.7 jobs per hour?

3. Customers arrive at the local sports stadium every 6 ± 1 seconds and join one of the two queues—queue 1 for non-ticket holder and queue 2 for ticket holders, who have priority over the others. Fifty-five per cent of the arrivals were found to be ticket holders. The gate is controlled by a single operator who can handle only one customer at a time. Ticket holders pass through the gate in 3 seconds, while the time taken by non-ticket holders was found to be exponentially distributed with a mean of 5 seconds. Simulate the system for complete processing of 1000 customers. What will be the effect of providing a second operator?
4. Write a SIMSCRIPT program to simulate problem 7 of Section 8.20.
5. Simulate the food processing plant discussed in problem 6 of Section 8.20. Use exponential distribution for processing times on machines.
6. A manufacturing system consists of two production lines, each consisting of three machines and two bins (Figure 9.5). The processing takes place in three stages and the complete manufacturing of an item requires operations on all the three machines in each production line. The total production is given by the sum of the output of machines 3 and 6. The ON/OFF state of machines is controlled by bin level conditions shown in Table 9.3. The machine breakdowns are classified into two categories— operator type and foreman type. The interarrival time of breakdowns and the speed of various machines are given in Table 9.4. There are two operators to service machines 1, 2, 4, and 5 and one operator to look after machines 3 and 6. There is one foreman who can act as operator if he is free and if all the operators are busy. It has been observed that 80% of the breakdowns are of operator-type and 20% of foreman-type. Operator-type breakdowns can be fixed by the foreman, but the reverse is not true. The repair of an operator-type breakdown takes 40 ± 25 seconds while a foreman-type breakdown requires 1000 ± 300 seconds. Using SIMSCRIPT, simulate the manufacturing system with a view to increasing the throughput. Investigate the effect of providing larger bins, faster machines, and additional operators on the throughput.
7. This exercise is concerned with the generation and passing of messages between tasks on a multi-microprocessor system. Due to various system constraints some of the messages generated are aborted, and our problem is to collect statistics on the aborted messages and possibly recommend system parameters that will reduce the number of aborted messages to a minimum.

There are six identical processor boards arranged in a loop (Figure 9.6) and each board can run several tasks. The messages generated by the tasks may be destined for a task on the same board or any other board. In cases where the message is destined for a board other than the immediate neighbour (on the right), the message is forwarded by the boards between the source and destination boards. For efficiency, tasks which communicate frequently with one another are placed as close as possible on the same board or on the neighbouring boards. We assume

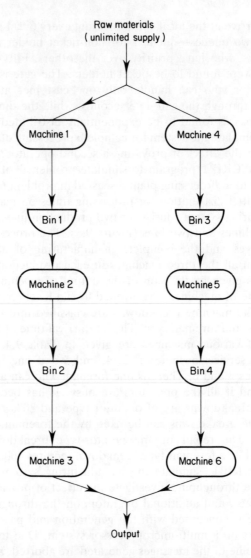

Figure 9.5   Manufacturing system with two production lines.

that the probability that the destination of the message is on the source board is 60%; if not on the source board, then the probability that it is on the immediate neighbour board is 80%, and if not on the immediate neighbour, then the destination will always be on the board next to it. Each board has 25 blocks of memory available for storing messages. Occasionally there may not be a sufficient number of blocks available for storing messages (messages are always stored before forwarding to its

Table 9.3 Bin levels and ON/OFF state of machines.

	Bin			
	1	2	3	4
Maximum capacity	6000	5000	4000	3500
Rundown level after overflow (preceding machine OFF until bin level drops to this value)	2500	2500	2000	2000
Fill-up level after emptying (succeeding machine OFF until bin level raises to this value)	400	300	400	400

Table 9.4 Breakdown characteristics and speed of machines.

Machine	Interarrival time of breakdowns (seconds)	Time to process an item (seconds)
1	350 ± 50	0.8
2	450 ± 100	1.1
3	300 ± 75	1.3
4	350 ± 30	1.0
5	425 ± 70	1.4
6	350 ± 50	1.5

destination) which vary from 1 to 5 blocks (uniform distribution) in length; in this case several '*wait for 50 microseconds and try again*' are attempted for free blocks, and if unsuccessful after 6 attempts, the message is aborted. Blocks on the source board are freed as soon as the message is copied across to another board or when the message is accepted (not stored) by the destination board.

The following data are available:

Interarrival time of messages: 3600 to 4500 microseconds (uniform distribution). Time for copying (reading) a message: 40 microseconds per block. Time for aborting a message: 40 to 80 microseconds (uniform distribution). Communication delay between neighbouring boards: 7 microseconds.

Write a SIMSCRIPT program to simulate the above system. Stop simulation after processing 1000 messages including aborted ones. Gather statistics on average message size, utilization of blocks on each board, number of tries for free blocks, number of aborted messages, and the number of cases where source and destination boards were the same.

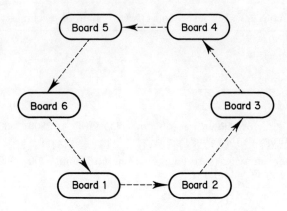

Figure 9.6   Multi-microprocessor system.

References

CACI (1985). *PC-SIMSCRIPT II.5 and SimAnimation User's Manual.* CACI, Los Angeles, CA. 90049.

Kiviat, P. J., Markowitz, H. M., and Villanueva, R. (1983). *SIMSCRIPT II.5 Programming Language.* CACI, Los Angeles, CA 90049.

Russell, E. C. (1983). *Building Simulation Models with SIMSCRIPT II.5. CACI, Los Angeles, CA 90049.*

10

Simulation Experiments in Practice

10.1 Collection and analysis of simulation output

The total simulation (discrete systems) process includes the construction, verification, and validation of the model as well as the verification of the associated computer programs and the validation of simulation data. The validation and verification of models have already been discussed in Chapter 4 and some aspects of statistical analysis of data are described in Chapters 5 and 6. Simulation is an experimental problem-solving technique and the main objective of a simulation exercise is to obtain reliable estimates of system performance measure (Schriber and Andrews, 1981) at reasonable cost. A simulation model is run several times using specified initial conditions and different streams of random numbers; this produces a series of values for each of the output variables and the true values of the output variables are estimated from these observed values. The statistical analysis of the output variables is usually carried out by fitting an approximate probability distribution to the observed data.

It is important to remember that even if the simulation is carried out correctly using a valid model, errors in the collection, analysis, and interpretation of results can lead to wrong conclusions and failure (Annino, 1979) of the simulation project. The *sample size* is a major factor that determines the accuracy of the statistical analysis of simulation results. But how do we compute the sample size or how many simulation *runs* are required in order to ensure the accuracy (Fishman, 1977) of simulation results? Similarly, how do we determine the *length* of each simulation run? There is no simple answer to these questions. A general guideline is to repeat the simulation until the *variance* of the estimated values of the variables is less than a specified value. The cost of simulation, together with the value of the information gained, should also be taken into consideration.

Sometimes we rely only on the output from a *single* simulation run for the estimation of various parameters of interest. *Non-terminating systems*, such as a 24-hour casualty department or a computer operating system, can be simulated for an infinite period of time, whereas the simulation of a *terminating system* such as post office or travel agency is terminated after a specific period of time (say 8 hours). In the case of a terminating system, *replication* is the only way of generating the necessary samples while sufficient data can be collected by controlling the *run length* of a non-terminating system.

In general, simulation results are not statistically independent, and the estimate of variables based on finite samples is influenced by *initial bias*. Simulation results suffer from these and other types of errors which must be controlled. There are standard statistical techniques available for analysis (e.g. mean, variance, confidence interval) of simulation output, provided the data collected satisfy certain well-defined characteristics. These and other methods, discussed in Chapters 4 and 5, form the basis for the validation of simulation results. Like any physical laboratory experiment, simulation experiments must be designed and executed in a systematic way and sufficient care must be taken in the collection, analysis, and interpretation of simulation data.

This chapter will discuss how simulation experiments are conducted in practice; what are the major sources of errors in simulation; how these errors can be controlled, and what general methodology is used in the statistical analysis of simulation results. For a thorough treatment of statistical methods in discrete system simulation, the reader is referred to Kleijnen, 1974, 1975; Fishman, 1978; Law and Kelton, 1982; and Friedman and Friedman, 1984.

10.2 Major sources of errors in simulation

Simulation of discrete systems invariably involves the use of random numbers. Thus simulation models are stochastic in nature and this is the cause for the *variability* of the observed results. In other words, different observations of the same system produce different values of a given variable, and the true value of the variable will have to be estimated from the measured values. In addition to the effects due to the stochastic elements in the model, the errors in the data used and the errors associated with the method of collection, analysis, and interpretation of the simulation output may also influence the final results.

10.2.1 Modelling errors

The use of invalid models may result in serious simulation errors, and in fact this is the cause for the failure of many simulation projects. A valid model is a necessary prerequisite in simulation. Verification and validation of models have already been discussed in Chapter 4.

10.2.2 Computer programming errors

The programming errors in computer implementation of a model may range from simple arithmetic errors to serious logical errors in the structure of the model. In Section 8.4.3 we have seen that the deletion of certain GPSS statements could lead to the simulation of entirely different systems. The truncation and round-off errors in numerical values can also cause problems. In addition to the usual program debugging aids, testing the model by simulating simple systems with known analytical solutions may help in detecting programming errors. Structured and modular programming designs would also be useful in minimizing errors.

10.2.3   Sampling errors

The validity of the assumed distribution for a given set of observations must be established before it is used in simulation experiments. Sampling from the appropriate distribution consists of two operations. First of all, *uniformly distributed* random *variates* are generated, and these are then used to generate random variates from the appropriate distribution (Section 6.9). Poor random number generators can cause serious errors in simulation. The characteristics of a good random number generator have been summarized in Section 6.2. In discrete systems simulation, random numbers are used not only to select *correct proportion* of the values from the distribution but also to produce the set of values in a *random sequence*. These processes produce sampling errors (Pidd, 1984) known as *'set effect'* and *'sequence effect'*. The set effect is due to the difference between the set of values produced by the sampling process and the theoretical distribution. The definition of probability distribution assumes the existence of an infinite population of values while discrete simulation can only produce finite samples, and this is the cause of the sequence effect. The set effect can be reduced by means of the variance reduction techniques discussed in Section 10.4, but the control of sequence effect is rather difficult.

10.2.4   Errors in parameter estimation

There are standard statistical techniques for the estimation of parameters from the observations on stochastic variables. However, the use of the central limit theorem in statistical analysis assumes that the random variables are drawn from an infinite population with a stationary probability distribution and finite values for mean and standard deviation, and that they are mutually independent. The central limit theorem assumes that the sum of n variables is approximately distributed as a normal variable and the *confidence interval* is given by

$$\bar{x} \pm C \frac{\sigma}{\sqrt{n}}$$

where $\bar{x}$ = sample *mean* of n independent observations
  σ = *standard deviation*

and C is the constant associated with the confidence level. It follows that the reliability of the estimate increases as the confidence interval reduces (i.e. n increases). Unfortunately, simulation outputs are not statistically independent and suffer from both *auto-correlation* and *cross-correlation*. For example, the queuing time of customer n depends on the waiting time of the preceding $n - 1$ customers. Therefore standard statistical methods cannot be directly applied for analysing simulation results.

Sometimes our interest is to compare two simulation results so as to evaluate alternative policies or system configurations (e.g. whether to use 4 or 5 phone lines). Here, precise estimate of output values is unnecessary as long as both policies are equally biased.

To complicate the matter further, the estimates of the *mean* and *variance* based on *finite samples* are seriously corrupted by the *initial bias* (i.e. effect of starting the simulation in a state not representative of the normal system behaviour). Methods for controlling the errors in the estimation of parameters are discussed in Section 10.3.

10.3   Error control in simulation

Let us now focus our attention on methods for controlling/reducing errors in simulation results. Various approaches are discussed below, and of course the cost of simulation and the usefulness of the results obtained do play a major role in the overall design and implementation of simulation experiments.

10.3.1   Detection and control of initial bias

The concept of *steady state* of a system was introduced in Chapter 2. When activated, most systems pass through a *transient period* (i.e. large fluctuations in the value of output variables) before settling down to a steady state. Some systems have no steady state (e.g. world economy) and here our interest may well be to study the transience. In simulation, some of these transients are caused by *starting conditions*. Very often simulation runs are initiated with the system in an *idle state* (e.g. no customers in the post office and postmaster idle) which is not representative of a state usually encountered during the normal operation of the system under study. The output of such simulations may undergo large fluctuations before achieving steady state. A simulated system is said to be in *steady state* if its current behaviour is *independent* of its starting *initial conditions* and the probability of being in one of its *states* is given by a *fixed* probability function.

Let us consider the small post office problem discussed in Section 7.4, with *Poisson* arrival and *exponential service* time distributions.

When $\lambda = 1/60$ and $\mu = 1/30$, we have (from Section 5.17.2), $\rho = 0.5$

$$\text{Mean waiting time in queue} \frac{\rho}{(1 - \rho)\mu} = 30$$

$$\frac{\text{Mean waiting time in queue}}{\text{Mean service time}} = \frac{30}{30} = 1 = \text{true value}.$$

The simulation of the post office system starting from idle state was carried out by writing a simple GPSS program. After serving every ten customers (i.e. measurements were made in steps of 10), the GPSS proram gave a printout of *mean service time* and *mean waiting time* and then the model was RESET before continuing the simulation. The data collected before each RESET were used to compute the *ratio* of the *mean waiting time* to the *mean service time* and the *mean* of these ratios was used for plotting the graph shown in Figure 10.1. The *variability* of sample *mean* and the effect of *initial bias* are clearly displayed. The sample mean settles to a *steady value* after serving about 1500 customers. Note that the individual waiting times will continue to show their inherent variability, but the variations of the sample mean will balance out.

In our post office simulation starting with no customers, the early arrivals will have a better chance of getting service than late arrivals. Therefore the sample mean that includes early arrivals will be biased if our interest is to estimate the steady state performance of the post office system. As the *sample size* increases (i.e. longer simulation run), the influence of initial bias will gradually die out. The effect of initial bias on simulation output can be reduced in several ways.

Method 1. Start the simulation in *idle state* and run for a sufficiently long period of time so that the effect of bias on estimates of mean and variance is negligibly small. The actual *length* (Fishman, 1977) of simulation will have

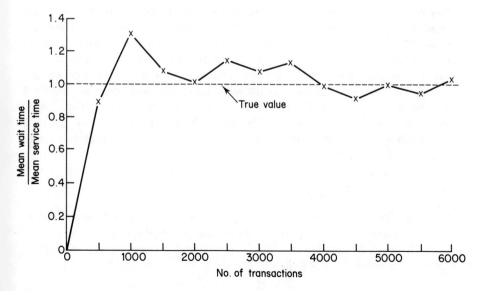

Figure 10.1 Initial bias and steady state.

238

to be determined by experimentation in conjuction with the intended level of confidence and the cost of simulation.

Method 2. Start the simulation nearer to the steady state (e.g. steady state or mean of the steady states obtained in the previous runs) of the system under study. This requires a good knowledge of the characteristics of a similar system which may or may not exist.

Method 3. Run simulation for a period of time called '*warming-up period*' or '*run-in period*' corresponding to the transient phase, during which no statistics are collected (or collected statistics are discarded) and the simulation proper begins by collecting statistics at the end of the warming-up period. Note that we are discarding part of the system statistics which will obviously decrease the accuracy of *variance* estimates that are needed for computing *confidence limits*. In general, the elimination of the initial statistics tends to reduce the bias of the output estimators, but increases the estimate of variance. Thus there is a need for compromise between bias reduction and variance reduction while evaluating the starting conditions (Wilson and Pritsker, 1978).

Different starting conditions are generally required depending upon the technique used in the estimation of the variance. If the estimate is based on a *single simulation run* (Section 10.3.3), then bias is eliminated only *once*. If replication (Section 10.3.2) is used, then bias is to be eliminated for each run and therefore great care must be exercised in the determination of the steady state. The elimination of bias is not required in *regenerative methods* (Section 10.3.4) where the *idle state* is taken as the *regenerative state*.

What should be the *length* of the *warming-up period*, or how do we detect the steady state so that the collection of statistics can begin? Several methods for detecting the steady state have been recommended by different authors (Gafarian *et al.*, 1978; Pritsker, 1984). Modern interactive computing facilities (plots, printouts, graphic displays) help us to closely monitor the values of variables as the simulation proceeds. The steady state is indicated by the absence of continuous changes in the value of variables in the same direction and the presence of only minor oscillations about a mean. For example, some versions of GPSS have a SSTATE block, which specifies that the simulation may be stopped if the value of the SNA stays in a specified range for a specified period of time.

10.3.2 Replication of simulation runs

We know that the estimation of sample mean and variance requires *independent samples*. Here, we repeat simulation K times for the same sample size with the same starting conditions, but with different streams of *random numbers* (e.g. use CLEAR in GPSS) so as to ensure that the *replications* are independent. The sample mean (e.g. mean queue length) is given by the overall mean of the K replications.

Suppose the simulation experiment (post office problem) is repeated K times with independent random number streams and let x_{ij} be the ith observation in the jth run. Then the estimates of the mean waiting time and its variance for large K are given by

$$M(n) = \frac{1}{K} \sum_{j=1}^{K} \bar{x}_j(n) = \frac{1}{nK} \sum_{j=1}^{K} \sum_{i=1}^{n} x_{ij}$$

$$\mathrm{var}(n) = \frac{1}{K-1} \sum_{j=1}^{K} [\bar{x}_j(n) - M(n)]^2$$

where $\bar{x}_j(n)$ = mean of jth run.

These estimates can be used to establish the confidence interval. The GPSS output (starting from idle state) given in Figure 10.2 shows the effect of utilization and initial bias on steady state when $K=1$. The true (theoretical) values are shown in Table 10.1. It can be seen from Figure 10.2 that, as the utilization increases, the length of the period of initial bias also increases.

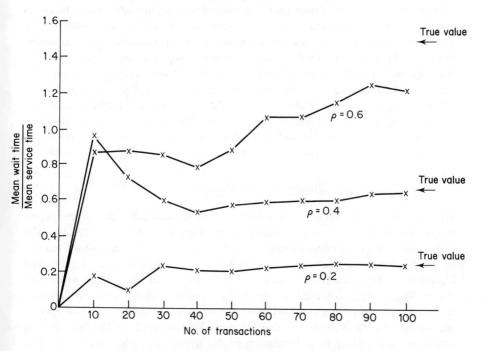

Figure 10.2 Effect of utilization on steady state.

Table 10.1 Theoretical values of ρ and the ratio R.

	1/60	1/60	1/60
Mean arrival rate, λ	1/60	1/60	1/60
Mean service rate, μ	1/12	1/24	1/36
Utilization, $\rho = \dfrac{\lambda}{\mu}$	0.2	0.4	0.6
Mean wait time in queue (time units/customer)	3	16	54
$\dfrac{\text{Mean wait time}}{\text{Mean service time}} = R$	0.25	0.667	1.5

10.3.3 Batch mean

After eliminating the initial bias the simulation is continued for a long period of time, and the output from this single simulation run is divided into segments or *batches* of equal size. If the *batch length* is sufficiently long, the individual batches can be treated as independent samples from measurements and thus sample mean and variance can be computed. The initial bias needs to be eliminated only *once* at the beginning of the simulation.

However, the assumption that the individual batches are independent is not strictly true. The *final state* of a batch becomes the *initial state* of the next batch, and thus *autocorrelation* exists between values of the variables. In order to reduce the autocorrelation, consecutive batches are separated by *intervals* in which the outputs from the simulation are discarded. Again, for the sake of independence, we are throwing away valuable information.

There is no simple formula to determine the *batch size* and the *length* of the interval separating consecutive batches. The results from experiments with the model for several batch sizes, human judgement, cost of simulation, and the value of the information gained should serve as a useful guide.

10.3.4 Regenerative method

The concept of state variables was discussed in Section 2.5. There are systems where identical system states recur at random intervals of time, i.e. the system or process *regenerates* itself at random intervals in time which cannot be predetermined. Such a system is said to be *regenerative* (Crane and Lemoine, 1977; Iglehart and Lewis, 1979); the point in time at which the system states recur is called a *regeneration point*, and the interval between two regeneration points is called an *epoch* or regeneration cycle. The epochs are similar to the batch size discussed in Section 10.3.3. The number of activities taking place in a simulation model during an epoch may vary. The regeneration points are computed with respect to a particular set of values of system variables chosen as a reference point. For example, the state of our post office system when there are no customers queuing or being served and the postmaster idle can be selected as a reference point.

It is quite possible that even if regeneration points exist, the parameters of the system are such that it may never reach them. A system starting from an idle state (regeneration point) may not reach that state again if interarrival times are too small and service times are too large. Regeneration implies that the sequences of activities that occur in a system during different epochs are independent. Therefore, sample statistics taken during different epochs in a simulation experiment should also be independent and free from initial bias. The central limit theorem can now be applied in the statistical analysis of the data collected.

10.3.5   Time series and spectral analyses

The replications of simulation runs, batch means, and regenerative methods are based on the fundamental assumption that the data used for estimating the true values of various parameters are *statistically independent*. The time series and spectral analyses assume that the simulation data are corrupted by autocorrelation, and the errors due to this in the estimated values are corrected by measuring the autocorrelation. The sequence of observations of any state variable of a stochastic system constitute a statistical *time series*. The *covariance* between events in a sequence can be studied by representing the time series as the sum of a number of sinusoidal waves of different frequencies. In time series analysis (Gordon, 1978; Box and Jenkins, 1976), we use a single simulation run, and observations are made at uniform time intervals. The method involves a series of lengthy computations and the storage of large amounts of data which must be available simultaneously.

In *special analysis* (Fitzsimmons, 1974) of simulation data, the computations are very similar to those in the time series analysis; however, the contributions of high and low frequencies are separated and highlighted. The spectral analysis (computation of sample spectrum or Fourier transform of covariance function) emphasizes the fact that two systems with the same mean value can have entirely different transient characteristics and the true difference between them can be studied by separating the low- and high-frequency components in the spectrum. This approach is extremely useful in the analysis of existing systems and in the design and implementation of future systems. Another advantage is that it is a *nonparametric* approach, and no assumption is made about the distribution of observations in the time series. The spectral analysis is mathematically complex and computationally expensive.

10.4   Variance reduction techniques

The variance reduction techniques (VRT) are useful in the analysis and validation of simulation output. The emphasis is on improving the reliability of estimates (e.g. reduce variance of mean wait time) without the need for collecting large samples (e.g. reduce variance without increasing sample size or achieve specified precision with a smaller sample size) and thus reduce the cost of simulation. The variance reduction is achieved by setting special experimental conditions or through the use of prior information about the system. There are several reduction techniques and their application depends on the particular model and our understanding of the model.

Antithetic sampling, common random number streams, control variates, stratified sampling, selective sampling, and importance sampling are some of the variance reduction techniques. Three of these methods are discussed below.

10.4.1 Antithetic sampling

The set effect and some of the sequence effect are controlled by antithetic sampling. We execute pairs of simulation runs, one with random numbers r_1 at time t_1, r_2 at time t_2, . . . r_n at time t_n and the second run with antithetic streams of random numbers $(1 - r_1)$ at time t_1, $(1 - r_2)$ at time t_2, . . . $(1 - r_n)$ at time t_n. The complementary sampling (antithetic sampling) is intended to produce negative correlation (i.e. a small observation in one run tends to be offset by a large observation in the other run) between output variables in the two simulation runs.

Suppose we repeat a simulation experiment K times and calculate an unbiased estimate x_j of some output variable on each run. Then the final mean and variance are given by

$$\bar{x} = \frac{1}{K} \sum_{j=1}^{K} x_j$$

$$\text{var}(\bar{x}) = \frac{1}{K} \left[\sum_{j=1}^{K} \text{var}(x_j) + 2 \sum_{i=1}^{K} \sum_{j=i+1}^{K} \text{cov}(x_i, x_j) \right]$$

If the runs are independent the covariance terms are zero; but if the sum of the covariance terms is negative, then the value of var $(\bar{x})$ will be reduced. Thus antithetic sampling (Fishman and Huang, 1983; Rubinstein and Samorodnitsky, 1985) is useful in reducing the variance estimates.

The generation of the antithetic streams of random numbers can be easily accomplished (Kleijnen, 1974) by using a multiplicative congruential random number generator. If

$$x_0 = \text{seed}$$
$$x_i = Cx_{i-1} \bmod M$$

are used for generating the first random sequence x_i, then the second random sequence x_i' generated by using the seed $x_0' = M - x_0$, will have the property that $x_i' = 1 - x_i$. Thus, the antithetic sequence can be generated simply by changing the initial value of the SEED.

10.4.2 Common random numbers (CRN)

In many simulations historical data (e.g. arrival time of customers in a post office) are used as simulation input. The historical arrival pattern is a single time series and therefore its repeated use should reduce the variation of the simulation output. Similar variance reduction can be achieved by starting different simulations (Rubinstein and Samorodnitsky, 1985) with the same random number seed (i.e. common random number stream). Almost complete control of *set effect* and partial control of *sequence effect* can be achieved by this method. This approach is particularly useful for comparing two *alternative* policies or system configurations under similar experimental conditions. Here the sampling variations are held constant (use separate random number generators for each source of variation in the model) so that the difference in the output variables can be interpreted as the effect due to the differences in system designs rather than due to changes in experimental conditions. Thus the estimates of the difference in the two sets of policies will be more accurate.

Suppose $\bar{x}_1$ to be the average waiting time obtained from a simulation (see Figure 8.7a) with one officer, and let $\bar{x}_2$ be the corresponding value associated with the system with two officers, then the variance of the difference is given by

$$\text{var}(\bar{x}_1 - \bar{x}_2) = \text{var}(\bar{x}_1) + \text{var}(\bar{x}_2) - 2\,\text{cov}(\bar{x}_1,\bar{x}_2)$$

If common random variates are used in the two runs, there will be correlation between $\bar{x}_1$ and $\bar{x}_2$, and if the covariance term can be made positive then the variance of their difference will be reduced.

SIMSCRIPT has ten and GPSS has eight different random number generators with unique seeds. In our travel agency problem of Figure 8.8, one could use one stream for arrivals and three other streams for generating service time of the three telephone lines. In many situations (e.g. Fortran, Pascal, microprocessors), there is only one random number generator available, and the random numbers from the same stream are selected at different points in time. This can introduce serious errors.

10.4.3 Control variates

This is another method (Kleijnen, 1974; Law and Kelton, 1982) for improving the reliability of estimates by controlling the set effect. The basic assumption is that the user has a good knowledge of the behaviour of the system being simulated. For example, if we can identify a control variable X that has *positive covariance* with the variable of interest Y, and if we can compute the theoretical expectations associated with the control variable, then a variance reduction for Y can be achieved. If we can establish positive correlation between the *input* (e.g. interarrival time, service time) and the *output* variables of the simulation model, then the input variable can be used as *control variate*. Even though this method is more difficult to implement, it tends to be more effective (Gaver and Shelder, 1971) than the other variance reduction techniques.

10.5 Design of simulation experiments

So far our emphasis has been to estimate the performance of a system for a given setting of its parameters. The next stage is to collect samples of observations corresponding to different parameter settings and draw conclusions through statistical analysis. One possible approach to the validation of simulations is to compare the results obtained from the real system with the output obtained from the simulator under identical conditions. The degree of confidence in such validations depends upon the number of experiments conducted and the range of parameter settings used in each experiment. The well-known '*experimental design*' methodology (Kleijnen, 1977; Ignall, 1972; Box *et al.*, 1978) can be applied to reduce the number of experiments required to achieve a specified level of *confidence*.

In simulation, the performance of the model may be influenced by a number of *factors* such as arrival rate, service rate, scheduling policies, etc. A *factor* (input parameters and structural assumptions) may be *qualitative* (e.g. priority of customers in a hospital) or *quantitative* (e.g. number of doctors). Some factors are *controllable* (e.g. number of doctors) while others are *uncontrollable* (e.g. arrival pattern of patients). There may be one or several *settings* or levels (e.g. one doctor or several doctors) for each factor, and a particular combination of a setting is generally known as a *treatment*. Simulation experiments can be designed to investigate the effect of these factors and each treatment gives a *sample* of observations. If there is no interaction between factors or levels, then an experiment may be designed to evaluate the output (response) for different input values and the results can be easily analysed by using standard statistical techniques (e.g. *Student's* t-*test* to compare two mean values). If there is only one factor, then all we have to do is to run the simulation at different levels of the factor and compute *confidence intervals* for the response at each level of the factor.

In practice there may be several factors at different levels and the factors may interact with each other. We would like to know whether the effect of these factors acting independently or jointly is *statistically significant*. There are several experimental design techniques available in the published literature (Cochran and Cox, 1957; Hicks, 1982). Our discussion will be confined to '*factorial design*', which is one of the simplest. Factorial experiments are conducted to compare the effects of the interaction between each level of each factor with each level of each of the other factors. Obviously, factorial experiments require many simulation runs. If there are K factors, each operating at L_f levels ($f = 1, 2, \ldots K$), then the number of possible designs in a fully factorial experiment is given by

$$\overset{K}{\underset{f=1}{}}\Pi L_f$$

In stochastic discrete system simulation each factor-level combination is repeated several times (say n times), then the total number of simulation runs required is given by

$$n \prod_{f=1}^{K} L_f$$

When $L_1 = L_2 = \ldots L_K = L$ and $n = 1$, the number of combinations become L^K. When $L = 2$ we have a 2^K factorial experiment.

In a factorial experiment there are two types of effects: the main effects and the interaction effects. A 2^3 factorial design with factors A, B, C is shown in Table 10.2, where $-$ and $+$ signs correspond (Law and Kelton, 1982) to the two levels associated with each factor, and R_i is the output from the simulation run with the ith combination of factor levels.

The main effects. Effects due to factor A, B, C as they are changed one at a time.

In Table 10.2 the main effect of factor j (j = A, B, C) is the average change in the response due to the movement of factor j from its $-$ level to its $+$ level while holding all other factors steady.

The interaction effects. These are the effects due to the simultaneous changes in two or more of the factors. If two factors are changed at the same time (e.g. changes in AB, AC, BC), they are called second-order effects, and if three factors are changed simultaneously (ABC), then they are called third-order effects.

In Table 10.2 the second-order interaction effect between factors A and B is defined to be half the difference between the average effect of factor A when factor B is at its $+$ level (C remains constant) and the average effect of factor A when factor B is at its $-$ level.

The third-order interaction effect between factors A, B, C is half the difference between the average two-factor interaction effect between factors A and B when factor C is at its $+$ level and the average two-factor interaction effect between factors A and B when factor C is at its $-$ level.

Table 10.2 2^3 Factorial design matrix.

Factor combination	Factor A	Factor B	Factor C	Response
1	$-$	$-$	$-$	R_1
2	$+$	$-$	$-$	R_2
3	$-$	$+$	$-$	R_3
4	$+$	$+$	$-$	R_4
5	$-$	$-$	$+$	R_5
6	$+$	$-$	$+$	R_6
7	$-$	$+$	$+$	R_7
8	$+$	$+$	$+$	R_8

The main effects of factors A, B, C can be written as

$$e_A = [(R_2 - R_1) + (R_4 - R_3) + (R_6 - R_5) + (R_8 - R_7)]/4$$

$$e_B = [(R_3 - R_1) + (R_4 - R_2) + (R_7 - R_5) + (R_8 - R_6)]/4$$

$$e_C = [(R_5 - R_1) + (R_6 - R_2) + (R_7 - R_3) + (R_8 - R_4)]/4$$

The second-order effects are given by

$$e_{AB} = \left[\frac{(R_4 - R_3) + (R_8 - R_7)}{2} - \frac{(R_2 - R_1) + (R_6 - R_5)}{2} \right]/2$$

$$e_{AC} = \left[\frac{(R_6 - R_5) + (R_8 - R_7)}{2} - \frac{(R_2 - R_1) + (R_4 - R_3)}{2} \right]/2$$

$$e_{BC} = \left[\frac{(R_7 - R_5) + (R_8 - R_6)}{2} - \frac{(R_3 - R_1) + (R_4 - R_2)}{2} \right]/2$$

The third-order effect is

$$e_{ABC} = \left[\frac{(R_8 - R_7) - (R_6 - R_5)}{2} - \frac{(R_4 - R_3) - (R_2 - R_1)}{2} \right]/2$$

The analysis of variance is used to split the observed variations in the output values into independent components which are usually expressed as the sum of squared deviations from the *means*. The effects of factors on the output variables are determined by performing statistical tests to establish the significance of these independent components.

The analysis of variance tells us whether a factor has any influence on the behaviour of the system or not; it does not identify any functional relationship between factor level and the corresponding system response. Such relationships would be very useful in predicting the performance at levels that have not been tested. *Linear* and *multiple regression techniques* are useful in establishing these relationships.

I mentioned that the main purpose of experimental design is to maximize the information gained from each simulation run. Another use of this method is in the selection of a best alternative by determining the *treatment levels* for all *factors* which produce an *optimum* (or near-optimum) response. The *response–surface* methodology (Myers, 1971) is generally used for *optimization* using simulations when all the factors are *quantitative*. A closer look at the statistical techniques associated with the design of experiments is beyond the scope of this book, and the interested reader should refer to (Kleijnen, 1975).

10.6 Validation of simulation results

The questions of verification and validation of models have already been discussed in Chapter 4. Verification implies that we have a thorough understanding of the model including inherent variability (due to changes in input data, model parameters, and the use of probability distributions) associated with the model. During validation, the output from the verified simulation model is subjected to the same statistical tests usually applied to the data obtained from the real system, and conclusions are drawn about the performance of the system.

The methods for the validation of models described in Chapter 4 and the statistical techniques developed in Chapters 5 and 6 form the basis for the validation of simulation models and simulation data. Several methods for improving the reliability of estimates by reducing possible errors due to initial bias and autocorrelation have already been discussed in this chapter. The time series analysis, spectral analysis, variance reduction methods, and experimental design techniques are useful aids in the validation process. *Sensitivity analysis* of simulation models can also be of some help in validation; this method relies on the fact that, in general, *reasonable changes* in model parameters or operating conditions should not lead to *unreasonable changes* in model performance.

Agreement between simulator output and measured data from the actual system is usually a good test of the validity of simulation results; however, simulation output and the output from many real-world systems are not statistically independent; hence the difficulty in directly applying conventional statistical tests. The size of the confidence interval, discussion with independent experts (other than those who developed the simulation model) in the field, human judgement, and consistency of results should also give valuable information (Van Horn, 1971) to the analyst during the validation phase.

The validity of simulation results varies from discipline to discipline. Chapter 4 discussed the *inductive* and *deductive* approaches to systems analysis. The *black box* approach to systems analysis (Section 3.4.4) is based on inductivism, and here the input and output of the system are *observable*, but the internal structure is unknown, i.e. prediction without explanation. The inductive information is derived from observations of system behaviour, statistical analysis, intuition, or a combination of these; thus the simulation model need not be an exact representation of the real system. On the other hand, the *white box* approach (deductive approach) to systems analysis implies that the system can be described completely by deductive information (mathematical relations, physical laws, etc.) and the input–output relations are based on *factual knowledge* of the internal structure of the system. Simulation models based on deductive approach are likely to be more representative of the real system. The validity and applicability of simulation results depend upon the *degree of deductivity* in a model. This explains why simulation has been more successful in the general area of engineering and physical sciences when compared to social, economic, environmental, and behavioural sciences.

10.7 Summary

Discrete system simulation is an experimental problem-solving technique using stochastic models. The simulation model is run several times using specified initial conditions and different streams of random numbers. This produces a series of values for the output variables and the *true values* are estimated from these observed values. The reliability of simulation output is established by estimating the variance of the sample mean. There are standard statistical techniques available for the analysis of simulation data provided the data collected satisfy certain statistical properties so that the *central limit theorem* can be applied. In general, simulation data are not statistically independent and the estimates of variables based on *finite samples* are influenced by *initial bias*. The simulation output suffers from several types of errors which must be eliminated (or controlled) before applying standard statistical techniques for analysis.

The major sources of simulation errors and procedures for reducing them are described in this chapter. Methods for the collection and analysis of simulation data so as to improve the accuracy and reliability of simulation results are presented. Variance reduction techniques which can be of some use in reducing the cost of simulation are introduced, and some aspects of *experimental design* in simulation and the general guidelines for the validation of simulation results are discussed. Like any other physical laboratory experiment, the simulation experiments must be designed and executed in a systematic way, and sufficient care must be taken in the collection, analysis, and interpretation of results.

10.8   Exercises

1. For exercise 7 of Chapter 8, investigate the effect of starting conditions on queue lengths. Identify the steady state point (if it exists) in each case.
2. For the example shown in Figure 8.7a, investigate the effect of starting conditions and server utilization on mean wait times.
3. For exercise 5 of Chapter 8, study the effect of initial conditions and various priority policies on steady state.
4. Modify the problem of Figure 8.8, so that calls are queued and no calls are lost. Calculate the mean and variance (see Section 10.3.2) of queuing time when $K = 25$. Compute a 90% confidence interval for the expected average waiting time of a call in the queue.
5. Compare the use of batch means and replications in the simulation of the system described in exercise 8 of Chapter 8.
6. Perform the following two simulation experiments, each consisting of 12 runs on the problem described in Figure 8.4.

Experiment 1   Use random number generator 4 for arrival times; use random number generator 5 for service times.
Experiment 2   Use antithetic values from generator 4 for arrival times; use antithetic values from generator 5 for service times.

Compare the output from the two experiments by plotting graphs. Compute the variance of the sample mean and comment on the usefulness of antithetic sampling.

7. The following data were obtained from the study of a manufacturing system output.

	1	2	3	4	5	6	7	8
Real system	32	33	32.5	34	33.5	34.5	—	—
Simulation model	29	31.5	34.5	30	28.5	35	33	32.5

Using α (significance level) $= 0.01$, test to determine if there is a significant difference between the means of the two results.

8. Using CRN, study the effect of adding a fourth telephone line to the system described in Figure 8.9 (modify the problem so that calls are queued and no calls are lost.). Compare the estimated values of mean wait times in queue in each case, and determine the number of replications required to produce a set of reasonably accurate and reliable results.

9. Use CRN to compare queuing delays associated with two priority policies in the immigration control problem discussed in Figure 8.7b.

10. Examine the definition of central limit theorem and its applicability to simulation data analysis.

11. What are the major sources of errors in simulation, and how are they overcome.

12. The output of a simulation experiment is influenced by two factors, each of which can take two levels. Discuss the general methodology used in the design of simulation experiments to test the effects. What treatment combinations would be used in the actual simulation runs. Comment on the value of the information gained through replication of experiments.

13. Investigate the sensitivity of average service time to average number of calls lost in the problem described in Figure 8.8 of Chapter 8.

14. Write short notes on the following
   (a) collection and analysis of simulation output,
   (b) elimination of initial bias,
   (c) variance reduction techniques,
   (d) experimental design,
   (e) sources of errors in simulation,
   (f) error control in simulation.

References

Annino, J. S., and Russell, E. C. (1979). 'The ten most frequent causes of simulation analysis failure—and how to avoid them', *Simulation*, **32**(6), 137–140.

Box, G. E. P., and Jenkins, G. M. (1976). *Time Series Analysis: Forecasting and Control*. Holden-Day, San Francisco, CA.

Box, G. E. P., Hunter, W. G., and Hunter, J. S. (1978). *Statistics for Experimenters: an introduction to design, data analysis and model building*. John Wiley, New York.

Cochran, W. G., and Cox, G. M. (1957). *Experimental Design*, 2nd edn. John Wiley, New York.

Crane, M. A., and Lemoine, A. J. (1977). 'An introduction to the regenerative method for simulation analysis'. *Lecture Notes in Control and Information Sciences*, Vol. 4. Springer-Verlag, New York.

Fishman, G. S. (1977). 'Achieving specific accuracy in simulation output analysis', *CACM*, **XX**(5), 310–315.

Fishman, G. S. (1978). *Principles of Discrete Event Simulation*. John Wiley, New York.

Fishman, G. S., and Huang, B. D. (1983). 'Antithetic variates revisited', *CACM*, **26**(1), 964–971.

Fitzsimmons, J. A. (1974). 'The use of spectral analysis to validate planning models,' *Socio-Econ. Plan. Sci.*, **VIII**(3), 123–128.

Friedman, L. W., and Friedman, H. H. (1984). 'Statistical considerations in computer simulation: the state of the art'. *J. Statist. Comp. Simul.*, **19**(3), 237–264.

Gafarian, A. V., Ancker, C. J., and Morisaku, T. (1978). 'Evaluation of commonly used rules for detecting "steady state" in computer simulation', *Nav. Res. Logist. Q.*, **25**, 511–529.

Gaver, D. P., and Shelder, G. S. (1971). 'Control variable methods in the simulation of a model of a multiprogrammed computer system', *Nav. Res. Logist. Q.*, **18**, 435–450.

Gordon, G. (1978). *System Simulation*. Prentice Hall, Englewood Cliffs, NJ.

Hicks, C. R. (1982). *Fundamental Concepts in the Design of Experiments*. Holt, Rinehart & Winston, New York.

Iglehart, D. L., and Lewis, P. A. W. (1979). 'Regenerative simulation with internal controls', *JACM*, **26**(2), 271–282.

Ignall, E. J. (1972). 'On experimental designs for computer simulation experiments', *Manag. Sci.*, **18**(7), 384–388.

Kleijnen, J. P. C. (1974). *Statistical Techniques in Simulation*, Part I. Marcel Dekker, New York.

Kleijnen, J. P. C. (1975). *Statistical Techniques in Simulation*, Part II. Marcel Dekker, New York.

Kleijnen, J. P. C. (1977). 'Design and analysis of simulations: practical statistical techniques', *Simulation*, **28**(3), 81–90.

Law, A. M., and Kelton, W. D. (1982). *Simulation Modelling and Analysis*. McGraw-Hill, New York.

Myers, R. H. (1971). *Response Surface Methodology*. Allyn & Bacon, Boston, MA.

Pidd, M. (1984). *Computer Simulation in Management Science*. John Wiley, London.

Pritsker, A. A. B. (1984). *Introduction to Simulation and SLAM II*. Systems Publishing Corp., West Lafayette, IN.

Rubinstein, R. Y., and Samorodnitsky, G. (1985). 'Variance reduction by the use of common and antithetic random variables', *J. Statist. Comp. Simul.*, **22**(2), 161–180.

Schriber, T. J., and Andrews, R. W. (1981). 'A conceptual framework for research in the analysis of simulation output', *CACM*, **24**(4), 218–232.

Van Horn, R. L. (1971). 'Validation of simulation results', *Manag. Sci.*, **17**(5), 247–258.

Wilson, J. R., and Pritsker, A. A. B. (1978). 'A procedure for evaluating startup policies in simulation experiments', *Simulation*, **31**(3), 79–80.

11

Continuous System Simulation

11.1 Introduction

In Chapter 1, I mentioned that there are two basic approaches (discrete and continuous) in system simulation depending upon our perception of the real system. The general characteristics of continuous systems and their model representations have been dealt with in Chapters 2 and 3. The *continuous simulation models*, where the values of the variable attributes change continuously, are generally described by deterministic differential and possibly some algebraic equations. In both continuous and discrete simulations, time is used as the independent variable, but the time advance mechanisms used for updating the simulation clock are different. Many discrete event simulation models include continuous subsystems, and vice-versa.

11.1.1 Direct digital versus digital analogue simulations

Earlier applications of simulation (Ragazzini, *et al.*, 1947) were in the analysis and design of engineering systems by using the continuous approach, and the actual simulation was carried out on *analogue computers*. Analogue computers are still being used for simulation (Bert and Pinder, 1982) in specialized areas; however, modern digital computers have become an attractive alternative in many situations because of their accuracy, reliability, flexibility, and the ability to mimic analogue machines under program control. Finding the numerical values of a set of problem variables at any point in time by solving a system of constrained equations representing the physical or conceptual system is the essence of continuous system simulation. In analogue simulation, problem variables are represented by continuously variable voltages (electrical analogues) whereas in digital simulation the numbers generated by electrical pulses are used for their representation. Continuous systems can be simulated on a digital computer in two ways (Brennan and Linebarger, 1964)—*direct digital simulation* and *digital analogue simulation*. In direct digital simulation the program is written directly from mathematical equations describing the model, whereas in digital analogue simulation the computer program virtually simulates an analogue com-

252

puter and the programming language contains special instructions to perform analogue functions such as additions, multiplications, summations, and integrations.

11.1.2 General characteristics of analogue and digital computers

It is important to observe the major characteristics of analogue and digital computers. The analogue computer is a special-purpose machine; it operates on all variables continuously in real time; it is a parallel device and solves simultaneous equations in the true sense of the word; it has built-in circuitry for summation, multiplication, integration, and function generation; it has no or very limited storage facility; it gives a solution immediately; it is less accurate due to amplifier drifts and invalid assumptions in the derivation of results; it cannot deal with very large and very small variables and hence scaling may be necessary; the input variables are continuous in nature and it is required to convert analogue voltages into numbers and vice-versa. The mathematical structure of the problem is apparent from the analogue flow diagram and the simulation results give deeper insight into the behaviour of the system under study. On the other hand, the digital computer is a general-purpose machine with logical ability; arithmetic and logical operations on numbers are performed sequentially; input variables are discrete in nature; it is more accurate and can handle very large and very small numbers using floating point arithmetic; direct mathematical integration is not possible; numerical integration may be difficult; it can store a vast amount of data; it is comparatively slow; and it is difficult to achieve real time operations.

11.1.3 Hybrid computers and hybrid simulations

The complementary nature of analogue and digital computers discussed in the previous section led to the development of the *hybrid computers* (Korn and Korn, 1972; Landauer, 1982) and hybrid simulations (Bekey and Karplus, 1968). The hybrid computer is basically an analogue computer which incorporates a small amount of digital logic. Hybrid computers are very useful (Volz, 1973) in simulating continuous–discrete systems. For example, the solution of differential equations in the problem can be carried out by the analogue subsystem and the logical operations, storing values, setting initial conditions, etc., can be performed by the digital logic. Hybrid simulation is not simulation on hybrid computers. In hybrid simulation the outputs of the analogue and digital computers are linked together through an interface for the purpose of simulation. The communication between analogue and digital computers is achieved through units which convert analogue signals into their digital equivalents and vice-versa (Korn, and Vichnevetsky, 1976; Hoeschle, 1968). Typically the analogue computer is used to obtain fast solutions to differential equations, and the digital computer is used for arithmetic and logical operations, storing of values, and more accurate numerical integrations which need not be in real time. The recent developments in cheaper and faster microprocessors have created a renewed interest in hybrid computers and hybrid simulations, especially for dedicated applications.

The simulation of continuous systems by using both analogue and digital computers are described in this chapter. In Section 11.2 simulation on analogue computers is discussed, and Section 11.3 presents the digital simulation of continuous systems by using CSMP (continuous system modelling program).

11.2 Analogue computer simulation

The *operatinal amplifiers* are the major components of analogue computers and these are connected to resistors, capacitors, potentiometers, and diodes to perform summation, integration, differentiation, multiplication, and function generation. The voltages (usually one of ±5, ±10, ±12, ±50, ±100) in the computer are related to the problem variables through scale factors, depending upon the range of problem variables. The analogue computer is ideal for solving simultaneous differential equations and, in particular, non-linear differential equations. The output of the analogue computer is displayed digitally and/or graphically, and the solution to the given problem is determined experimentally by repeating the simulation several times.

The operational amplifier consists of a high voltage gain, direct-couplied, inverting amplifier; an input impedance and an output impedance. The ideal operational amplifier must have infinite gain (ratio of output voltage to input voltage), infinite bandwidth (same gain at all frequencies), infinite input impedance, zero output impedance, zero drift (zero output for zero input at all times), and zero phase shift. It is not necessary to understand the electrical details in order to simulate continuous systems on analogue computers. Without going into the electrical circuitry and theoretical derivations, the basic analogue operations and their notations required for our discussions are given in the next section and the reader is referred to Bennett, 1974 and Ricci, 1972, for further details.

11.2.1 Basic operations and notations

The analogue computer programs are written in the form of analogue flow diagrams using special symbols, and the programs are implemented by making the necessary connections (patching) on the machine. The analogue computer representation of a problem need not be unique. There may be several programs for the same problem, depending upon the variables and scale factors chosen.

(a) The operational amplifier. The symbol and the operation of the '*operational amplifier*' is shown in Figure 11.1. Note that the sign of the output

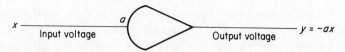

Figure 11.1   The operational amplifier (a = gain or amplification).

voltage is reversed or inverted. An operational amplifier with unit gain is called an inverter, which simply reverses the sign of the ouput.

(b) Summer. The *summing amplifier (adder)* is shown in Figure 11.2.

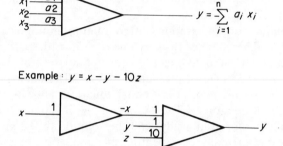

$$y = \sum_{i=1}^{n} a_i x_i$$

Example: $y = x - y - 10z$

Figure 11.2   Summing amplifier.

(c) Integrator. The operation and the notation of the *integrator* are shown in Figure 11.3. The initial condition (IC) is the value of the integrator output when the time $t = 0$.

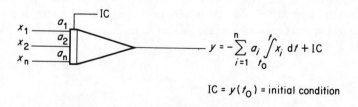

$$y = -\sum_{i=1}^{n} a_i \int_{t_0}^{t} x_i \, dt + IC$$

IC = $y(t_0)$ = initial condition

Example: $y(t) = \int_{t_0}^{t}(x-y+10z)dt$
$y(t_0) = 1$

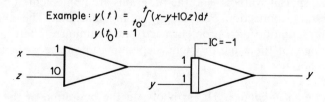

Figure 11.3   Integrator.

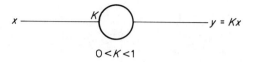

Figure 11.4 Potentiometer (pot).

(d) Potentiometer (pot). The *potentiometer* or the coefficient multiplier is shown in Figure 11.4.

(e) Multiplier and function generator. These are shown in Figure 11.5.

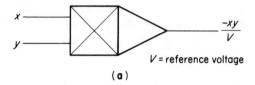

(a)

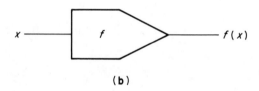

(b)

Figure 11.5 (a) Multiplier; (b) function generator.

11.2.2 Linear systems

Let us consider the model of the mechanical system discussed in Section 3.6.5:

$$M\ddot{x} + D\dot{x} + Kx = F(t)$$

where $M = 10$ kg;

$D = 2.5$ newton-second/metre

$K = 1.25$ newton/metre;

$F(t) = 10$ newtons;

$\dot{x}(0) = x(0) = 1$

Rearranging the equations so that the highest-order derivative is on the left-hand side, we get

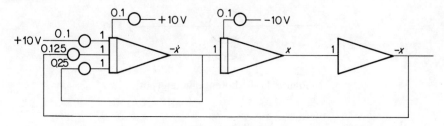

Figure 11.6   Analogue computer diagram for linear system.

$$\ddot{x} = -(1/4)\dot{x} - (1/8)x + 1$$

The analogue computer flow diagram is shown in Figure 11.6, where 1 volt represents a displacement of 1 metre as well as a velocity of 1 metre/second.

11.2.3   Simultaneous equations

Consider a linear system represented by

$$\ddot{x} + 2\dot{x} - 5y = 0$$

$$g + y + 4x = 0$$

and $\qquad x = y = 0; \dot{x} = 2$ at time $t = 0$

Rearranging the terms, we get

$$\ddot{x} = 5y - 2\dot{x}$$
$$\dot{y} = -4x - y$$

and the corresponding analogue program is shown in Figure 11.7.

11.2.4   Nonlinear systems

The equations involving terms of the form

$$a_m \left(\frac{dy}{dx}\right)^n$$

where $n \neq 1$ or a_m is not a constant, are said to be nonlinear. The analytical or numerical solution of nonlinear equations is generally difficult. However, the analogue computer solution of nonlinear equations does not pose any major problems; hence this method is very attractive. Special analogue computer elements are available for simulating nonlinearities which appear in the form of multiplications, divisions, powers, and functions of dependent variables.

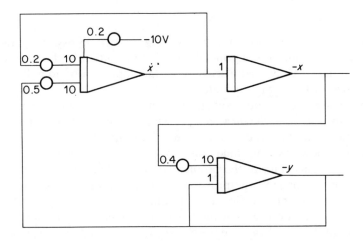

Figure 11.7   Program for solving simultaneous equations.

The predator–prey model described in Section 3.6.1 is an example of nonlinear systems and the equations (3.8) can be rewritten as

$$\frac{dN_1}{dt} = \lambda_1 N_1 - K_1 N_1 N_2$$

$$\frac{dN_2}{dt} = -\lambda_2 N_2 + K_2 N_1 N_2$$

where $K_1 = \lambda_1 \alpha$ and $K_2 = \lambda_2 \beta$

The analogue computer program for simulating the predator–prey problem is shown in Figure 11.8, where V is the reference voltage.

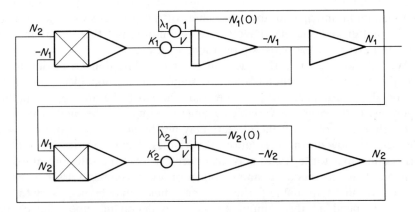

Figure 11.8   Program for simulating nonlinear system.

11.2.5 Magnitude and time scaling

The *magnitude* (amplitude) and *time scaling* are two necessary operations in analogue simulation. Basic principles behind magnitude and time scaling are described here. A detailed discussion of this topic can be found in Bennet, 1974 and Charlesworth and Fletcher, 1974.

The analogue computer voltage is limited to a specified value (e.g. ± 10 V) known as the *reference voltage*, while the magnitude of the range of the problem variables could be any finite quantity. The reference voltage is sometimes known as 1 machine unit or 1 MU. This means that 1 volt cannot always represent 1 unit of the problem variable; therefore we must have an estimate of the range of the problem variables, and this is used to scale the variables so that their analogue representation never exceeds 1 MU. The *magnitude scaling* ensures that the maximum anticipated values of the problem variables are always represented by the maximum (or less than maximum) allowable amplifier ouput voltages. Depending upon the values of the problem variables, scaling up or scaling down may be necessary. The magnitude scaling is done by appropriate amplifier and potentiometer settings. If the estimated absolute maximum value of the problem variable $x(x \geq 0)$ is $\bar{x}$ metres/second, then the magnitude scale factor S can be computed as follows:

$$1\ MU = S \cdot \bar{x} \text{ metre/second}$$
$$S = (1/\bar{x})\ MU/metre/second.$$

The unscaled analogue program can now be rewritten so that instead of x, the variable $x/\bar{x}$ appears at the output of the amplifier as a machine variable and the solution to the original problem is obtained by multiplying the simulation result by $\bar{x}$. Too small (when variable range is too large) and too large (when variable range is too small) scale factors may lead to very small and very high output voltages, and this may introduce errors in the solution. The selection of satisfactory scale factors depends upon our knowledge of the maximum absolute values of the problem variables. The estimation of the maximum anticipated absolute values of the problem variables is not a trivial matter and one may have to use common sense, theoretical analysis, trial-and-error methods, or combinations of these.

We will now examine the question of time scaling that arises due to the fact that the natural phenomenon being simulated may take place too quickly or too slowly compared to the time frame in which the analogue computer operates. If the problem variables change too quickly, the analyst may not get a chance to observe; the plotters may not be able to record, and hence the need to slow down the solution. If variables change too slowly, amplifier drifts and capacitor leakages may introduce errors in the solution; moreover it is necessary to speed up simulation in order to complete a set of experiments within a reasonable period of time. Thus it may be necessary to slow down or speed up the computer simulation depending upon the characteristics of the particular model.

The time scale factor β is defined as the ratio of the computer time to the problem time. If $\beta > 1$ the computer solution is slower than the process being simulated. The systems which have faster response time than the computer itself are simulated in *expanded time* by slowing down ($\beta > 1$) the computer solution. In some cases simulation is carried out in *compressed time* by speeding up the computer solution (i.e. $\beta < 1$) in order to improve the accuracy and to save time and money.

All the components except integrators are unaffected by time scaling, as time is involved only in the description of the integrators. It can be shown (Ricci, 1972) that the computer solution can be speeded up or slowed down by a factor β (i.e. integration takes place with respect to machine time and not with respect to problem time) by dividing every integrator input by β.

11.2.6   Analogue computer operations

The analogue computer programs are implemented on the machine by making the necessary connections as described in the analogue program (diagram). The operational amplifiers are connected by patch cords to act as adders, integrators, and function generators. The potentiometers (pots) are used to set the initial values of integrators, and they also serve as coefficient multipliers. Associated with each amplifier there is an overload indicator which lights up whenever the output of the amplifier exceeds the reference voltage (i.e. 1 MU) at any time during the computations. Improper scaling of variables is one of the major causes for overloads. The conditions which cause the overloads must be isolated and eliminated before the computations are continued. The operation of the analogue computer is controlled by a three-way switch: RESET–HOLD–COMPUTE. In RESET mode the computer gives the static solution to the problem at $t = 0$ (i.e. initial conditions); in COMPUTE mode the problem is solved continuously for a preset period of time, and in HOLD mode the input is disconnected and the current solution is 'frozen'. Thus the solution can be interrupted and examined at any point in time and afterwards the solution can be either continued or RESET and started again from the beginning. The solution variables and the output of the individual amplifiers are recorded on digital voltmeters, oscilloscopes, or plotters.

11.2.7   Analogue computer simulation—summary of steps

Various steps involved in the analogue computer simulation of a given system can be summarized as follows:

(a) Derive the mathematical model of the system in terms of differntial and algebraic equations.
(b) Rewrite each differential equation with its highest-order derivative on the left-hand side.

(c) Select suitable variables for measurement and draw an unscaled analogue flow diagram for each equation and interconnect them wherever necessary.

(d) Estimate the maximum anticipated absolute values of the problem variables.

(e) Select the reference voltage and determine the magnitude and time scale factors, initial condition voltages, amplifier gains, and potentionmeter settings.

(f) Draw scaled analogue flow diagram showing all the input voltages initial conditions, amplifier gains and pot settings.

(g) Patch the machine according to the scaled analogue program and test the system with initial conditions.

(h) Run simulation; isolate and eliminate overloads and other errors, if any; repeat simulation and record/display results.

(i) Translate analogue voltages into numerical values of the problem variables and interpret results. Repeat simulation until the solution is satisfactory.

11.3 Digital computer simulation using CSMP (Continuous System Modelling Program)

11.3.1 Historical background

In digital analogue simulation the user could program the digital computer just like an analogue computer. Gradually, advanced digital features were added to the digital analogue simulation languages and some of the analogue features were dropped. This led to the development of *direct digital simulation* languages. In direct digital simulation, digital computer programs are written directly from mathematical equations describing the system without using the analogue representation. Several continuous system simulation languages have been reported in the published literature (Brennan and Linebarger, 1964; Nilsen and Karplus, 1974). A block-oriented digital analogue simulation language, PACTOLUS, was developed for IBM 1620 in 1964 and equation-oriented direct digital simulation languages MIMIC (Control Data Corp., 1968) and DSL/90 (IBM, 1965) followed. In 1966 IBM developed CSMP/360—continuous system modelling program—which is an extension of DSL/90.

In order to promote and coordinate the development of simulation languages, the SCI (now the SCS, Society for Computer Simulation) set up a simulation software committee, which in 1967 produced a CSSL report defining the desirable characteristics of a good simulation language. CSMP/360, which is a non-procedural language, satisfies most of the CSSL standards. CSMP-III is an extension of CSMP/360 and includes better integration methods, graphic displays, plot facilities, and double precision arithmetic. CSSL-III (Prog. Sci. Corp., 1970), CSSL-IV (Nilsen, 1976) and ACSL (Mitchell and Gauthier, 1985) are some of the languages developed according

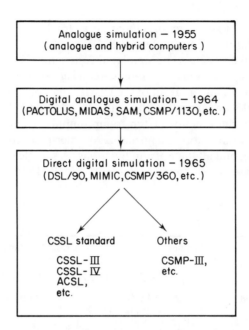

Figure 11.9   Evolution of continuous system simulation methods.

to CSSL specifications. The languages have several advanced features including better integration methods, file handling routines, and I/O facilities. An outline of the evolution of continuous system simulation methods and languages is shown in Figure 11.9. Several other languages, including large-scale subroutine packages such as LINPACK and FORSIM (Dongarra *et al.*, 1982; Carver *et al.*, 1978), are also available for simulation. DYNAMO (Pugh, 1973) is a structured problem-oriented programming language developed around 1962 for simulating systems dynamics and, as mentioned in Chapter 7, GASP-IV and SLAM can be used for continuous and combined continuous–discrete simulations (Ören, 1977).

The discussions in the following sections of this chapter are confined to CSMP/360 (CSMP for short), which is one of the most popular continuous system simulation languages. Most of the CSMP/360 programmes will run under CSMP-III as well. CSMP (IBM, 1972) is written in Fortran, and is particularly suitable for simulating systems which can be modelled in terms of differential and algebraic equations. Only important features of CSMP are considered here, and for further details the reader is referred to (IBM, 1972; Speckhart and Green, 1976).

11.3.2   Overview of CSMP

Numerical integration algorithms are at the heart of every digital simulation (continuous systems) language. The selection of correct integration method and step size is crucial for accuracy, stability, and speed of computations.

Both variable and fixed step size integration methods with built-in error-checking procedures are available in CSMP.

The model of the system to be simulated is specified in terms of equations, functional blocks, and Fortran statements. The power and flexibility of Fortran are retained, and a subset of the CSMP functional blocks corresponds to the usual analogue computer elements. In addition, CSMP has facilities for generating special functions (step, ramp, impulse, random signals, etc.), hybrid elements (comparators, quantizers, zero-order-hold, etc.), digital elements (AND, OR, etc.), and all the Fortran functions. A sample of the 34 functional blocks and 18 Fortran functions available in CSMP (IBM, 1972) is shown in Figure 11.10.

Name of function	Function	CSMP format
Integration	$Y = \int_0^t X \, dt + IC \; ; \; Y(0) = IC$	$Y = \text{INTGRL}(IC, X)$
Zero-order hold	$Y = X2$ if $X1 > 0$ $Y =$ last output, if $X1 \leqslant 0$ $Y(0) = 0$	$Y = \text{ZHOLD}(X1, X2)$
Function switch	$Y = X2$ if $X1 < 0$ $Y = X3$ if $X1 = 0$ $Y = X4$ if $X1 > 0$	$Y = \text{FCNSW}(X1, X2, X3, X4)$
Comparator	$Y = 0$ if $X1 < X2$ $Y = 1$ if $X1 \geqslant X2$	$Y = \text{COMPAR}(X1, X2)$
Limiter	$Y = P1$ if $X < P1$ $Y = P2$ if $X > P2$ $Y = X$ if $P1 \leqslant X \leqslant P2$	$Y = \text{LIMIT}(P1, P2, X)$
Step function	$Y = 0$ if $t < P$ $Y = 1$ if $t \geqslant P$	$Y = \text{STEP}(P)$
AND function	$Y = 1$ if $X1 > 0$ and $X2 > 0$ $Y = 0$ otherwise	$Y = \text{AND}(X1, X2)$
NOT AND	$Y = 0$ if $X1 > 0$ and $X2 > 0$ $Y = 1$ otherwise	$Y = \text{NAND}(X1, X2)$
Exponential	$Y = e^x$	$Y = \text{EXP}(X)$
Natural logarithm	$Y = \log(X)$	$Y = \text{ALOG}(X)$
Sine	$Y = \sin(X)$	$Y = \text{SIN}(X)$
Square root	$Y = \sqrt{X}$	$Y = \text{SQRT}(X)$
Absolute value	$Y = |X|$	$Y = \text{ABS}(X)$
Largest value	$Y = \max(X1, X2, \dots X_n)$	$Y = \text{AMAX1}(X1, X2, \dots X_n)$
Smallest value	$Y = \min(X1, X2, \dots X_n)$	$Y = \text{AMIN1}(X1, X2, \dots X_n)$

Figure 11.10   A sample of CSMP functions.

CSMP is a non-procedural (i.e. effectively parallel computations result) language; most of the statements can be written in any order, and they are sorted into correct sequence before the program is executed. The flexibility of CSMP is further enhanced by the provision of SORT/NOSORT options in program segments.

Three types of statements may appear in a CSMP program. The *structure* statements describe the system to be simulated in terms of equations and functional blocks; the *data statements* assign numerical values to problem parameters, system constants, and initial conditions for integration; and the *control statements* specify the program execution options, sequence of simulation, integration method, error checks, stopping criteria, and the choice, format, and frequency of the output. The program structure of CSMP consists of three segments: INITIAL, DYNAMIC, and TERMINAL. In simple CSMP programs all the three segments may be merged into a single segment which will be interpreted as DYNAMIC and there is no need for labelling the segment. The debugging facilities in CSMP are good and it is easy to learn the language.

11.3.3 Symbolic names, constants, and source statement format

Most of the Fortran programming conventions apply to CSMP. The symbolic names should not be more than six characters long and the first character must be alphabetic. Unless otherwise specified, all symbolic names will be treated as floating point variables. Floating point numbers can be written directly (not more than a total of 12 characters and not more than 7 significant decimal digits) with a decimal point or in E format. The arithmetic operators and the order of operations are exactly the same as in Fortran. CSMP programs are written only in column 1 through 72; a statement can be continued on as many as 8 lines and the continuation of a statement is indicated by three consecutive periods (. . .) at the end of the information on a line. An asterisk (*) in the first column denotes comments and the structure statements can begin in any column.

11.3.4 A simple CSMP simulation—example 1

The distance x in metres travelled by an elevator between stops in a mine is described by the differential equation

$$\ddot{x} = -1.7(t - 2)^3$$

where t = time in seconds, $\dot{x}(0) = x(0) = 0$ and $0 \leqslant t \leqslant 4$.

Compute the value of x as a function of time.

The CSMP program is shown in Figure 11.11a. Let us briefly examine the CSMP statements and their function in the program. The TITLE allows the user to specify a title which appears at the top of each page of printed output; the CONSTANT statement, which is an example of data statement, is used to assign constant values to symbolic names. The statements, starting with variable names X2DOT, XDOT and X, are structure statements which describe the elevator model to CSMP. The INTGRL functions on the right-hand side of the structure statements perform numerical integration. The TIMER, TITLE, PRINT, PRTPLT, and LABEL are control statements. The parameters which control the simulation run are specified on the TIMER statement. The length of the simulation run is specified by FINTIM, the interval between printouts is defined by PRDEL, the print–plot interval is specified by OUTDEL, and DELT indicates the integration interval. The LABEL statement allows the user to specify a title to each page of the print–plot output and the names of the variables to be printed and plotted are indicated on PRINT and PRTPLT statements respectively. The END statement signals the end of the description of the simulation model and causes the model to run. The STOP denotes the end of simulation and the end of the job is indicated by ENDJOB. There is no explicit mention of INITIAL, DYNAMIC, and TERMINAL segments in the program and therefore the whole program is interpreted as a DYNAMIC segment. The output produced by the program is shown in Figure 11.11b, where X, the distance travelled, is represented by the horizontal axis of the plot, the time by the vertical axis, and the origin of the plot is at the top left-hand corner. The RKS (Runge–Kutta) method of numerical integration and the minimum allowable integration interval defined by DELMIN are default options.

11.3.5 Data, structure, and control statements—example 2

The role of data, structure, and control statements in CSMP has already been mentioned in Section 11.3.2. I will now illustrate the format and use of these statements in CSMP simulations.

```
TITLE  A SIMPLE CSMP PROGRAM *********
* SIMULATION OF DISTANCE TRAVELLED BY AN ELEVATOR
   CONSTANT K  = -1.7
           X2DOT  = K*(TIME-2.0)**3
           XDOT  = INTGRL(0.0,X2DOT)
           X  = INTGRL(0.0,XDOT)
TIMER FINTIM = 4.0,PRDEL = 0.4,OUTDEL = 0.2,DELT = 0.01
PRINT X,XDOT,X2DOT
PRTPLT X
LABEL  DISTANCE TRAVELLED  VERSUS  TIME  ******
END
STOP
ENDJOB
```

Figure 11.11(a) CSMP program listing for example 1.

```
Timer Variables
  DELT  = 1.0000E-02
  DELMIN= 4.0000E-07
  FINTIM= 4.0000E+00
  PRDEL = 4.0000E-01
  OUTDEL= 2.0000E-01


******  RKS   integration  ******
     TIME          X           XDOT          X2DOT
  0.0000E+00   0.0000E+00   0.0000E+00    1.3600E+01
  4.0000E-01   8.9129E-01   4.0147E+00    6.9632E+00
  8.0000E-01   2.9315E+00   5.9187E+00    2.9376E+00
  1.2000E+00   5.4679E+00   6.6259E+00    8.7040E-01
  1.6000E+00   8.1609E+00   6.7891E+00    1.0880E-01
  2.0000E+00   1.0880E+01   6.8000E+00    5.6248E-24
  2.4000E+00   1.3599E+01   6.7891E+00   -1.0880E-01
  2.8000E+00   1.6292E+01   6.6259E+00   -8.7040E-01
  3.2000E+00   1.8828E+01   5.9187E+00   -2.9376E+00
  3.6000E+00   2.0869E+01   4.0147E+00   -6.9632E+00
  4.0000E+00   2.1760E+01  -2.0862E-07   -1.3600E+01


     DISTANCE TRAVELLED  VERSUS   TIME ********

                               MINIMUM          X   VERSUS  TIME              MAXIMUM
                              0.0000E+00                                     2.1760E+01
     TIME          X          I                                              I
  0.0000E+00   0.0000E+00    +
  2.0000E-01   2.4613E-01    +
  4.0000E-01   8.9129E-01    --+
  6.0000E-01   1.8172E+00    ----+
  8.0000E-01   2.9315E+00    ------+
  1.0000E+00   4.1650E+00    ---------+
  1.2000E+00   5.4679E+00    -------------+
  1.4000E+00   6.8066E+00    ---------------+
  1.6000E+00   8.1609E+00    ------------------+
  1.8000E+00   9.5200E+00    ---------------------+
  2.0000E+00   1.0880E+01    -------------------------+
  2.2000E+00   1.2240E+01    ---------------------------+
  2.4000E+00   1.3599E+01    -------------------------------+
  2.6000E+00   1.4953E+01    ----------------------------------+
  2.8000E+00   1.6292E+01    ------------------------------------+
  3.0000E+00   1.7595E+01    ----------------------------------------+
  3.2000E+00   1.8828E+01    -------------------------------------------+
  3.4000E+00   1.9943E+01    ---------------------------------------------+
  3.6000E+00   2.0869E+01    -----------------------------------------------+
  3.8000E+00   2.1514E+01    ------------------------------------------------+
  4.0000E+00   2.1760E+01    -------------------------------------------------+
```

Figure 11.11(**b**) Elevator distance as a function of time—example 1.

(*a*) *Data statements*. These are used for model initialization; can appear in any order; may be intermixed with structure statements; and need not start in column 1. CONSTANT, PARAMETER, and arbitrary functional blocks AFGEN and NLFGEN for handling functions of one variable are the most important data statements.

The CONSTANT statement assigns a constant value to a variable. Several equations separated by commas may appear in a CONSTANT statement and several CONSTANT statements may be used.

CONSTANT   A = 23.2,   B = 12.0   OHM = 232.5

The PARAMETER and CONSTANT statements may be used inter-
changeably. However, only one multiple value parameter may be used for
each simulation run. The multiple values of the parameter are used for
successive simulation runs.

PARAMETER   VELCTY = 23.2,   C = 3.0
PARAMETER   OHM = (200.0, 225.5, 260.0)

The function AFGEN performs linear interpolation between points whereas
NLFGEN uses quadratic interpolation. These functions are defined in data
statements and used in structure statements. The data points on the curve
are given in pairs of x and y; and the x values in the sequence, must be
monotonically increasing.

AFGEN   CURVE x_1, y_1, x_2, y_2, x_3, y_3, x_4, y_4
AFGEN   CURVE = −3.1, 1.5, −1.6, 2.3, 0.5, 1.1, 0.9, 1.9

(b) *Structure statements.* These are used to define the model to CSMP. The
structure statements are written in Fortran equation form and the expression
on the right-hand side consists of constants, variables, and output from
functions (see Figure 11.10) and subroutines. Examples of structure statements are:

CODE = K*(A + B) + C
Y   = ZHOLD(X1, X2)
X   = INTGRL(1.0, 2*A**2 + C)
FN   = AFGEN(CURVE,X1)
VEL = Y + (−FN + D*X)/(A + C) + INTGRL(2.0, XDOT)

The INTGRL function in an expression must appear at the right-most part
of that expression and the initial condition of an INTGRL function may not
be an expression.

(c) *Control statements.* The control statements are divided into translation,
execution, and output control statements. These statements are used to
control the sequence of simulation. In general, control statements may start
in any column except a few including ENDJOB, which must start in column
one.

The translation control statements define how the structure statements are
to be translated by the compiler. INITIAL, DYNAMIC, TERMINAL,
END, ENDJOB, RENAME, SORT, NOSORT, and STOP are examples
of translation control statements. The RENAME statement is used to change
the reserved names such as TIME, DELT, DELMIN, FINTIM, PRDEL,

and OUTDEL so as to make the description of problem variables more meaningful. For example, the default option in CSMP is to use TIME as the independent variable and this can be changed to X by means of RENAME statement. The RENAME statement must appear before the TIMER statement and the new names must be used in the structure statements

RENAME   TIME = X, DELT = DELTX

The INITIAL, DYNAMIC, TERMINAL statements are discussed in Section 11.3.6 and the use of SORT, NOSORT is explained in Section 11.3.7. The first occurrence of END statement signifies the end of the model description and causes the simulation run. Successive END statements terminate specifications for successive models. The END statement resets the independent variable (TIME) to zero, resets the initial conditions, and initiates a new run after incorporating the changes (data and control statements) specified between the two consecutive END statements. The last END statement must be followed by STOP and ENDJOB.

The execution control statements define parameter values which control the simulation run. The use of TIMER and FINISH is described below and METHOD is dealt with in Section 11.3.8. As mentioned in Section 11.3.4, the TIMER statement is used to assign values to system variables such as DELT, FINTIM, PRDEL, OUTDEL, and DELMIN (minimum allowable integration interval for variable step methods). The default values of TIMER parameters are described in Section 11.3.8. The value of DELT specifies integration interval for numerical integration. The simulation by successive solution of model equations is done after each increment in time defined by DELT. A decrease in the value of DELT generally tends to increase both computing time and the accuracy of results.

TIMER   DELT = 0.01, FINTIM = 2.5, DELMIN = 0.0001

The FINISH statement allows the user to specify additional criteria for stopping a simulation run. The length of a simulation run is controlled either by the elapsed time set by FINTIM on the TIMER statement or by one of the specified conditions defined on the FINISH statement, whichever occurs first. The use of FINISH is optional and multiple FINISH statements are allowed.

TIMER   FINTIM = 2.6
FINISH   VEL = 0.0, DIST = 12.5, X = Y

With the above statements the simulation is terminated before TIME = 2.6 if VEL = 0.0 or DIST = 12.5 or X = Y. The RESET (see below) statement must be used to nullify FINISH specifications between successive runs.

The output control statements specify details of variables to be printed and plotted. LABEL, PRINT, PRTPLT, RANGE, RESET, and TITLE are examples of output control statements. The use of LABEL, PRINT, PRTPLT, and TITLE has already been mentioned in Section 11.3.4. The RANGE statement can be used to obtain the minimum and maximum values of specified problem variables and their time of occurrence during a run.

    RANGE   VEL, ACCEL

The RESET statement nullifies previous specifications on control statements such as PRINT, RANGE, LABEL, PRTPLT, and FINISH. The TITLE cannot be RESET. The RESET can be used in two ways

    RESET
    RESET   PRTPLT, RANGE, LABEL

A RESET statement with only RESET on it nullifies all previous PRINT, PRTPLT, RANGE, and LABEL statements. The following example illustrates the use of data, control, and structure statements.

Example 2

In Section 3.6.5 the automobile suspension system was characterized by

$$M\ddot{x} + D\dot{x} + Kx = F \qquad (11.1)$$

where we have assumed that the damper force is proportional to velocity and the spring force is proportional to the displacement. In practice, the behaviour of the spring is not linear, and for a particular spring let us assume that the spring force (in Newtons) is given by

$$S = K_1 x - (K_1 - K_2)(x - a) + R \quad \text{when } x \geq a$$
$$= K_1 x + R \quad \text{when } x < a$$

where K_1, K_2, and a are constants, and R (Newtons) is a function of x (centimetres), which is available only as a table of experimental results. Figure 11.12a shows the characteristics (excluding the effect of R) of the nonlinear spring. Equation (11.1) now reduces to

$$M\ddot{x} + D\dot{x} + S = F$$

The CSMP program which simulates the above system is shown in Figure 11.12b. The value of R as a function of x is given by the function AFGEN CURVE, and the appropriate value of S is computed by using COMPAR(X,A) which gives an output of one, only when $X \geq A$. The purpose of the simulation is to select the best value of D from a set of values for fixed values of M, F, and S so as to minimize the oscillations. The simulation is repeated for three different values of D and the graph of the

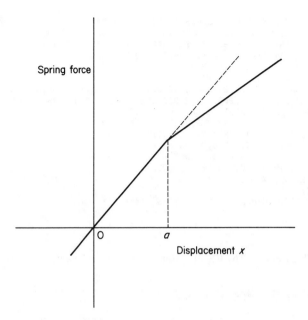

Figure 11.12(**a**) Nonlinear spring characteristics.

displacement versus time for $D = 25$ is shown in Figure 11.12c. Note that $X \geqslant A$ only when TIME $= 0.2$ to 0.3, and here the nonlinear characteristic of the spring comes into play.

11.3.6 INITIAL, DYNAMIC, and TERMINAL segments—example 3

The program structure of CSMP consists of INITIAL, DYNAMIC, and TERMINAL segments (Figure 11.13) and the explicit labelling of segments may be necessary to control the sequence of simulation in complex models. The DYNAMIC segment is required while the other two are optional.

The computations to be performed only once at the beginning of a simulation run are included in the INITIAL segment. The structure statements within INITIAL segments are executed only when TIME $= 0$. The INITIAL segment is optional and, if it appears, then it must be the first segment in the program. Of course the results of this section are available to the rest of the program at all times.

The DYNAMIC segment appears immediately after INITIAL segment and usually consists of structural statements for describing the model. The actual simulation is carried out here by solving a set of simultaneous equations numerically, and this involves a series of discrete calculations over a large number of very small time intervals. This segment includes all statements to

```
TITLE   SIMULATION OF SUSPENSION SYSTEM********
* ILLUSTRATION OF DATA,STRUCTURE AND CONTROL STATEMENTS
        CONSTANT   F = 950.,K1 = 400.0,K2 = 200.0,A = 2.5,M =1.25
        PARAMETER  D = (15.0,25.0,20.0)
* LINEAR INTERPOLATION OF DATA
        R = AFGEN(CURVE,X)
AFGEN   CURVE = -1.0,2.1,-0.5,4.32,0.0,0.0,0.5,3.2,1.0,-2.7,...
1.5,6.23,2.0,-4.12,2.5,2.0,3.0,2.6,3.5,-3.78,4.0,6.15
* SPRING CHARACTERISTICS CHANGE WITH TIME
        S = K1*X-COMPAR(X,A)*(K1-K2)*(X-A)+R
        X2DOT = (1.0/M)*(F-S-D*XDOT)
        XDOT  = INTGRL(0.0,X2DOT)
        X     = INTGRL(0.0,XDOT)
TIMER FINTIM = 1.0,PRDEL=0.05,OUTDEL=0.05
PRINT X,XDOT,X2DOT
PRTPLT X
LABEL  DISPLACEMENT  VERSUS  TIME *********
END
STOP
ENDJOB
```

Figure 11.12(**b**) CSMP program listing for example 2.

DISPLACEMENT VERSUS TIME *********

```
                        MINIMUM        X   VERSUS   TIME      MAXIMUM
                        0.0000E+00                            2.6735E+00
 TIME        X          I                                     I
0.0000E+00  0.0000E+00  +
5.0000E-02  6.5613E-01  ------------+
1.0000E-01  1.7099E+00  ---------------------------------+
1.5000E-01  2.4121E+00  -------------------------------------------------+
2.0000E-01  2.6590E+00  ----------------------------------------------------------+
2.5000E-01  2.6473E+00  ----------------------------------------------------------+
3.0000E-01  2.5431E+00  -------------------------------------------------------+
3.5000E-01  2.4322E+00  -------------------------------------------------+
4.0000E-01  2.3632E+00  ----------------------------------------------+
4.5000E-01  2.3430E+00  ----------------------------------------------+
5.0000E-01  2.3506E+00  ----------------------------------------------+
5.5000E-01  2.3647E+00  ----------------------------------------------+
6.0000E-01  2.3744E+00  ----------------------------------------------+
6.5000E-01  2.3777E+00  ----------------------------------------------+
7.0000E-01  2.3770E+00  ----------------------------------------------+
7.5000E-01  2.3753E+00  ----------------------------------------------+
8.0000E-01  2.3739E+00  ----------------------------------------------+
8.5000E-01  2.3734E+00  ----------------------------------------------+
9.0000E-01  2.3734E+00  ----------------------------------------------+
9.5000E-01  2.3737E+00  ----------------------------------------------+
1.0000E+00  2.3738E+00  ----------------------------------------------+
```

Figure 11.12(**c**)   Characteristics of a suspension system—example 2.

be executed at each integration step repetitively until a termination condition is met. If INITIAL segment is specified, then DYNAMIC segment must appear; otherwise the program segment is interpreted as DYNAMIC and no labelling is necessary.

The TERMINAL segment consists of statements for display and evaluation of simulation runs as well as the computations required for the initiation of additional runs. The control statements usually appear in the TERMINAL

INITIAL
   Statements for computations to be performed at the beginning of simulation
   (automatically sorted).

DYNAMIC
   Statements for computations to be performed during simulation run. These
   statements may be executed several times (automatically sorted).

TERMINAL
   Statements for computations to be performed at the end of simulation run
   (not sorted).

Figure 11.13   CSMP program structure.

segment, which is optional and appears after the DYNAMIC segment. This segment is automatically entered when TIME equals FINTIM or when FINISH criterion is satisfied.

Example 3

Consider the elevator problem of Section 11.3.4, restated as follows

$$\ddot{x} = -K(t - 2.0)^3$$
$$\dot{x}(0) = x(0) = 0; \quad 0 \leqslant t \leqslant 4$$

The elevator takes exactly 4 seconds to travel between stops, and the value of K which makes the velocity of the elevator zero at time $t = 4$ is known (from trial simulations) to be in the range $1.4 < K < 1.9$. We want to develop a CSMP program to compute

(a) value of K which makes $\dot{x}(4) = 0$,
(b) maximum velocity and the corresponding value of t,
(c) maximum and minimum acceleration and the corresponding time,
(d) time at which the acceleration is zero.

The CSMP program demonstrating the use of INITIAL, DYNAMIC, and TERMINAL segments is shown in Figure 11.14a. Initially the value of K is set to (LOW + HIGH)/2 in the INITIAL segment where LOW is the lower and HIGH is the upper bounds on K. At the end of a simulation run the value of (HIGH − LOW) is tested in the TERMINAL segment and if it is less than $1.0E - 4$, then the simulation is repeated once again with the current value of K plus the parameters on the second TIMER statement and the results printed/plotted. FINTIM = 4 is still in force as it is not redefined on the second TIMER statement. The RKS method (default option—see Section 11.3.8) is used for numerical integration during the evaluation of K, and Milne's method is used for the final run.

At the end of a simulation run let us consider the situation when (HIGH − LOW) is greater than or equal to $1.0E - 4$. Now a negative value of XDOT indicates that the current value of K is too small and therefore we set LOW = K; a positive value of XDOT implies that K is too large and

272

therefore set HIGH = K in the TERMINAL segment before the simulation is repeated by CALL RERUN. The correct value of *K* is always trapped between HIGH and LOW. We know that the velocity $\dot{x}$ of the elevator is maximum when its acceleration $\ddot{x}$ is zero, and this information is used to track the maximum velocity and its time of occurrence using the ZHOLD function. The three LABEL statements are associated with the three PRT-PLT statements according to the order in which they appear in the program. The WRITE,IF,FORMAT statements are typical examples of mixing Fortran statements in a CSMP program. The computed value of *K* at the end of 14 iterations was found to be *K* = 1.6032. The velocity of the elevator as a function of time is shown in Figure 11.14b; the maximum velocity of XDOT = 6.4129 occurred (Figure 11.14c) at TIME = 2; the maximum and minimum accelerations were ± 12.826 (Figure 11.14d) and the acceleration became zero at TIME = 2.

```
TITLE    SIMULATION OF AN ELEVATOR *********
* ILLUSTRATION OF INITIAL,DYNAMIC AND CONTROL SEGMENTS
INITIAL
    CONSTANT  HIGH=1.9,LOW=1.4
* INITIAL ESTIMATE OF  K
            K=0.5*(HIGH+LOW)
DYNAMIC
            X2DOT = -K*(TIME-2)**3
            XDOT  = INTGRL(0.0,X2DOT)
            X     = INTGRL(0.0,XDOT)
* TRACKING MAXIMUM VELOCITY
            MXDOT=ZHOLD(X2DOT,XDOT)
TERMINAL
            WRITE (6,5)K
5  FORMAT(' K ' ,F12.4)
            IF((HIGH-LOW).LT.1.0E-4) GO TO 3
            IF(XDOT.LT.0.0) GO TO 10
* VALUE OF K IS TOO LARGE
            HIGH=K
            GO TO 2
* VALUE OF K IS TOO SMALL
10          LOW=K
* REPEAT SIMULATION WITH NEW VALUE OF LOW OR HIGH
2           CALL RERUN
3           CONTINUE
* RKS METHOD OF INTEGRATION USED--DEFAULT
TIMER       FINTIM=4.0
END
TIMER       OUTDEL=0.125,DELT=0.0125,PRDEL=0.125
METHOD      MILNE
PRINT       X
PRTPLT      XDOT
PRTPLT      MXDOT
PRTPLT      X2DOT
LABEL ELEVATOR VELOCITY  VERSUS  TIME **********
LABEL MAXIMUM VELOCITY USING ZHOLD FUNCTION *******
LABEL ELEVATOR ACCELERATION VERSUS TIME *******
END
STOP
ENDJOB
```

Figure 11.14(a) CSMP program listing for example 3.

ELEVATOR VELOCITY VERSUS TIME **********

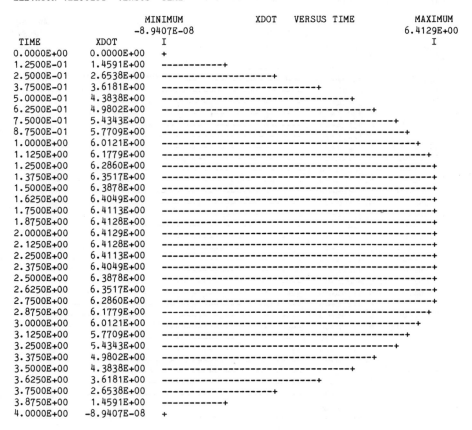

```
                         MINIMUM              XDOT   VERSUS TIME              MAXIMUM
                       -8.9407E-08                                         6.4129E+00
     TIME        XDOT     I                                                  I
0.0000E+00   0.0000E+00   +
1.2500E-01   1.4591E+00   -----------+
2.5000E-01   2.6538E+00   --------------------+
3.7500E-01   3.6181E+00   ------------------------------+
5.0000E-01   4.3838E+00   ---------------------------------------+
6.2500E-01   4.9802E+00   --------------------------------------------+
7.5000E-01   5.4343E+00   -------------------------------------------------+
8.7500E-01   5.7709E+00   ----------------------------------------------------+
1.0000E+00   6.0121E+00   -------------------------------------------------------+
1.1250E+00   6.1779E+00   ---------------------------------------------------------+
1.2500E+00   6.2860E+00   ----------------------------------------------------------+
1.3750E+00   6.3517E+00   -----------------------------------------------------------+
1.5000E+00   6.3878E+00   -----------------------------------------------------------+
1.6250E+00   6.4049E+00   ------------------------------------------------------------+
1.7500E+00   6.4113E+00   ------------------------------------------------------------+
1.8750E+00   6.4128E+00   ------------------------------------------------------------+
2.0000E+00   6.4129E+00   ------------------------------------------------------------+
2.1250E+00   6.4128E+00   ------------------------------------------------------------+
2.2500E+00   6.4113E+00   ------------------------------------------------------------+
2.3750E+00   6.4049E+00   ------------------------------------------------------------+
2.5000E+00   6.3878E+00   -----------------------------------------------------------+
2.6250E+00   6.3517E+00   -----------------------------------------------------------+
2.7500E+00   6.2860E+00   ----------------------------------------------------------+
2.8750E+00   6.1779E+00   ---------------------------------------------------------+
3.0000E+00   6.0121E+00   -------------------------------------------------------+
3.1250E+00   5.7709E+00   ----------------------------------------------------+
3.2500E+00   5.4343E+00   -------------------------------------------------+
3.3750E+00   4.9802E+00   --------------------------------------------+
3.5000E+00   4.3838E+00   ---------------------------------------+
3.6250E+00   3.6181E+00   ------------------------------+
3.7500E+00   2.6538E+00   --------------------+
3.8750E+00   1.4591E+00   -----------+
4.0000E+00  -8.9407E-08   +
```

Figure 11.14(b)   Velocity of elevator as a function of time—example 3.

When $K = 1.6$ it can be shown that the analytical solution to our problem is given by

$$x(t) = 6.4t - 0.08(t - 2)^5 - 2.56$$

and the verification of the simulation results is left as a student exercise.

11.3.7   SORT and NOSORT options—example 4

The CSMP statements are interpreted as equations and therefore proper ordering of statements is essential for correct program execution. In our elevator problem of Section 11.3.4, the equations for X2DOT, XDOT and X are required in that order for correct solution of the differential equation. *Automatic sorting* of equations according to correct order before program

MAXIMUM VELOCITY USING ZHOLD FUNCTION *******

		MINIMUM 0.0000E+00	MXDOT VERSUS TIME	MAXIMUM 6.4129E+00
TIME	MXDOT	I		I
0.0000E+00	0.0000E+00	+		
1.2500E-01	1.4591E+00	------------+		
2.5000E-01	2.6538E+00	--------------------+		
3.7500E-01	3.6181E+00	------------------------------+		
5.0000E-01	4.3838E+00	-------------------------------------+		
6.2500E-01	4.9802E+00	--+		
7.5000E-01	5.4343E+00	---+		
8.7500E-01	5.7709E+00	--+		
1.0000E+00	6.0121E+00	--+		
1.1250E+00	6.1779E+00	--+		
1.2500E+00	6.2860E+00	---+		
1.3750E+00	6.3517E+00	--+		
1.5000E+00	6.3878E+00	--+		
1.6250E+00	6.4049E+00	--+		
1.7500E+00	6.4113E+00	--+		
1.8750E+00	6.4128E+00	--+		
2.0000E+00	6.4129E+00	--+		
2.1250E+00	6.4129E+00	--+		
2.2500E+00	6.4129E+00	--+		
2.3750E+00	6.4129E+00	--+		
2.5000E+00	6.4129E+00	--+		
2.6250E+00	6.4129E+00	--+		
2.7500E+00	6.4129E+00	--+		
2.8750E+00	6.4129E+00	--+		
3.0000E+00	6.4129E+00	--+		
3.1250E+00	6.4129E+00	--+		
3.2500E+00	6.4129E+00	--+		
3.3750E+00	6.4129E+00	--+		
3.5000E+00	6.4129E+00	--+		
3.6250E+00	6.4129E+00	--+		
3.7500E+00	6.4129E+00	--+		
3.8750E+00	6.4129E+00	--+		
4.0000E+00	6.4129E+00	--+		

Figure 11.14(c) Tracking maximum velocity using ZHOLD function—example 3.

execution is one of the important features of CSMP, and the programmer is free to write most of the structure statements in any order provided certain rules are followed. Normally all statements in the INITIAL and DYNAMIC segments are automatically sorted while those in the TERMINAL segment are not sorted (Figure 11.13). To specify a change, SORT or NOSORT sections are introduced into the appropriate program segment. The statements in the NOSORT sections are not sorted and executed in the order in which they appear. The SORT section cannot include certain types of statements. In particular, the equation-oriented structure of CSMP demands that the same variable must not appear on both sides of the equal sign of a statement in a SORT section. For example, X = X + 1 would be invalid. Similarly, some Fortran statements consisting of IF and GO TO, WRITE and FORMAT, combinations cannot be placed in SORT sections. The use

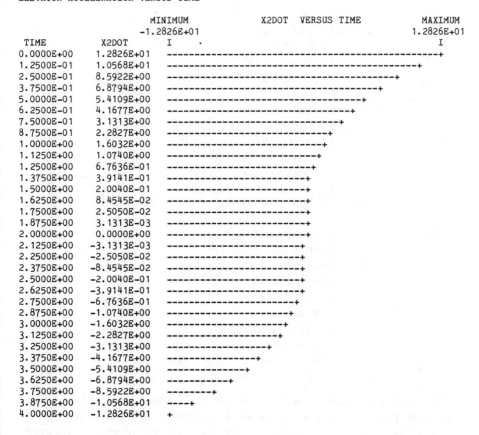

ELEVATOR ACCELERATION VERSUS TIME *******

TIME	X2DOT		MINIMUM -1.2826E+01 I	X2DOT VERSUS TIME	MAXIMUM 1.2826E+01 I
0.0000E+00	1.2826E+01		---+		
1.2500E-01	1.0568E+01		---+		
2.5000E-01	8.5922E+00		--+		
3.7500E-01	6.8794E+00		-------------------------------------+		
5.0000E-01	5.4109E+00		---------------------------------+		
6.2500E-01	4.1677E+00		-----------------------------+		
7.5000E-01	3.1313E+00		--------------------------+		
8.7500E-01	2.2827E+00		-----------------------+		
1.0000E+00	1.6032E+00		---------------------+		
1.1250E+00	1.0740E+00		-------------------+		
1.2500E+00	6.7636E-01		-----------------+		
1.3750E+00	3.9141E-01		----------------+		
1.5000E+00	2.0040E-01		---------------+		
1.6250E+00	8.4545E-02		---------------+		
1.7500E+00	2.5050E-02		--------------+		
1.8750E+00	3.1313E-03		--------------+		
2.0000E+00	0.0000E+00		--------------+		
2.1250E+00	-3.1313E-03		--------------+		
2.2500E+00	-2.5050E-02		--------------+		
2.3750E+00	-8.4545E-02		---------------+		
2.5000E+00	-2.0040E-01		---------------+		
2.6250E+00	-3.9141E-01		----------------+		
2.7500E+00	-6.7636E-01		-----------------+		
2.8750E+00	-1.0740E+00		-------------------+		
3.0000E+00	-1.6032E+00		---------------------+		
3.1250E+00	-2.2827E+00		-----------------------+		
3.2500E+00	-3.1313E+00		--------------------------+		
3.3750E+00	-4.1677E+00		-----------------------------+		
3.5000E+00	-5.4109E+00		---------------------------------+		
3.6250E+00	-6.8794E+00		-------------+		
3.7500E+00	-8.5922E+00		--------+		
3.8750E+00	-1.0568E+01		----+		
4.0000E+00	-1.2826E+01		+		

Figure 11.14(d) Acceleration of elevator as a function of time—example 3.

of SORT and NOSORT options is illustrated in the following example, which also highlights the applications of STEP, RAMP and LIMIT functions in CSMP.

Example 4

How much to buy and when to buy so as to minimize the cost of acquiring the inventory, the cost of holding the inventory and the cost of failing to supply the customers is the essence of inventory control. Ideally, one would also like to see a steady inventory level (desired level) which would simplify considerably the problem of inventory management.

A simple inventory control system can be described by:

$$\dot{X} = V - S$$
$$\dot{Y} = U - V$$
$$Z = S + C(D - X)$$
$$U = 2 \text{ when } Z < 2$$
$$\quad = 13 \text{ when } Z > 13$$
$$\quad = Z \text{ when } 2 \leqslant Z \leqslant 13$$
$$V = 0.6Y \text{ when } t < 5$$
$$\quad = 0.7Y \text{ when } 5 \leqslant t < 15$$
$$\quad = 0.8Y \text{ when } t \geqslant 15$$
$$S = L \text{ when } t < 4$$
$$\quad = L + 2 \text{ when } 4 \leqslant t < 10$$
$$\quad = L + 4 \text{ when } 10 \leqslant t < 15$$
$$\quad = L + 4 + 0.1\,(t - 15) \text{ when } t \geqslant 15$$
$$X(0) = 25; \; Y(0) = 10; \; D = 25; \; C = 1.3, 1.5, 1.0, 0.5$$

where
X = current inventory level
D = desired inventory level
Y = outstanding level of orders
U = rate of ordering
V = rate of delivery
S = rate of sales
C = ordering constant
t = time in weeks
L = 4 for the first simulation run
$\quad$ = 5 for all other runs

The *number of items* is used as a measure of various *rates* and *levels*, and the *plan period* is taken as 52 weeks. It is obvious from the model that the rate of sales, the rate of delivery, and the rate of ordering are piecewise continuous functions. The rate of ordering can not exceed a maximum of 13 per week and should never be less than 2 per week.

Our problem is to find the value of C for a given value of D so as to minimize the oscillations of the current inventory level about the desired inventory level, and in doing so we hope to strike a balance between inventory costs and shortage costs.

The CSMP program which demonstrates the use of INITIAL, DYNAMIC, TERMINAL, and NOSORT options is shown in Figure 11.15a. The program can be simplified by using STEP functions for generating the values of S. For example,

$$S = 4.0 + 2.0*\text{STEP}(4.0) + 2.0*\text{STEP}(10.0)$$

will generate

$$S = 4 \quad \text{when } 0 \leqslant t < 4$$
$$\quad = 6 \quad \text{when } 4 \leqslant t < 10$$
$$\quad = 8 \quad \text{when } t \geqslant 10$$

```
TITLE SIMULATION OF INVENTORY SYSTEM ********
* ILLUSTRATION OF SORT AND NOSORT OPTIONS
INITIAL
                S = L+B
   CONSTANT  X0=25.0,Y0=10.0,L=4.0,B=0.0,D=25.0
   PARAMETER C=1.3
DYNAMIC
                XDOT=V-S
                YDOT=U-V
* DELIVERY RATE CHANGES WITH TIME
                V=Y*(0.6+STEP(5.0)*0.1+STEP(15.0)*0.1)
                Z=S+C*(D-X)
* LIMIT ON ORDERING RATE
                U=LIMIT(2.0,13.0,Z)
                X=INTGRL(X0,XDOT)
                Y=INTGRL(Y0,YDOT)
  NOSORT
                B=0.0
                IF (TIME.LT.4.0) GO TO 20
                B=2.0
                IF (TIME.LT.10.0) GO TO 20
                B=4.0
* SALES RATE CHANGE WITH TIME
     20         S=L+B+RAMP(15.0)*0.1
TERMINAL
                IF (L.GE.5.0) GO TO 30
                L=5.0
CALL RERUN
  30            CONTINUE
TIMER           DELT=0.1,FINTIM=52.0,OUTDEL=2.0, PRDEL=2.0
PRINT           X,Y,U,V,Z ,S
PRTPLT          X
LABEL INVENTORY LEVEL  VERSUS  TIME *******
END
                PARAMETER  C=1.5
END
                PARAMETER  C=1.0
END
                PARAMETER  C=0.5
END
STOP
ENDJOB
```

Figure 11.15(a) CSMP program listing for example 4.

and the actual implementation of this feature is left as an exercise to the reader.

Figure 11.15b shows the current inventory level with respect to time when $L = 5$, $C = 1.3$ and FINTIM $= 52$. It is clear from the plot that the inventory level undergoes minor oscillations during the first few days and then gradually settles down to a steady level of 24.9. The CSMP program shows the use of multiple END statements to repeat simulation after changing the value of the parameter C. In all, the program goes through five simulation runs corresponding to $L = 4$ and $C = 1.3$; $L = 5$ and $C = 1.3$; $L = 5$ and $C = 1.5$; $L = 5$ and $C = 1$; $L = 5$ and $C = 0.5$. The amplitudes of the oscillations about the desired inventory level vary for different runs, and the result shown in Figure 11.15b was found to be the best of the lot.

INVENTORY LEVEL VERSUS TIME *******

TIME	X	MINIMUM 2.3455E+01 I	X VERSUS TIME	MAXIMUM 2.5952E+01 I
0.0000E+00	2.5000E+01	--------------------------------+		
2.0000E+00	2.5658E+01	---+		
4.0000E+00	2.4934E+01	-------------------------------+		
6.0000E+00	2.4228E+01	----------------+		
8.0000E+00	2.5455E+01	--+		
1.0000E+01	2.5099E+01	-------------------------------------+		
1.2000E+01	2.3771E+01	------+		
1.4000E+01	2.5223E+01	---+		
1.6000E+01	2.5950E+01	---+		
1.8000E+01	2.4909E+01	-------------------------------+		
2.0000E+01	2.4691E+01	-------------------------+		
2.2000E+01	2.4960E+01	----------------------------------+		
2.4000E+01	2.4932E+01	-------------------------------+		
2.6000E+01	2.4886E+01	-----------------------------+		
2.8000E+01	2.4903E+01	------------------------------+		
3.0000E+01	2.4908E+01	-------------------------------+		
3.2000E+01	2.4904E+01	------------------------------+		
3.4000E+01	2.4903E+01	------------------------------+		
3.6000E+01	2.4904E+01	------------------------------+		
3.8000E+01	2.4904E+01	------------------------------+		
4.0000E+01	2.4904E+01	------------------------------+		
4.2000E+01	2.4903E+01	------------------------------+		
4.4000E+01	2.4904E+01	------------------------------+		
4.6000E+01	2.4905E+01	------------------------------+		
4.8000E+01	2.4903E+01	------------------------------+		
5.0000E+01	2.4904E+01	------------------------------+		
5.2000E+01	2.4903E+01	------------------------------+		

Figure 11.15(b) Current inventory level as a function of time—example 4.

11.3.8 Integration methods in CSMP

Numerical integration is the most important operation in digital simulation of continuous systems. In CSMP the user has a choice of *seven* integration methods (Figure 11.16) ranging from rectangular and trapezoidal rule techniques to variable step-size methods that adjust step size during each integration step so as to strike a balance between accuracy and computing time. The default option is the RKS (Runge–Kutta, variable step size) method, but any of the integration methods including *user-supplied Fortran subroutines* can be selected under program control. The following CSMP statement selects Milne's method for integration.

METHOD MILNE

The RKS method is suitable for most applications. The integration step size is defined by assigning a value to DELT on the TIMER statement. If DELT· is not specified, then its initial value is automatically set to 1/16 of PRDEL or OUTDEL, whichever is smaller. If DELT is specified, it is automatically adjusted, if necessary, to be a sub-multiple of PRDEL or OUTDEL. If both PRDEL and OUTDEL are not specified, then DELT is adjusted to be a sub-multiple of FINTIM/100. The minimum allowable step size for variable step integration methods can be specified on TIMER by assigning a value to DELMIN. The default value for DELMIN is FINTIM $\times$ 10^{-7}.

For certain types of problems, fixed step integration methods may give more accurate results. However, the selection of an integration method and suitable step size consistent with the accuracy and computational speed is not straightforward. Several simulation runs with different step sizes and integration methods (Dickie and Ricketts, 1978) may be necessary to identify the correct method and step size for certain types of problems. In general, if a smaller integration step size produces a significantly different answer, then the step size being used is probably too large.

11.3.9 Some features of CSMP different from Fortran

Unless otherwise stated all variables in CSMP are treated as real variables. $I, J \ldots M, N$ are not automatically treated as integer variables. To specify I, A, B as integers, the following CSMP statement is required

CSMP name	Integration method	Step-size
MILNE	Fifth-order predictor-corrector	Variable
RKS	Fourth-order Runge-Kutta	
ADAMS	Adams-second-order	Fixed
RECT	Rectangular integration	
RKSFX	Fourth-order Runge-Kutta	
TRAPZ	Trapezoidal rule	
SIMP	Simpson's rule	
CENTRL	Dummy routine for user-supplied method	

Figure 11.16   Integration methods in CSMP.

FIXED   I, A, B

The PRINT and PRTPLT statements operate only with real variables. If A is integer and C is real, then A should be printed in CSMP as follows:

C = A
PRINT C

Another special feature of CSMP is that it is a non-procedural language with built-in SORT and NOSORT options. Unlike Fortran, statements of the form $X = X + 1$ cannot be used in the SORT sections of a CSMP program.

11.3.10   CSSL on microprocessors

Even though CSMP has not been implemented on micros, there are several other continuous system simulation languages (CSSL) currently available on desktop computers. ACSL/PC can be used for modelling and analysis of continuous systems described by time dependent nonlinear differential equations or transfer functions. A full implementation of ACSL is (Mitchel and Gauthier, 1985), running on IBM PC or compatible personal computers. ISIM is another CSSL which can run (Hay and Crosbie, 1984) on a small 8-bit micro with CP/M operating system, 48K bytes of memory, and floppy disks. It also runs on 16-bit micros operating under CP/M 86 or MS-DOS, and on IBM PC operating under PC-DOS. Models are defined by means of a natural differential equation notation and the results may be either tabulated or plotted. Flexible-run control features of ISIM provide a comprehensive, interactive simulation environment which gives the user full control of the simulation. The simulation run can be interrupted and the user can display or change values of variables and plot results of simulation. SLAM-II and MicroPASSIM are two other recently reported microprocessor implementations (see Section 12.4) of CSSL. A catalogue of micro, mini, and mainframe simulation software can be found in SCS, 1985.

11.4   Summary

Earlier applications of simulation were in engineering, and the simulation was carried out on analogue computers. Direct digital simulation (or simply, digital simulation) and digital analogue simulation are the two methods used for the simulation of continuous systems on digital computers. The complementary nature of the analogue and digital computers led to the development of hybrid computers and hybrid simulations. Even though analogue and hybrid computers are still being used for special applications, digital computers are more attractive because of their accuracy, flexibility, reliability, and ability to mimic analogue machines under program control. The development of cheaper and faster micros has further enhanced the popularity of digital simulations.

The operational amplifier is the major component of an analogue computer. The analogue computers operate in real time, can solve simultaneous equations in the true sense of the word, and they are particularly suitable for simulating nonlinear systems. Comparatively poor accuracy, inability to handle very large and very small variables, problems associated with the estimation of variable ranges and scale factors, and the difficulties in storing data are some of the drawbacks of the analogue computers.

The digital analogue simulation languages are block-oriented, whereas the direct digital simulation languages are equation-oriented. CSMP- and CSSL-based languages such as CSSL-III, CSSL-IV and ACSL, are direct digital simulation languages. Large-scale subroutine packages, such as FORSIM, LINPACK, etc., can also be used for the simulation of continuous systems. CSMP is one of the most popular continuous system simulation languages. It is based on Fortran; it incorporates several analogue functions and a variety of integration methods. Various features of the CSMP language and several examples to illustrate the use of CSMP for practical applications are presented in this chapter.

11.5 Exercises

1. Draw analogue computer diagrams for simulating the following systems:
   (a) $3\ddot{x} + 4\dot{x} + 6x = 1$; $\dot{x}(0) = 1/2$, $x(0) = 0$
   (b) $4\ddot{x} + K\dot{x} + 3x = 3$; $\dot{x}(0) = x(0) = 0$; $0 < K < 5$
   (c) $5\dot{x} + x = 4$; $x(0) = 1/4$

2. Develop analogue computer program to solve the following simultaneous equations:
   (a) $4\dot{x} + 2y = 0$
   $$3x + \ddot{y} + 3\dot{y} = 6$$
   $$\dot{y}(0) = 0;\ x(0) = 1/4;\ y(0) = 1$$
   (b) $\ddot{x} + 3\dot{x} + 5\dot{y} + 6x = 2$
   $$\ddot{y} + 4\dot{y} + \dot{x} + 2y = 0$$
   $$\dot{x}(0) = \dot{y}(0) = 1;\ x(0) = y(0) = 0$$

3. Draw analogue computer diagrams to simulate the following nonlinear systems:
   (a) $\ddot{x} - 2\dot{x} + 2x^2\dot{x} + x = 0$
   $$\dot{x}(0) = 2;\ x(0) = 0$$
   (b) $\ddot{x} + 4\dot{x}^2 + 6x = 1$
   $$\dot{x}(0) = 0;\ x(0) = 1$$

4. Compare and contrast the general characteristics of analogue and digital computers.

5. Write short notes on
   (a) magnitude and time scaling,
   (b) hybrid computers and hybrid simulations,

(c)   direct digital simulation versus digital analogue simulation.
6. Starting from the definition of a system, explain how you would go about simulating the system on an analogue computer.
7. Using CSMP, experiment with the problem of Section 11.3.4 with a view to study the following:
   (a)   effect of integration step size on accuracy of results and computational speed,
   (b)   accuracy of simulation by using different integration methods.
8. The behaviour of a mass spring system (Figure 11.17) with softening spring is characterized by

$$M\ddot{x} = -K_1(x - 0.6) - 0.6K_2; \text{ when } x > 0.6$$
$$= -K_2x; \text{ when } -0.5 \leqslant x \leqslant 0.6$$
$$= -K_3(x + 0.5) + 0.5K_2; \text{ when } x < -0.5$$

Simulate the system, for $M = 2$; $K_1 = 160$, $K_2 = 500$, $K_3 = 150$, $\dot{x}(0) = 0$; $x(0) = 1$
9. The current flowing through the electrical circuit shown in Figure 11.18 can be described by the differential equation

$$R_1\frac{dq}{dt} + \frac{q}{c} + R_1i_2 = V$$
$$L\frac{di_2}{dt} + R_2i_2 - \frac{q}{c} = 0$$

where $\dot{q} = i_1$; $i = i_1 + i_2$, $i_2(0) = q(0) = 0$.

Simulate the system to compute q, i_2, and i_1 as functions of time when, $R_1 = 8$ ohms, $R_2 = 15$ ohms, $C = 0.005$ farad, $L = 0.1$ henry, and $V = 12$ V.

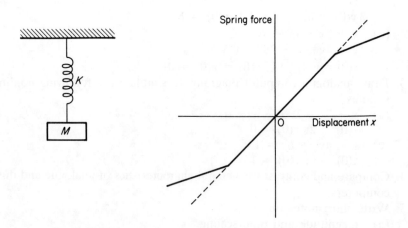

Figure 11.17   Vibrating system with nonlinear spring.

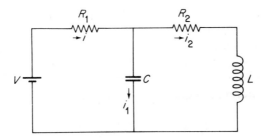

Figure 11.18   LCR electrical circuit.

10. A special form of Mathieu's equation, which describes the behaviour of sinusoidally excited mechanical systems, is given by

$$\ddot{x} + K(1 - \cos 2t)x = 0$$
$$x(0) = 2; \ \dot{x}(0) = 0$$

Simulate the system by using CSMP for

$$3 \leqslant K \leqslant 4 \text{ in steps of } 0.2$$
and
$$0 \leqslant K \leqslant 1 \text{ in steps of } 0.2$$

11. The radioactive decay of a substance A to B, B to C, and C to the stable substance D is given by

$$\dot{x}_1 = -K_1 x_1$$
$$\dot{x}_2 = K_1 x_1 - K_2 x_2$$
$$\dot{x}_3 = K_2 x_2 - K_3 x_3$$
$$\dot{x}_4 = K_3 x_3$$

where x_1, x_2, x_3, x_4 are the amount of substances A, B, C, D present at time t and K_1, K_2, K_3 are the decay rates. Develop a CSMP program to simulate the decay process, when

$$K_1 = 0.02 \text{ per day}$$
$$K_2 = 0.025 \text{ per day}$$
$$K_3 = 0.019 \text{ per day}$$
$$x_1(0) = 2 \text{ grams}$$

$$x_2(0) = x_3(0) = x_4(0) = 0$$

Compute the time to complete the decay process (i.e. when $\dot{x}_4 = 0$).

12. Write CSMP program to simulate the following systems:
    (a) $\ddot{x} + \dot{x} + 24x = 24 \cos\theta; \ -2\pi \leqslant \theta \leqslant 2\pi; \ \dot{x}(0) = 0; \ x(0) = 0$
    (b) $\dddot{x} + 3\ddot{x} + 2\dot{x} + x + 5\ddot{y} + y = 1.0$
         $\dddot{y} + \ddot{y} - 1.3\dot{y} - 1.6\dot{x} + 2y = 2.5$
         with zero initial conditions

(c) $\ddot{x} + 20x + 3x^3 = 0; \ \dot{x}(0) = 2.5; \ x(0) = 0$

(d) $3\dot{x} = 1 - 7x + 2y$

       $3\dot{y} = 11 + 4x - 5y$

       $x(0) = 2; \ y(0) = 0$

13. The growth of a rare species of birds in an island is described by the following differential equation:

$$\ddot{x} + \dot{x} + 1.25x = 1.25K$$

where $x(t)$ = number of birds on the island at time t in years,

         K = maximum number of birds that can live on the islands,

         $x(0)$ = $0.2K; \ \dot{x}(0) = 0.05K$

Simulate the growth of the bird population using CSMP and compare the results with the analytic solution given by

$$x(t) = K[1 - (0.8 \cos t + 0.35 \sin t) \ e^{-0.5t}]$$

14. The vibration of the mass spring system shown in Figure 11.19 can be described by

$$M_1\ddot{x} = -K_1x_1 + K_2(x_2 - x_1)$$
$$M_2\ddot{x} = -K_2(x_2 - x_1)$$

where x_1 = downward displacement of mass M_1 from its equilibrium position,

         x_2 = downward displacement of mass M_2 from its equilibrium position,

   K_1, K_2 are spring constants.

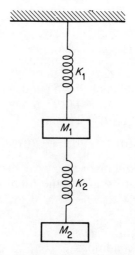

Figure 11.19   Mass–spring system.

Write a CSMP program to simulate the system, when $\dot{x}(0) = \dot{x}_2(0) = x_1(0) = x_2(0) = 0$

$$K_1 = 5 \text{ newton/metre}$$
$$K_2 = 2.5 \text{ newton/metre}$$
$$M_1 = 2 \text{ kg}$$
$$M_2 = 1.5 \text{ kg}$$

15. Write CSMP programs to solve problems 7, 10c, and 12 of Section 3.8.
16. Give suitable numerical values to various parameters of problems described in Sections 3.6.1, 3.6.4, and 3.6.6, and solve them by using CSMP. Compare the simulation results with analytical solutions.

References

Bekey, G. A., and Karplus, W. J. (1968). *Hybrid Computations*. John Wiley, New York.
Bennett, A. W. (1974). *Introduction to Computer Simulation*. West Publishing, New York.
Bert, J. L., and Pinder, K. L. (1982). 'Analogue simulation of the human microvascular exchange system', *Simulation*, **39**(3), 89–95.
Brennan, R. D., and Linebarger, R. N. (1964). 'A survey of digital simulation: digital analogue simulator programmes', *Simulation*, **3**(6), 22–36.
Carver, M. B., Stewart, G. D., Blair, J. M., and Selander, W. N. (1978). *The FORSIM VI simulation package for the automated solution of arbitrarily defined and partial and/or ordinary differential equation systems*. Report No. AECL-5821, Atomic Energy of Canada Ltd, Chalk River, Ontario, Canada.
Charlesworth, A. S., and Fletcher, J. R. (1974). *Systematic Analogue Computer Programming*. Pitman, London.
Control Data Corporation (1968). *MIMIC Digital Simulation Language Reference Manual*. Sunnyvale, CA.
Dickie, A. A., and Ricketts, I. W. (1978). 'An operational comparison of 13 numerical integration methods suitable for Minicomputer applications', *Proc. UKSC Conference on Computer Simulation*, Chester (UK), pp. 307–311.
Dongarra, J. J., Bunch, J. R., Moler, C. B., and Stewart, C. W. (1982). *LINPACK User's Guide*. SIAM, Philadelphia, PA.
Hay, J. H., and Crosbie, R. E. (1984). 'ISIM—a simulation language for microprocessors', *Simulation*, **43**(3), 133–136.
Hoeschle, D. F. (1968). *Analogue-to-Digital, Digital-to-Analogue Conversion Techniques*. John Wiley, New York.
IBM (1965). *DSL/90 Digital simulation Language User's Guide*. IBM corporation, San Jose, CA.
IBM (1972). *System/360 Continuous System Modelling Programme, User's Manual and CSMP III (with Graphic Features) Manual*. IBM corporation, White Plains, NY.
Korn, G. A., and Korn, T. M. (1972). *Electronic Analogue and Hybrid Computers*. McGraw-Hill, New York.
Korn, G. A., and Vichnevetsky, R. (1976). 'Analogue/hybrid computation and digital simulation', *IEEE Trans. on Comp.*, **C-25**, 1312–1320.
Landauer, J. P. (1982). 'Using a multiprocessing hybrid computer for flight simulation', *Simulation*, **39**(1), 23–26.
Mitchell, E. E., and Gauthier, J. S. (1985). *ACSL: Advanced Continuous Simulation*

Language User's Guide, and *ACSL/PC Users Manual*. Mitchel & Gauthier Associates Inc., Indy Pommers, 290 Baker Ave., Concord, MA 01742.

Nilsen, R. N., and Karplus, W. J. (1974). 'Continuous system simulation languages: a state of the art survey', *Proc. Int. Assoc. Analogue Comput.* **XVI**(1), 17–25.

Nilsen, R. N. (1976). *CSSL-IV: the successor to CSSL-III*. Young Lee & Associates, 2710, W. 23rd St, Torrance, CA.

Ören, T. I. (1977). 'Software for simulation of combined continuous and discrete systems: a state of the art review', *Simulation*, **28**(2), 33–46 and **29**(4), 125–126.

Pugh, A. L. (1973). *DYNAMO II User's Manual*. MIT Press, Cambridge, MA.

Programming Sciences Corporation (1970). *CSSL-III User's Guide and Reference Manual*. Los Angeles, CA.

Ragazzini, J. R., Randall, R. H., and Russell, F. A. (1947). 'Analysis of problems in dynamics by electronic circuits', *Proc. IRE* (May), pp. 444–452.

Ricci, F. J. (1972). *Analogue/Logic Programming and Simulation*. Spartan Books, New York.

Sci Software Committee (1967). 'The Sci Continuous System Simulation Language, CSSL', *Simulation*, **9**(6), 281–303.

SCS (1985). 'Catalog of simulation software', *Simulation*, **45**(4), 196–209.

Speckhart, F. H., and Green, W. L.(1976). *A Guide to using CSMP—The Continuous System Modelling Programme*. Prentice Hall, Englewood Cliffs, NJ.

Volz, R. A. (1973). 'Examples of function optimisation via hybrid computation', *Simulation*, **XXI**(2), 43–48.

12

Trends in Simulation

12.1 Introduction

Previous chapters discussed the construction and implementation of simulation models. The growing interest in the use of simulation as an aid in the study of non-experimentally verifiable systems is an indication of our confidence in simulation results and the importance we attach to simulation as a problem-solving technique. The trend towards the application of more and more *quantitative methods* in the social, behavioural, and environmental sciences will produce more complex models which are likely to be more related to reality. In complex situations, simulation is probably the only effective way of presenting information so that it may be easily understood by many, and better understanding will certainly lead to better decision-making. However, one must always remember the fact that the concepts conveyed by a model are basically the concepts held by the modeller; hence the need for exercising caution.

This chapter lists a few recent applications of simulation from various disciplines and discusses the general trends in simulation by examining some of the current and proposed research activities. Current research areas include simulation methodology, simulation software, computer graphics, computer hardware, and artificial intelligence.

12.2 Some recent simulation applications

Simulation models are widely used for problem-solving in many areas. It would be a formidable task even to attempt to list simulation studies that have been conducted during the past few years. The reader may get an idea of the vastness of the field by examining some of the recently reported applications of simulation under the following selected headings.

1. Agriculture (Oddson and Aggarwal , 1985)
2. Aircraft industries (Cook, 1984; Murphy and Butler, 1984; Lin and Hsu, 1984)

3. Biology and medicine (Vansteenkiste and Kerckhoffs, 1984; Düchting and Vogelsaenger, 1984; Taha and Stephen, 1984)
4. Computer networks (Sorensen, 1984; Chlamtac and Jain, 1984)
5. Distributed systems (Melman and Livny, 1984)
6. Hospital administration (Rao and Davis, 1984; Dumas, 1984)
7. Financial modelling (Coats and Chesser, 1982; Naylor, 1980; Gray, 1984)
8. Inventory systems (Banks and Malave, 1984; Ebrahimzadeh, *et al.*, 1985)
9. Maintenance process (Czajkiewicz, 1985)
10. Manufacturing industries (Bassett and Kochhar, 1984; Brennan *et al.*, 1984; Arumugam, 1985)
11. Policy decisions and planning (Moffatt, 1984; Blakley *et al.*, 1982; Wang and Sterman, 1985; Ward, 1984)
12. Process industries (Tucker, 1984; Wood *et al.*, 1984; Upadhye *et al.*, 1985)
13. Resource allocation (Caroll, 1982)
14. Robotics (Novak, 1984; Jayaraman, 1984)
15. VLSI design (Neubauer and Akers, 1984; Hayes, 1982)

12.3 Simulation methodology and software

Simulation must become easier for ordinary users, and there is an urgent need for user-friendly software for all stages of simulation including the definition, development, and validation of simulation models. The simulation practitioners should be users and not expert programmers. Modelling techniques should be such that complex models can be created by people with very little mathematical expertise. There must be better communication between the modeller and the model user and complex mathematical models should not stand in the way. A considerable amount of current research is directed towards making computers and simulation software more friendly and acceptable. Cellier (1983) has implemented a menu-driven interactive command procedure in ACSL, in which the tasks of editing, linking, and compilation are done automatically. In order to reduce the complexity of the simulation software, he recommends a separation of simulation functions into independent modules that communicate through a database management system.

12.3.1 The development of specification languages

There is an ongoing debate among users, designers, and implementors of simulation languages on international *standarization* (Nance, 1984) of simulation languages. In general, the purpose of standardization is to reduce the cost and time both for producers and customers. But many simulation practitioners argue that model portability is not going to save large sums of money; more savings can be achieved by improved communication of models, techniques, and concepts. In other words we should concentrate our efforts on developing methods to communicate model characteristics and experimental results with the help of SMSDL (simulation model specification and documentation language) rather than attempting to standardize at the programming language level. The SMSDL is intended to reduce modelling cost by introducing an intermediate specification form between a conceptual model (the model as it exists in the mind of the modeller) and an executable representation of that model, i.e. *separation between model description and program execution.*

Currently, a shift in emphasis from program to model development is gradually taking place. It appears that a large section of the simulation community are now more concerned about the conceptual problem description rather than the guidelines prescribed by the languages, which often impose constraints on the expression and realization of concepts. Research papers (Nance and Overstreet, 1985) are beginning to appear on the development of specification languages to assist in the construction and analysis of discrete event simulation models.

12.3.2 The credibility and acceptability of simulations

Proper analysis of simulation output is absolutely essential for making inferences about the properties of the system being simulated, and we have discussed the need for building *confidence intervals* on the mean of the output variables. The presence of serial correlation makes that estimate difficult. Further research is needed in constructing and evaluating reliable confidence interval procedures which are easy to use.

The *verification* and *validation* procedures currently in use are completely unsatisfactory, and independent verification and validation support software are badly needed. Continued research in '*proving programs correct*' will have an impact on the verification process. The definition and validation of models are still considered to be difficult. Current research interests include the development of systematic methods for model validation (especially the validation of unique systems) and the analysis of *type 1* and *type 2* errors (model builder's risk and model user's risk).

There is considerable interest in formulating a methodology (Balci and Sargent, 1981) for constructing the relationship among model user's risk, model builder's risk, range of acceptable validity, sample size, and the cost of data collection and simulation. Such a methodology would be of great help to *model sponsor*, *model builder* and *model user*, who can then select the appropriate relationship with respect to the intended application. Simple criteria to assess the *credibility* (i.e. confidence in the model) of models is essential for wider acceptance of simulation as an aid in decision-making. This is particularly important in today's world of large and complex systems, partly due to the cost of simulation and partly due to the increasing trend in the use of simulation for practical applications. The credibility of models must be assessed both by model builders and model users.

The *acceptability* of simulation studies can be expressed (Ören, 1981) in terms of the acceptability of different components of simulation study such as simulation results, data, model, experimental frames, and the programming techniques used. The acceptability of individual components may be assessed with respect to the goal of study, the structure and data of the real system, the model parameters, experimental frame, modelling methodology, simulation methodology, and the software engineering. Although some research has been devoted to this area, the progress is slow, and new concepts and better criteria to assess the overall acceptability of simulation studies are needed.

12.3.3   ROSS and ESL simulation languages

In general, the definition, modelling, validation, modification, and analysis of large-scale systems are difficult. The developments in *expert systems* (Hayes–Roth *et al.*, 1983) and *object-oriented languages* (see Sections 12.3.5 and 12.3.6) can be of great help in overcoming some of these difficulties. This approach has already been applied to the design and implementation of a new simulation language and environment called ROSS (rule-oriented simulation system) which is centred around objects, messages, and behavioural rules (Klahr, 1984). The motivation for developing ROSS was to produce intelligible, flexible, and efficient simulation specifications which meet the user's needs. In ROSS, a simulation is defined as a series of objects which communicate via messages which, in turn, trigger certain actions associated with an object. Routines are provided for good colour graphics output. The object-oriented languages allow replacement of an object by humans, either to train the human or for the human to excite the simulation in a particular way. Even though ROSS was developed primarily for military combat simulations, it has several features suitable for other domains as well.

An advanced continuous system simulation language called ESL (supported by the European Space Agency) is currently undergoing evaluations (Crosbie *et al.*, 1985). ESL provides a new computer tool to assist engineers in the design, diagnosis, evaluation, and understanding of complex dynamic systems including those containing nonlinearities and discontinuities. The main features of the language are: (a) building models from submodels, (b) separation of model and experiment, (c) advanced discontinuity handling, and (d) a parallel segment feature. An interpreter translates the user's program into an intermediate code which is then interpreted at run time. The translator may be used to convert the intermediate code to Fortran-77 to generate a more efficient executable program for production runs. ESL may be used to model even complex discontinuous systems with ease and guaranteed accuracy.

12.3.4 Graphics and Animation

We all know that graphic display is considerably more striking and meaningful than printed summary statistics. The humans can manipulate complex information more efficiently in the form of pictorial images. Graphics, and in particular colour graphics, provide enhanced visualization of simulation objects; for example, static graphics can be used to support views of network diagrams and animated graphics to support views of transaction movements. However, one must be careful not to confuse the information displayed on a graphic screen with the actual data stored inside the machine; it is the model that is more important, and graphic display is only a representation based on some or all of the data.

In simulation the number of possible alternative that could be simulated is large, and each run may be expensive. Repeating simulation runs for various parameter settings so as to produce optimum results is difficult and time-consuming. A pictorial representation of variables of interest (Nelson and Ravindran, 1985) would be helpful in reducing the number of alternatives to be simulated. Simulation experiments can then be performed for detailed analysis of the selected subset of likely candidates and the behaviour of the system being simulated over time can be displayed and interpreted. Pictures contain vital information about the system and graphical analysis is extremely useful as a tool for exposing the behaviour of various system configurations under peak loads and under unexpected operating conditions.

Many applications of computer graphics involve the representation of three-dimensional shapes. A three-dimensional solid may be represented as a *closed surface* or directly with solid objects (i.e. solid modelling) using as *primitives* solids such as cubes, cones, spheres, and cylinders which are added and subtracted to form desired shapes. Solid model-based simulation is found to be particularly attractive in robotics. General Motors have developed a computer system called RoboTeach,which integrates robotics, solid modelling, and simulation. RoboTeach has several applications including the selection of the right robot for a specific task, and programming the robot to perform the tasks in the most efficient way.

Animated graphics is considered to be a highly desirable feature in simulation software. Animation can be used to visualize and explain how programs and algorithms work by creating graphical snapshots and movies correlated with the program's actions. Such a facility provides visual feedback as a program and its parts are being executed, and this would be extremely useful (London and Duisberg, 1985) in program design, development, and debugging. Animated colour displays give dramatic evidence to the fact that the simulation model is indeed simulating the desired system, and this can be used for convincing potential sponsors and users of simulation we have already mentioned (sections 1.4.3 and 9.16) the use of CINEMA and SimAnimation for animated graphics. ANDES (Joyce *et al.*, 1984) is a *simulation environment* which is part of the JADE *software environment*. ANDES can animate not only the behaviour of the simulation model, but also the underlying mechanisms of the simulation. The user can enhance the predefined views of ANDES with their own views tailored to specific applications in two-dimensional colour graphics.

Both static graphics and animated graphics are becoming standard features in many simulation packages; however, high-resolution graphics is still expensive. For some applications such as flight simulations, real-time animation is required. In real-time (i.e. elapsed time between the display of two images is the same as that which would elapse in reality between the attainment of the two positions) animation, the speed of computations required to provide continuous animation is very high indeed.

12.3.5 Ada as a simulation language

The problems associated with the development of large-scale simulation software are complex and significantly different from those of small programs; hence the need for applying methods of software engineering (Sheppard, 1983). The software engineering methods can reduce the cost of developing large and complex software and also improve the quality and flexibility of the product. Simulation-oriented programming languages (incorporating discrete, continuous, or combined discrete–continuous simulation) should be designed to support software engineering methods (Golden, 1985) including *modular design* and *structured programming*. So far, the use of software engineering methodologies in simulation software has not been taken seriously, and only a few current simulation languages have the ability to support these methodologies.

Ada programming language (US Department of Defence's proposed standard system implementation language for embedded systems) was developed (Downes and Goldsack, 1982; Unger *et al.*, 1984) specifically to lower the cost of software systems by providing a language and environment that would be a vehicle for the practice of software engineering, especially in the area of embedded computer systems. Simulation models are large software systems whose requirements are very similar to the embedded systems; thus Ada should provide a better tool for designing and implementing complex simulation software. Ada provides a rich base of constructs, including data and program abstraction, for the implementation of simulation models, and offers promise in terms of execution on parallel architectures. Another attraction to Ada is that it incorporates the key concepts of an object-based language. Object-based computing raises the level of abstraction available in the design process. In addition, simulation has several applications in the software life-cycle; hence it is reasonable to provide it as part of an integrated software engineering environment.

At present there is a growing interest in combined discrete–continuous simulations, and there are relatively few simulation languages (GASP-IV, SLAM, SIMAN) to support this. Future simulation languages must be flexible and powerful, and the use of Ada as a simulation language (Antonelli *et al.*, 1986) is currently receiving active attention.

12.3.6 Artifical intelligence and Expert systems

The term AI (*artificial intelligence*) is frequently used to describe a range of advanced projects involving complex problem-solving, perception, reasoning, planning, and other functions usually associated with human thought. *Expert systems* (Shannon *et al.*, 1985) address only part of the problem addressed by the AI systems. Expert systems (knowledge-based systems) are concerned with the automation of tasks that are normally performed by specially trained or talented people; the emphasis is on consistently duplicating the results of a human expert, and not on understanding the basic mechanism used by the human expert to arrive at a given result. A simpler definition of an expert system is that it is a computer software system that can achieve an expert-level performance in a specialized field. There are no generally accepted definitions of an expert system. Expert systems have already been implemented for several specific problem-solving tasks with limited complexity. Currently there are over 50 existing or developing (Gevarter, 1983) expert systems. Predictions indicate that half the computers sold in 1995 will contain not only arithmetic components but also AI components, and such machines will be known as '*logic machines*'.

The major difference between an *expert system software* and *conventional software* is in the methodology used for problem-solving. Unlike the conventional software, there is no predetermined sequence of operators to solve a problem, and the expert system is required to synthesize the suitable operators for a given task. Since the synthesis mechanism is very similar to human intelligence, expert system is classified as a branch of AI.

The knowledge of an expert system consists of *facts* and *heuristics*. The *facts* constitute a body of information that is widely shared, publicly available, and generally agreed upon by experts in a particular field. The *heuristics* are mostly private knowledge and rules of good judgement that characterize expert decision-making in the field. The performance of the expert system depends very much on the quality of the *knowledge base* it possesses. For example, the knowledge base may include expert knowledge for the definition, development, verification, and validation of simulation models.

In order to implement an expert system, the domain of knowledge must be well defined and codifiable. The problem of how to acquire and organize knowledge about the various domains of interest must be solved satisfactorily before one can make progress towards the implementation of practical expert systems.

Simulation is an iterative experimental problem-solving technique, and the analyst is responsible for translating the problem into a series of program statements which are sequentially executed by the computer. The user has to plan various phases of modelling and simulation including model-building, verification, validation, experimental design, and collection and analysis of simulation output; i.e. the user must have the expertise in mathematics, probability theory, statistics, experimental design, modelling, computer programming, simulation languages, etc. In an expert simulation system the user would simply declare the knowledge about the system and define the goal; the '*logic machine*' will then come up with the solution to the problem. Expert simulation systems (O'Keefe, 1986) of tomorrow would make it possible for the user to perform simulation correctly and easily without being an expert in several fields. LISP and Prolog are the two most widely used AI programming languages. Prolog as a programming language is a powerful tool and provides a simple abstract notation which is independent from an underlying machine architecture. Prolog has many features (Adelsberger and Neumann, 1985) which make it an ideal language for simulation. The technology is still in its infancy, and a bright future is forecast for AI.

12.4 Simulation on microprocessors

The work practices of microcomputer users differ from those of mainframe users in many ways. Microprocessor-based simulation packages are designed to provide a programming environment for the user, including screen editor, automatic linking, loading, and recompilation of changed modules. A variety of simulations can be done on micros and a sample of some recent applications can be found in Browne *et al.* (1983), Laughery (1985), Schrefler (1984), Schroer *et al.* (1985), and Vayda and Wear (1985). A growing trend in the computer industry is the transition from the use of remote terminals connected to a central computer to distributed local processing of data. In several cases micros are being used in conjunction with mainframe computers for model development and simulation. For example, model development and modifications are done on a microcomputer; the model is run on the mainframe and the results are downloaded on to the micro, which is used for displaying the results in both printed and graphical form. However, one should be aware of the merits and demerits of the micros (slower, smaller, and cheaper) and the problems associated with the sharing of workloads.

Data security is another issue to be looked into. Usually there are several users and several phone lines connected to a typical central computing system. With micros, the owner has full control over the micro and the floppy disks; but the possibility of someone stealing a floppy disk still remains. DEC/PRO allows one to query a serial number and design the software to not run if it is not the right serial number. This helps the developers of software to control the distribution of their product.

A highly desirable feature in any computing system is the provision of a *voice keyboard* module that can be interfaced with the application package. With voice keyboard, one could talk to the computer and the voice module translates the recognized commands to the application package as if they had come from the keyboard. Voice recognition systems which are '*speaker-independent*' are designed to recognize the speech of most speakers. However, the current state of the art is such that a higher recognition reliability is achieved with '*speaker-dependent*' systems. These systems are trained by the user by repeating each word or command in the vocabulary several times. Such a system has been developed by Texas Instruments.

Voice or speech recognition systems together with artificial intelligence, in general, will have probably the greatest commercial applications in the near future.

The influence of micros will be considerably more widespread within the next few years. Faster microprocessors are needed for certain types of applications such as continuous system simulation and real-time applications; 16-bit micro is already here; 32-bit micros are beginning to appear and optical disks with virtually unlimited read-only storage are just around the corner.

The increase in speed and memory size have resulted in the implementation of several simulation languages on microprocessors. Some of these are adaptations of mainframe simulation languages, while others are specially designed for use on micros. The microprocessor implementation of GPSS, SIMSCRIPT, SIMAN, ACSL, and ISIM has already been discussed briefly in Sections 1.4.3, 8.18, 9.16 and 11.3.10. SLAM-II is a Fortran-based simulation language that provides the power of three different (network, discrete event, or continuous) modelling approaches. Micro PASSIM is a modelling package for combined simulation (discrete-event and continuous) using Turbo Pascal.

A good interactive simulation language must provide facilities not only for user interaction with the running model, but also for interactive model development. In compiler-based simulation languages even the smallest changes cannot be made on the spot, and one has to go through a set of procedures. Inter-SIM is an interactive *menu-driven* interpreter that provides (O'Keefe, 1985) rapid development and immediate execution of visual interactive simulation models on microprocessors. Model changes can be incorporated easily and quickly.

Animated simulation using CINEMA and SimAnimation on micros has been dealt with in Sections 1.4.3 and 9.16. The use of the GPSS/H for animated simulation graphics has been reported by Barta (1985). Current research activities indicate that we can expert significant advances in animated simulation in colour within the next five years.

Several versions of Prolog (artificial intelligence language) are currently available on micros. Prolog can be considered to be a very high-level language best suited for rapid prototyping. It has several qualities which make it attractive for goal-oriented simulation modelling.

A catalogue of microprocessor-based simulation software is given in SCS (1985). Another source of information is the annual conference publication of SCS on modelling and simulation on microcomputers. Whether one likes it or not, micros are becoming an integral part of our life; therefore there is an urgent need for having access to, and the ability to use, microprocessors, if one is to be competitive in the kind of society that is evolving.

12.5   The era of supercomputers

The major limitation of the conventional digital computer is in the so-called Von Neumann bottleneck—i.e. the need to extract data and program instructions, one word at a time, sequentially, from the main memory and only one arithmetic operation may be performed at any one time. The speed of simulation of large and complex systems is constrained by the number-crunching capability of the sequential digital computers. This is particularly significant in simulations involving a large number of runs, solution of differential equations, and real-time applications. The limitations of the conventional digital computers can be overcome (Karplus, 1984) by the use of supercomputers, a network of microprocessors, or peripheral array processors. Through extensive parallelism and pipelining, peripheral array processors can greatly enhance the capabilities of the host computer to process numerical data at very high speed.

Enormous computing power and massive data management are required (Absar, 1985) in finding and developing oil and gas reserves. Supercomputers are being used to store, classify, and interpret large amounts of geophysical seismic data obtained during the explorations for oil and gas. Cray and Cyber-200 machines have functional units which can overlap action over multiple operands, and thus produce more than one result per clock cycle. Hitachi and Fujitsu have already delivered machines which claim to surpass the peak performance of the current US supercomputers.

NASA's (Ames Research Centre, California) numerical aerodynamic simulation (NAS) system is intended to produce (NASA, 1985) the world's most powerful supercomputer system. The NAS system is expected to reach continuous, high speeds of one billion computations per second in 1988. The goal for the system in the 1990s is ten billion calculations per second. High-speed supercomputers will be used to solve complex aerodynamical equations and, in effect, aircraft configurations can be tested by flying (simulating) the aircraft in the computer. Thus the time and cost of development of new aircraft will be drastically reduced. In addition, these supercomputers will be used for supporting research in weather prediction, genetic engineering, and computational astrophysics. The initial NAS network consists of a Cray 2 supercomputer with an operating speed of 250 million calculations per second. Crowded chips in a computer can build up enough heat to damage each other, and Cray 2 is the first computer to have its chips totally immersed in a fluid that draws heat away.

A discussion of the present state and future directions of supercomputers can be found in Davis (1984) and Lundstrom and Larsen (1985).

12.6 Summary

The development of tools and techniques required for the application of simulation for solving large and complex problems is receiving attention. Microprocessors are no longer a luxury. We have object-oriented languages, colour graphics, animation capabilities, and database systems to support simulation. Better techniques are being developed for the definition, development, verification, and validation of simulation models. More and more research is being directed towards improving experimental design techniques and methods for collection and analysis of simulation output. Artificial intelligence has become a usable tool, and supercomputers are just around the corner. We are now in a better position to provide the simulation practitioners with the tools and techniques they need. However, it will take many years before all the objectives of the current research efforts are fully realized.

References

Absar, I. (1985). 'Applications of supercomputers in petroleum industry', *Simulation*, **44**(5), 247–251.

Adelsberger, H. H., and Neumann, G. (1985). 'Goal oriented simulation modelling using Prolog', in *SCS Conference on Modelling and Simulation on Microcomputers* (ed. R. G. Lavery), pp. 42–47.

Antonelli, C.J., Volz, R. A., and Mudge, T. N. (1986). 'Hierarchical decomposition and simulation of manufacturing cells using Ada', *Simulation*, **46**(4), 141–152.

Arumugam, V. (1985). 'Priority sequencing in a real world job shop', *Simulation*, **45**(4), 179–186.

Balci, O., and Sargent, R. G. (1981). 'A Methodology for cost–risk analysis in the statistical validation of simulation models', *CACM*, **24**(11), 190–197.

Banks, J., and Malave, C. O. (1984). 'The simulation of inventory systems: an overview', *Simulation*, **42**(6), 283–290.

Barta, T. A. (1985). 'Animated simulation graphics with GPSS', in *SCS Conference on Modelling and Simulation on Microcomputers* (ed. R. G. Lavery), pp. 51–54.

Bassett, G., and Kochhar, A. K. (1984). 'Evaluation of material requirements planning strategies by computer simulation', *Proceedings of the 1984 UKSC Conference on Computer Simulation*, pp. 302–312.

Blakley, D. L., Cohen, K. J., Lewin, A. Y., and Morey, R. C. (1982). 'Assessing defence procurement policies', *Simulation*, **38**(3), 75–83.

Brennan, L., Browne, J., and Davies, B. J. (1984). 'The development of an interactive simulation model for management decision making', *Proceedings of the 1984 UKSC Conference on Computer Simulation*, pp. 313–326.

Browne, J., Regan, S., *et al.* (1983). 'The design of microcomputer based net change MRP system', *Computers and Industry*, **4**(3), 243–252.

Caroll, J. M. (1982). 'Digital simulator for allocating fire fighting resources', *Simulation*, **38**(1), 1–12.

Cellier, F. E. (1983). 'New problems in software complexity, simulation', *Simulation*, **41**(3), 118–119.

Chlamtac, I., and Jain, R. (1984). 'A methodology for building a simulation model for efficient design and performance analysis of local area networks', *Simulation*, **42**(2), 57–66.

Coats, P. K., and Chesser, D. L. (1982). 'Coping with business risk through probabilistic financial statements', *Simulation*, **38**(4), 111–121.

Cook, M. V., and Malik, I. A. (1984). 'The dynamic simulation of aircraft using actively controlled models in a wind tunnel', *Proceedings of the 1984 UKSC Conference on Computer Simulation*, pp. 258–274.

Crosbie, R. E., Javey, S., Hay, J. S., and Pearce, J. G. (1985). 'ESL—a new continuous system simulation language', *Simulation*, **44**(5), 242–246.

Czajkiewicz, Z. J. (1985). 'Optimisation of the maintenance process', *Simulation*, **44**(3), 137–141.

Davis, D. B. (1984). 'Supercomputers: a strategic imperative', *High Technology*, May, pp. 44–52.

Downes, V. A., and Goldsack, S. J. (1982). *Programming Embedded Systems with Ada*. Prentice Hall, Englewood Cliffs, NJ.

Düchting, W., and Vogelsaenger, T. (1984). 'The present status of simulating three-dimensional tumor growth and treatment', *Proceedings of the 1984 UKSC Conference on Computer Simulation*, pp. 219–227.

Dumas, M. B. (1984). 'Simulation modelling for hospital bed planning', *Simulation*, **43**(2), 69–78.

Ebrahimzadeh, M., Barnoon, S., and Stern, Z. A. (1985). 'A simulation of multi-item drug inventory system simulation', *Simulation*, **45**(3), 115–121.

Gevarter, W. B. (1983). 'Expert systems: limited but powerful', *IEEE Spectrum*, August.

Golden, D. G. (1985). 'Software engineering considerations for the design of simulation languages', *Simulation*, **45**(4), 169–178.

Gray, P. (1984). 'Using the interactive financial planning system (IFPS) for stochastic simulation', *Simulation*, **43**(6), 286–292.

Hayes, J. (1982). 'A fault simulation methodology for VLSI', *Proceedings of the ACM–IEEE, 19th Design Automation Conference*, pp. 393–399.

Hayes-Roth, F., Waterman, D. A., and Lenat, D. B. (1983). *Building Expert Systems*. Addison Wesley, Reading, MA.

Jayaraman, R. (1984). 'Simulation of robotic applications', *IBM Research Report*, RC10714, No. 48003.

Joyce, J., Birtwistle, G., and Wyvill, B. (1984). 'ANDES—an environment for animated discrete event simulation', *Proceedings of UKSC Conference on Computer Simulation*, pp. 93–100.

Karplus, W. J. (1984). 'Selection criteria and performance evaluation methods for peripheral array processors', *Simulation*, **43**(3), 125–131.

Klahr, P. (1984). 'Artificial intelligence approaches to simulation. *Proceedings of UKSC Conference on Computer Simulation*, pp. 87–92.

Laughery, K. R. (1985). 'Modelling human operators on a microcomputer: a micro version of SAINT', *Simulation*, **44**(1), 10–16.

Lin, C. F., and Hsu, K. L. (1984). 'Digital simulation of guidance and control system of an advanced supersonic fighter', *Simulation*, **42**(1), 21–30.

London, R. L., and Duisberg, R. A. (1985). 'Animating programmes using SMALLTALK', *IEEE Computer*, **18**(8), 61–71.

Lundstrom, S. F., and Larsen, R. L. (1985). 'Computer and information technology in the year 2000—A projection', *IEEE Computer*, **18**(9), 68–79.

Melman, M., and Livny, M. (1984). 'The DISS methodology of distributed system simulation', *Simulation*, **42**(4), 163–176.

Moffatt, I. (1984). 'Environmental management models and policies', *Proceedings of the 1984 UKSC Conference on Computer Simulation*, pp. 182–190.

Murphy, L. N., and Butler, G. F. (1984). 'The software design for a real-time air-to-ground flight simulator', *Proceedings of the 1984 UKSC Conference on Computer Simulation*, pp. 505–516.

Nance, R. E. (1984). 'To be, or not to be—is that the question?', *ACM Simuletter*, **15**(1), 5–7.

Nance, R. E., and Overstreet, C. M. (1985). 'A specification language to assist in analysis of discrete event simulation models', *CACM*, **28**(2), 190–201.

NASA (1985). 'NASA numerical aerodynamic simulation facility', *Simulation*, **44**(5), 257–258.

Naylor, T. (1980) 'Third generation corporate simulation models'. In *Simulation with Discrete Models: A State-of-the-Art View*. IEEE, New York, pp. 131–141.

Nelson, B., and Ravindran, A. (1985). 'A hybrid graphical-simulation analysis of a health system application', *Simulation*, **44**(5), 219–224.

Neubauer, C. M., and Akers, L. A. (1984). 'Automatic VLSI layout simulation', *Simulation*, **42**(6), 276–282.

Novak, B. (1984). 'Robotic simulation facilitates assembly line design', *Simulation*, **43**(6), 298–299.

Oddson, J. K., and Aggarwal, S. (1985). 'Discrete–event simulation of agricultural pest management system', *Simulation*, **44**(6), 285–293.

O'Keefe, R. M. (1985). 'Truly interactive simulation: inter-SIM'. In *SCS Conference on Modelling and Simulation on Microcomputers* (ed. R. G. Lavery), pp. 131–137.

O'Keefe, R. M. (1986), 'Simulation and expert systems—a taxonomy and some examples', *Simulation*, **46**(1), 10–16.

Ören, T. J. (1981). 'Concepts and criteria to assess acceptability of simulation studies: a frame of reference', *CACM*, **24**(4), 180–189.

Rao, G., and Davis, R. H. (1984). 'The development and evaluation of system simulation models for patient admission policies', *Proceedings of the 1984 UKSC Conference on Computer Simulation*, pp. 191–197.

Schrefler, B. A. (1984). *Engineering Software for Microcomputers*. Pineridge Press, Swansea, UK.

Schroer, B. J., Black, J. T., and Zhang, S. X. (1985). 'Just-in-time (JIT), with Kanban, manufacturing system simulation on a microcomputer', *Simulation*, **45**(2), 62–70.

SCS (1985). 'Catalog of simulation software', *Simulation*, **45**(4), 196–209.

Shannon, R. E., Mayer, R., and Adelsberger, H. H. (1985). 'Expert systems and simulation', *Simulation*, **44**(6), 275–284.

Sheppard, S. (1983). 'Applying software engineering to simulation', *Simulation*, **40**(1), 13–19.

Sorensen, S. A. (1984). 'Performance studies of computer networks', *Proceedings of the 1984 UKSC Conference on Computer Simulation*, pp. 477–487.

Taha, H. A., and Stephen, F. M. (1984). 'Modelling with imperfect data: a case study simulating a biological system', *Simulation*, **42**(3), 109–115.

Tucker, P. (1984). 'An approach to industrial process modelling, and application to a spiral separator for minerals', *Proceedings of the 1984 UKSC Conference on Computer Simulation*, pp. 346–357.

Unger, B. W., Lomow, G. A., and Birtwistle, G. M. (1984). *Simulation Software and Ada*. Society for Computer Simulation, La Jolla, CA.

Upadhye, R. S., Anselmo, K. J., and Schiesser, W. E. (1985). 'Developing generalised reactor models for a process simulator', *Simulation*, **44**(3), 149–153.

Vansteenkiste, G. C., and Kerckhoffs, E. J. H. (1984). 'Information base support in simulation of biological systems', *Proceedings of the 1984 UKSC Conference on Computer Simulation*, pp. 198–218.

Vayda, T. P., and Wear, L. L. (1985). 'Simulation of an ethernet interface using micro PASSIM', *Simulation*, **45**(3), 129–137.

Wang, Q., and Sterman, J. D. (1985). 'A disaggregate population model of China', *Simulation*, **45**(1), 7–14.

Ward, M. D. (1984). 'Modelling the USA–USSR arms race', *Simulation*, **43**(4), 196–202.

Wood, R. K., Thambynayagam, R. K. M., Noble, R. G., and Sebastian, D. J. (1984). 'DPS—a digital simulation language for the process industries', *Simulation*, **42**(5), 221–233.

Index

304